FOCUS ON BIPOLAR DISORDER RESEARCH

FOCUS ON BIPOLAR DISORDER RESEARCH

MALCOMB R. BROWN
EDITOR

Nova Science Publishers, Inc.
New York

Editorial Production Manager: Donna Dennis
Senior Production Editor: Susan Boriotti
Office Manager: Annette Hellinger
Graphics: Andrea Charles, Magdalena Nuñez and Annemarie VanDeWater
Editorial Production: Marius Andronie, Maya Columbus, Keti Datunashvili, Melissa Diaz, Joan Flynn, Andrew Kallio, Vladimir Klestov, Lorna Loperfido, Joann Overton and Rusudan Razmadze
Circulation: Ave Maria Gonzalez, Vera Popovic, Luis Aviles, Alexandra Columbus, Raymond Davis, Cathy DeGregory, Marlene Nuñez, Jeannie Pappas, Lauren Perl and Katie Sutherland

Library of Congress Cataloging-in-Publication Data
Available upon request

ISBN 1-59454-059-4

400 Oser Ave, Suite 1600
Hauppauge, New York 11788-3619
Tele. 631-231-7269 Fax 631-231-8175
e-mail: Novascience@earthlink.net
Web Site: http://www.novapublishers.com

Printed in the United States of America

CONTENTS

PREFACE

Bipolar disorder is episodic and recurrent with a high degree of inter-individual variation and heterogeneity between patients. Longitudinal studies are an optimal approach to investigating the highly variable course of bipolar disorder, but are expensive and often have a significant amount of missing data. Chapter 1 will review the incorporation of technology in longitudinal studies of patients with mood disorders and describe the authors experience with the development, validation and use of an automated instrument for data collection and analysis in several research studies of patients with bipolar disorder. Chapter 2 will show the role of cations such as sodium, potassium, calcium and lithium in bipolar disorder, which has been studied extensively in the past. Ionic gradients exert significant influence on the neurons by affecting the resting membrane potentials, action potentials, neurotransmitter release, signaling and signal transduction. Clinical measurements show that the membrane potentials of leucocytes in bipolar patients are significantly hyperpolarized whereas they are slightly depolarized in euthymic patients on lithium. During the past twenty years, considerable research has demonstrated that neuropsychological dysfunction is a common correlate of bipolar disorder (cf. Martinez-Aran, Vieta, Colom, Reinares, Benabarre, Gasto, & Salamero, 2000). Yet, the nature and severity of these abnormalities, remains unsettled, and numerous conundrums exist, and are discussed in Chapter 3.

Migraine and depression are both common disorders in the general population, and epidemiological studies have shown a substantial co-morbidity between them. The present investigation was undertaken to examine the prevalence of migraine in patients presenting with major affective disorders and to study the clinical characteristics of these patients and is outlined in Chapter 4. Despite vast research from multifaceted points of view, the biochemical abnormalities underlying the predisposition to, and the pathophysiology of, affective disorders have not yet been fully understood. Although it appears difficult to interpret universally numerous results from different laboratories, often controversial and sometimes even contrasting, continuous research efforts aiming at elucidating the intracellular molecular mechanisms related to affective disorders and already established mood stabilizing agents will lead to our newer conceptualization of biological aspects of affective disorders as well as to development of novel therapeutic drugs for these disorders and is discussed in Chapter 5.

Numerous neurological conditions may be complicated by behavioral symptoms such as aggression, mania and psychosis. The authors will describe in Chapter 6 the results of a retrospective chart review and a prospective clinical trial of two different AEDs, sodium divalproex and oxcarbazepine, and discuss the pathophysiology of these syndromes and the role of AEDs in effective treatment. The Bech-Rafaelsen Mania and Melancholia Scales are the psychometrically most validated rating scales for mood disorders as they have been accepted for dimensionality (total score being a sufficient outcome statistic) by item response models. Clinical trials in which the two scales have been used as outcomes have been reviewed in Chapter 7 to evaluate the efficacy of the various treatments.

Nearly 40% of depressed patients do not improve with the first pharmacological treatment, even with adequate time, dose and compliance; 20% of patients with major depressive disorder do not improve even with a two year treatment, and 12% never improve. In Chapter 8, the authors first present a case report, and then we make a review between narcissistic personality disorder, hypertimic personality, bipolar disorder and resistant depression, discussing its therapeutic implications.

Bipolar Disorder among older adults is a problem that has gained recognition due to changes in population demographics and growing sophistication in the assessment and diagnosis of bipolar illness. Treatments for late-life bipolar disorder include pharmacologic as well as psychosocial interventions. There are very few published, controlled studies on drug treatments of bipolar disorder in older adults. The limited literature suggests that lithium, a mainstay of treatment in younger bipolar populations, may have limited usefulness due to poor tolerability in older populations and possibly less efficacy in secondary manic states and is discussed in Chapter 9.

In: Focus on Bipolar Disorder Research
Editor: Malcomb R. Brown, pp.1-14
ISBN 1-59454-059-4

Chapter 1

NEW TECHNOLOGY FOR LONGITUDINAL STUDIES OF PATIENTS WITH BIPOLAR DISORDER

Michael Bauer
Department of Psychiatry and Psychotherapy, Charité - University Medicine Berlin, Campus Charité-Mitte (CCM), Germany
Neuropsychiatric Institute & Hospital, University of California Los Angeles (UCLA), Los Angeles, CA
Tasha Glenn
ChronoRecord Association, Inc., Fullerton, CA
Natalie Rasgon
Neuropsychiatric Institute & Hospital, Stanford School of Medicine, Palo Alto, CA
Paul Grof
University of Ottawa, Royal Ottawa Hospital, Ottawa, Canada
Laszlo Gyulai
University of Pennsylvania School of Medicine, Philadelphia, PA
Peter C. Whybrow
Neuropsychiatric Institute & Hospital, University of California Los Angeles (UCLA), Los Angeles, CA

ABSTRACT

Bipolar disorder is episodic and recurrent with a high degree of inter-individual variation and heterogeneity between patients. Longitudinal studies are an optimal approach to investigating the highly variable course of bipolar disorder, but are expensive and often have a significant amount of missing data. The tools used for daily self-assessment in longitudinal studies of mood disorders are traditionally paper based. Automation of long-term data collection can reduce missing data, eliminate errors associated with data entry, provide ongoing feedback for patients and clinicians during a long study and allow the use of interim data for clinical decision support. This article will review the incorporation of technology in longitudinal studies of patients with mood disorders and describe our experience with the development, validation and use of an automated instrument for data collection and analysis in several research studies of patients with bipolar disorder. ChronoRecord is software that patients install on a home computer to report mood, medications, sleep, life events, weight and menstrual data. 80 of 96 (83%) patients with bipolar disorder showed high acceptance of this computerized approach to daily self-reporting, entering 8662 days of data for a 3-month period during the validation study (mean of 114.7 ± 32.3 SD days). The mean percent of days missing for mood data was 6.1% ± 9.3 SD, equivalent to missing 7.3 day out of the 114.7 days. The widespread acceptance of computer technology by the general public can be leveraged to improve the design of longitudinal studies.

INTRODUCTION

Bipolar disorder is the most expensive behavioral health care diagnosis in the United States for both patients and their insurance plans [1] and is frequently disabling. [2] The lifetime prevalence for the entire spectrum including bipolar I and II, cyclothymia and bipolar not otherwise specified is estimated to be between 2.6-6.5% of the general population. [3] Almost all patients who suffer this disorder have multiple episodes, with the relapse rate by 5 years being estimated at around 90%. [4] The course of bipolar disorder is episodic and recurrent and associated with both inter-individual variation and heterogeneity between patients. [5, 6] Thus over a lifetime any one patient may experience many forms of the illness including mixed emotional states, psychosis, depressive and manic or hypomanic episodes, and the rapid cycling among those episodes. [7] There is also great variation among patients in the severity of symptoms, the duration and number of episodes, the degree of recovery between episodes, the intervals between episodes and the pattern of polarity. Furthermore, current research suggests that a spectrum or continuum of bipolar disorder exists that includes predisposing temperaments such as hyperthymic, dysthymic and cyclothymic traits. [8, 9] Given the wide range of phenotypic expression associated with bipolar disorder, rapidly changing and complex medication regimens are commonplace. [10, 11] Finally, despite modern treatments full recovery is infrequent and incomplete symptomatic remission with a high degree of individual variability is the accepted clinical norm. [12]

SELF-REPORTING IN BIPOLAR DISORDER

Because of the variability and heterogeneity in the expression of bipolar disorder, the optimal approach to understanding the natural course of the illness, and to evaluating treatment outcomes is prospective longitudinal studies. However, such studies are expensive, and thus are often viewed as impractical. The need for long-term commitment and participation makes it difficult to recruit subjects and to motivate them, especially when feedback of the results must be delayed until the end of the study. In an effort to overcome some of these difficulties several paper-based self-report data collection instruments have been developed for use in the study of patients with bipolar disorder, including the Life Chart Methodology [13] and the STEP-BP Mood Chart. [14] A third instrument, the ChronoSheet, [15] grew out of a simple system of self-report developed by one of us (PCW) during the 1980s to follow the clinical course of patients with the rapid-cycling variant of the illness. In its paper and pencil form it was used successfully both as a research tool and as a method of increasing patient understanding of their illness, and thus their compliance with the treatment regimen. We soon discovered, however, that a significant problem with paper based reporting is that patients often complete the forms sporadically, or just before a clinic visit when the retrospective recall of events may be inaccurate and biased. [16] Furthermore, with no time log of when recordings are made such errors are often overlooked or ignored. Capturing the information from paper documents for computer analysis is also labor intensive, expensive, slow and prone to errors in data entry. And even when accurately transposed longitudinal data frequently suffer from significant missing values, differential attrition, inconsistent assessment intervals and a variable number of observations for each participant. [17]

New Technologies for Data Collection

The rapid incorporation of computer technology into everyday life by the general public has provided an opportunity to improve the quality of data collection in longitudinal studies of bipolar illness. With this in mind, ChronoRecord is an automated electronic version of the self-report ChronoSheet, which has been previously validated against two observer-rated scales [18] the Young Mania Rating Scale (YMRS) [19] and Hamilton Depression Rating Scale (HAMD). [20] We describe here our experience from an ongoing study using ChronoRecord software on a home computer to collect self-reported data from patients suffering bipolar disorder. The data from 80 patients, who each entered data for a 3-month period, have been analyzed to determine the feasibility of the concept and to validate the ChronoRecord software instrument. Examples of how the data collected with ChronoRecord software may be used in research are also provided, specifically an evaluation of the influence of antidepressants and of gender upon the clinical course of bipolar disorder in these patients.

Methods

The study participants were consecutively recruited from the mood disorders clinics at three academic centers. After a complete explanation of the study, 96 patients signed the written consent form approved by the Institutional Review Board at their respective institution. All patients met the DSM-IV criteria for bipolar disorder, diagnosed by clinical interview and confirmed with the MINI International Neuropsychiatric Interview. [21] Other inclusion criteria were: age 18 years or older, daily access to a personal computer and the skills to use it, and the ability to read and write English. Patients with antisocial personality disorder or dementia were excluded. No other inclusion or exclusion criteria were used to avoid creating a bias in the patient sample.

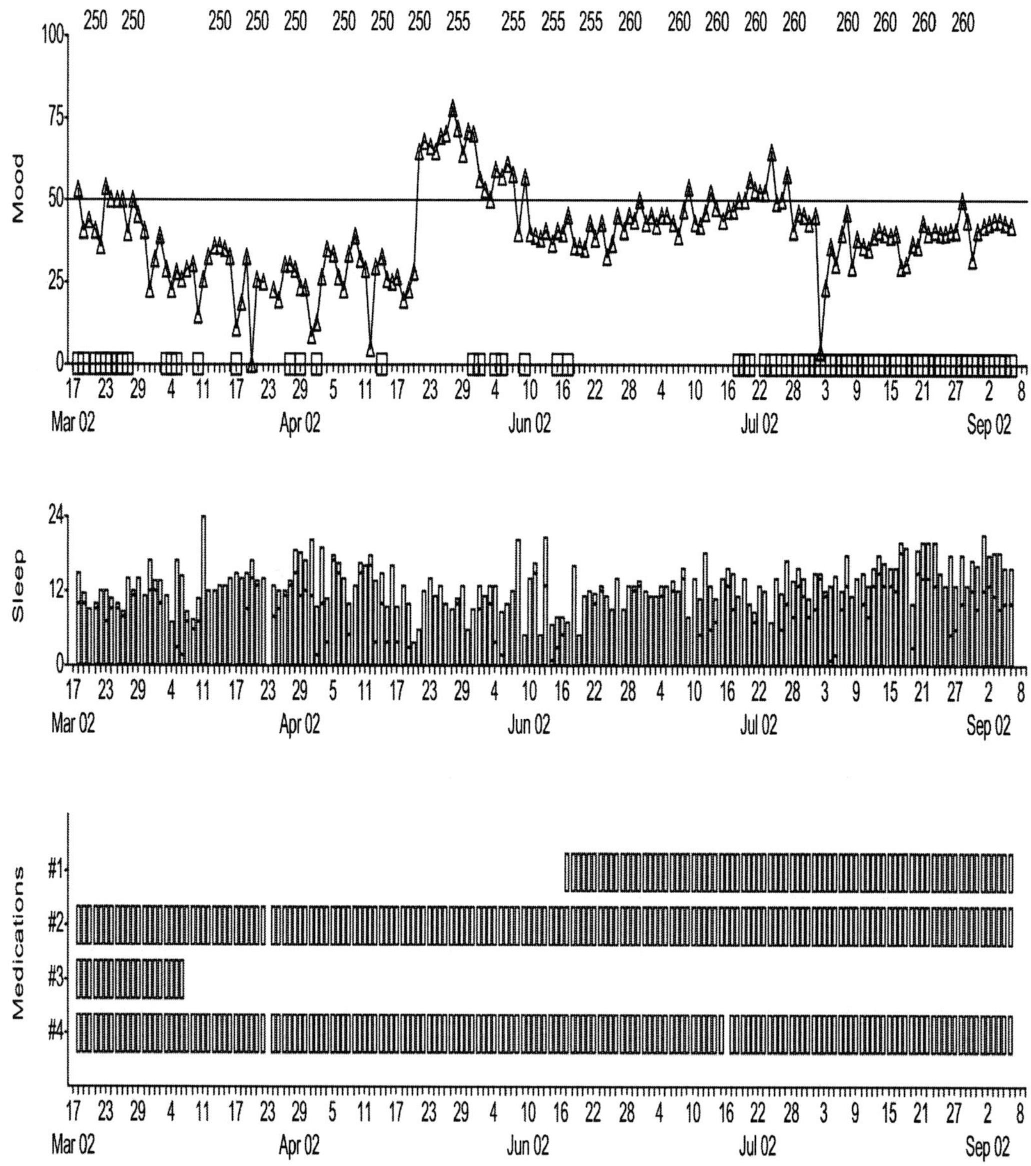

* Color charts are also available.

Drug Legend:

#1 Lithium Carbonate capsules 300 mg
#2 Depakene capsules (valproic acid) 250 mg
#3 Zoloft (sertraline) 50 mg
#4 Synthroid (levothyroxine – T4) 125 mcg

Figure 1. 180-Day Mood Chart From a 47 Year Old Male With Bipolar I Disorder*

ChronoRecord

The ChronoRecord data collection software presents the patient with large, colorful icons for mood, medication and sleep to facilitate data entry. For recording mood ChronoRecord uses a 100-unit visual analog scale between the extremes of mania and depression that the patient marks proportionately. During the patient's training, personal anchor points were set by the patient describing the most depressed and most manic states they ever experienced. Patients were told to describe the predominant features of the extreme state in addition to mood, and often depicted a mixed episode as the most manic experience. Instructions to the patient for mood entry were: 1) Enter a single rating that best describes your overall mood for the prior 24 hours, 2) Carefully review the entire 24-hour period, 3) Try not to let previous day influence how the current day is rated, 4) Calibrate the rating to the anchor points set during enrollment, and 5) Try to enter data at the same time every day. If a patient did not enter data on one day, they were instructed that it could be entered later, but noted as such. (The data collection software is available in German, English [for both North America and the U.K.] and Spanish, and is currently being translated into Polish and Norwegian.)

After one-half hour of training, the patients were given ChronoRecord software to install on their home computers. For a 3-month period, the patients entered mood, sleep, menstrual data, psychiatric medications, and life events daily. Weight was entered weekly (Figure 1). 80 of the 96 patients returned 8662 days of data by e-mail or diskette in over 240 data transfers without incident. The demographics for the 80 patients are shown in Table 1. The mean number of days of data returned by the 80 patients was 114.7 ± 32.3 SD (range 24-189 days). For mood entries, the mean percent of days missing was 6.1% ± 9.3 SD, equivalent to missing 7.3 days out of the 114.7 days. The primary reasons cited by those 16 patients who did not return any data during the study were: a) discontinued coming to the clinic, b) lost access to a computer, c) changed mind about charting and d) moved from the area.

Table 1. Characteristics of the Patients with Bipolar Disorder Using ChronoRecord Software (N=80)

Age (years)	38.67 ± 10.86 SD
N (%) Male: N (%) Female	35 (43.8%): 45 (56.3%)
BPI: BP II	58 (72.5%):22 (27.5%)
Onset (years)	23.0 ± 9.8
Years of illness	15.4 ± 10.7 SD
Single: Married: Divorced: Other	40%: 39%: 13.8%: 7.5%
Number of hospitalizations	2.43 ± 3.71 SD
N (%) Receiving government disability	(23) 28.8%
Years of education	15.2 ± 1.8 SD
Number of medications	3.76 ± 1.82 SD
Taking mood stabilizer Y: N	73 (91.3%): 7 (8.8%)
5 or more hospitalizations (%)	(23) 28.8%

RESULTS

Validation Study

The validation study [22] compared self-reported ChronoRecord mood ratings with clinician mood ratings on HAMD and YMRS, and self-reported ratings on the paper-based Beck Depression Inventory (BDI). [23] To assess concurrent validity, the ratings for the same date at 4 visits over the 3-month study period were evaluated using Pearson correlation, linear regression and general linear mixed model analyses. The Pearson correlation coefficient between HAMD and ChronoRecord was -0.683 ($p < .001$), between BDI and ChronoRecord was -0.673 ($p < .001$) and between YMRS and ChronoRecord was 0.395 ($p < .001$). Both the results of estimating a linear regression and a general linear mixed model that includes a patient factor were significant and remarkably consistent. The strong correlation coefficient together with the results of the regression and mixed model showed concurrent validity for HAMD. YMRS was not validated with ChronoRecord due to insufficient days when clinician YMRS ratings indicated mania in the outpatient sample.

77 (96%) of the 80 patients completed an evaluation questionnaire at the end of the study to rate their comfort with the ChronoRecord software on a 5-point scale (0=not usable, 5= excellent). The mean overall rating was 4.65.

The pattern of missing ChronoRecord mood data was analyzed and found to be missing completely at random (MCAR). There was no relationship among the missing data, the patients' demographic characteristics and the patients' mood, including the extremes of mania or depression.

Influence of Antidepressants

For the 80 patients who returned data for the 3-month period, the frequency of mood changes was compared between the 47 patients that took antidepressants and the 33 that did not. [24] (Figure 2). The distribution of time spent in mood categories (normal, depressed, hypomanic/manic) differed significantly using the χ^2 statistic. Patients taking antidepressants were depressed more frequently (29.0% vs 13.8%) ($p<.001$). The mean switches from depression to mania for those taking (0.80%) or not taking antidepressants (0.37%) were compared by t-test and no significant difference was found ($p=.152$). The percentage of depressed-to-manic switches was independent of the diagnosis of bipolar I (0.6%) or II disorder (0.8%) using a t-test ($p=.677$). Most of the depressive symptoms experienced by both groups were mild, similar to the residual or inter-episode depressive symptoms reported in other longitudinal studies of bipolar disorder. [25, 26, 27]

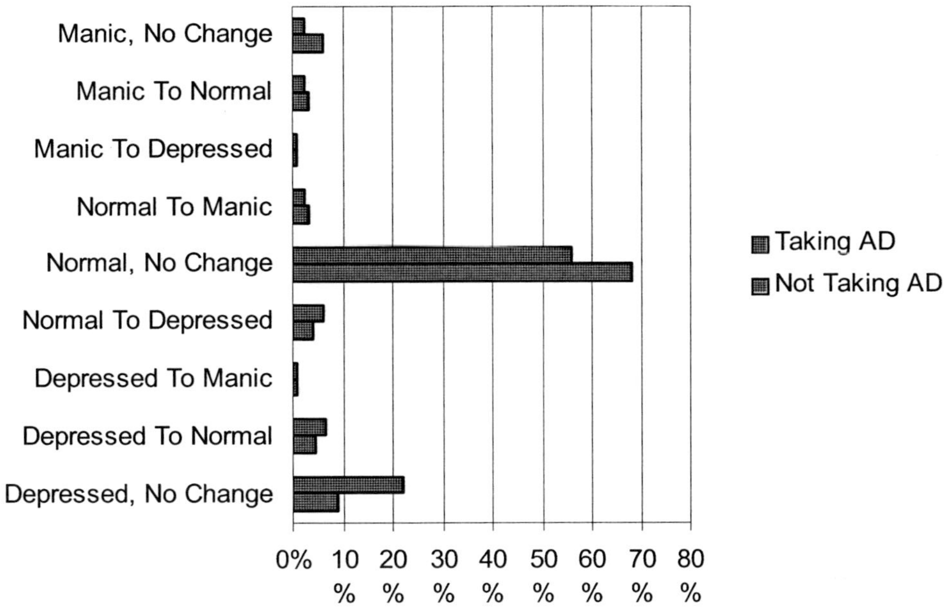

Figure 2. Distribution Of All Mood Category Switches For The Groups Taking (N=47; 4822 days) Or Not Taking (N=33; 3543 days) Antidepressants (p<.001)

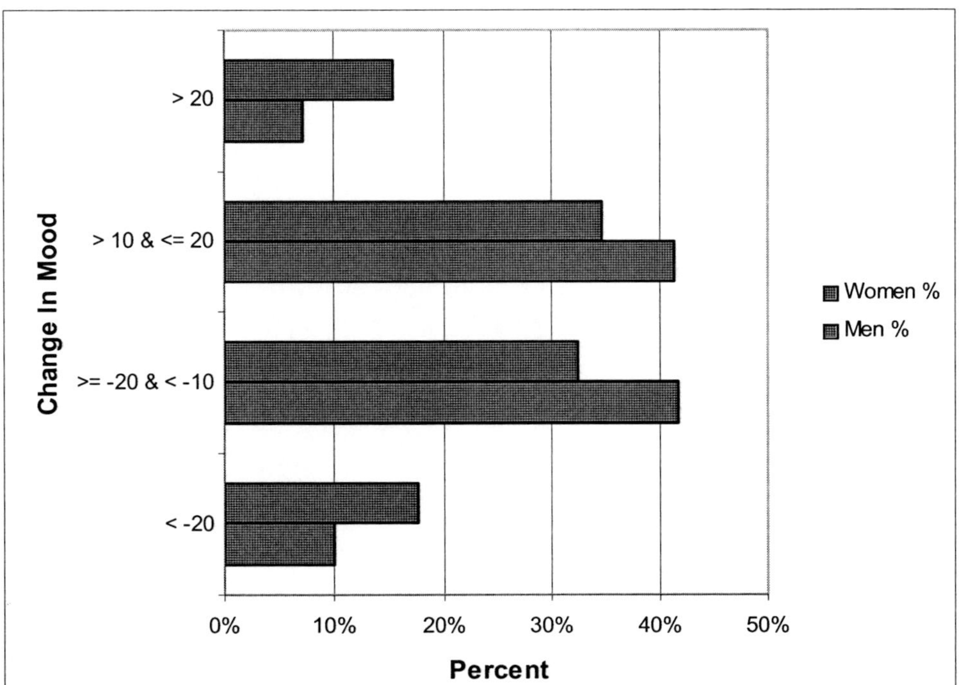

Figure 3. Distribution Of All Mood Changes Greater Than 10 on a 100-unit Scale Between Men (N=35; 3483 days) and Women (N=45; 5179 days) (p<.001)

Gender Differences in Mood Patterns

Of the 80 patients returning data, 3483 days of data were received from 35 men and 5179 days from 45 women. [28] Women were depressed more frequently than men (29.2% vs 17.6%) using a t-test (p=.046). When the severity of depressed symptoms and manic were compared, using the χ^2 statistic, women had severe mood symptoms more frequently than did men (for depression: 17.1% vs 10.9%; for mania: 18.7% vs 3.2%) ($p<.001$). Women reported large mood fluctuations (greater than 20 in either direction on the 100-unit scale) more frequently than men (33.0% vs. 17.2%) using the χ^2 statistic (p=.001). (Figure 3) Out of the 31 pre-menopausal women, 12 (39%) reported long menstrual cycles, 3 (10%) had oligomenorrhea, and the majority, 20 (65%) reported significant mood changes across the menstrual cycle when the mean mood in the first 7 days of the menstrual cycle was compared with the mean mood in the last 7 days. Eight women (26%) had significant mood changes in more than one cycle. However, as with prior findings, there was no pattern or consistent direction to the mood changes associated with the menstrual cycle. [29, 30]

Discussion

To our knowledge, ChronoRecord is the first automated system to employ patient friendly software on a home computer to aid the long-term monitoring of patients with mood disorder. Other examples of automated systems for reporting affective symptoms include the use of a palmtop computer to enter life charts, [31] employing an interactive voice response system over the telephone to administer the HAMD scales, [32] and using a PC to administer a modified version of the HAMD. [33] With the phenomenal worldwide growth in the percentage of households with personal computers the automation of longitudinal studies with software such as the ChronoRecord now becomes feasible. In 2002, 57.2% of households in Germany had a personal computer, an increase from 47.3% in 2000.[1] Similarly in 2001, 56% of U.S. households had at least one computer, and 88% of households with computers subscribe to the Internet. [35] With the Windows operating system now employed in greater than 85% of personal computers worldwide, [36] software for the public can be developed to run on a standard interface. Over the same time period, the cost of personal computers has dropped dramatically, with complete systems now costing less than $500 USD. In short, home computers are becoming standard household appliances throughout the industrialized world.

Prior studies have shown that patients will reliably report medication, sleep and mood on paper-based instruments. Patient self-reporting of medications taken has been shown to agree with physician records for a variety of medications including antidepressants, [37] hormone replacement therapy [38, 39] and oral contraceptives. [40] Paper diaries have been found to be a reliable method to obtain medication data in a variety of conditions including diabetes, [41] asthma [42, 43] and substance abuse. [44] The process of self-recording medications may even serve as a reminder that improves patient compliance. [45] Sleep research also

1 Statistisches Bundesamt Deutschland. Ausstattung privater Haushalte mit Informationstechnik – Duetschland. 2003. Available at: www.destatis.de/basis/d/evs/budtab2.htm. Accessed 6/22/2003.

makes extensive use of patient self-reporting instruments, [46, 47] including sleep diaries and questionnaires. [48, 49]

Multiple studies have shown that patients can reliably evaluate their own mood. A variety of paper tools have been validated with clinician ratings for self-reporting depression. [50, 51, 52] Self-reporting of mania poses an additional challenge in that many patients are prone to underestimate the severity of an episode, especially during the hypomanic phase. Nonetheless, although patients experiencing mania often have less insight into their illness than do those in other phases of bipolar disorder, [53] several self-reported paper-based rating scales have been validated against clinician ratings of mania and consistently correlate across severity levels. [54, 55, 56]

Results from validation of the self-reported Internal State Scale [57, 58] and recent investigations into the phenomenology of mania [59, 60] have found that the scores on both clinician and self-rating instruments are highly correlated with activation-related features and not with mood, suggesting that increased activity rather than elevated mood constitutes the core feature of mania. [61] In the ChronoRecord the charting of the patients sleep-wake activity easily tracks this distinction between activity and mood. Similarly, by personalizing the calibration of the anchor point for mania in the ChronoRecord a dysphoric mood does not confound the patient's reporting of the extreme of his or hers most manic state.

Evidence shows that patient compliance with reporting onto paper diaries does not vary with age, gender or race. [62, 63] Other studies, however, suggest that electronic diaries such as ChronoRecord offer a significant advance in effectiveness when compared with paper-based diaries. Thus in patients with chronic pain, 75-80% of the date and time entries in the paper diaries were falsified (backfilled prior to office visits) while the actual compliance rate with the electronic diary was 94%. [64] Patients with asthma [65] and chronic low back pain [66] were also found to be more compliant with electronic than with paper diaries. Several studies have directly investigated the patient perspective of computerized assessment tools to see if the use of technology created a feeling of general anxiety. Computers did not produce anxiety in both male and female patients with obsessive-compulsive disorder [67] or alcoholism [68] who had different educational backgrounds. All these studies reflect the broad acceptance we found for the automated ChronoRecord in patients suffering bipolar disorder.

Since much of the data involved in longitudinal studies of mood disorders is numerical or categorical, it is ideally suited for collection using computer technology. [69] Additionally, a further benefit of patients entering data directly into a computer is the elimination of the need to transpose the data into an electronic form for analysis. Such data entry is not only expensive, estimated to constitute 5-10% of the total project cost, [70] but also slow and error prone. Handwritten documents are the most difficult for a data entry staff to handle, requiring good procedures and operator intelligence to determine what is useful in a partially legible, incomplete or "noise filled" hand written document. In contrast, the ChronoRecord is designed to prevent some data entry errors, and requires the patient correction of others at the time of data collection. For example, ChronoRecord requires that the patient enter weight once a week before the mood data are accepted, requires confirmation (before the sleep entry is accepted) if the patient enters 0 hours of sleep and a similar validation before the medication entry is accepted if the patient records a large change in the number of pills being taken. As an added precaution ChronoRecord also prevents modification of previously entered data and of data entry a priori to a future date.

Another benefit of automated data collection systems is the reduction in missing data. In this ChronoRecord study in over 80% of patient less than 10% of the daily data were missing. In addition since data can be collected daily, rather than weekly or monthly, a small number of missing values typically have only a minimal impact on the statistical methods used in the analysis. Other common problems found in longitudinal data analysis, such as correlation between repeated measurements for individual patients and irregularly timed data, can be resolved using analytical techniques such as general estimating equations and general linear mixed models. [71, 72, 73] However, since both missing values and the strategies used for dealing with missing values can create a potential bias or loss or statistical power, [74, 75] and there are no universally applicable methods of handling missing values in clinical trials, [76] it is preferable to emphasize techniques, such as automating self-reporting, that can minimize the amount of missing data. [77]

An automated electronic system helps standardize data collection in studies at multiple centers, enabling the rapid development of large databases that are consistent and reliable. Also, in paper-based longitudinal studies, the time required for collecting and processing data often prevents their use in the immediate management of the patient, thus giving little reward for patient or researcher. [78] In contrast, automated systems can provide immediate, on-going feedback for both the study participant and the researcher, improving subject motivation to complete the protocol. This continued feedback available in an automated study also provides the timely use of the clinical information that is captured during a longitudinal study, [79] as is exemplified by the ChronoRecord mood charts (Figure 1). ChronoRecord charts can be printed on demand and used as decision support tools for clinicians and educational materials for patients.

In conclusion, we believe that the widespread acceptance of home based computer technology can be leveraged to improve the design of longitudinal studies in mood disorder. Automation of data collection may decrease missing data, improve data quality and expand the number of subjects participating in a standardized protocol across centers, with minimal increased cost.

References

[1] Peele PB, Xu Y, Kupfer DJ. Insurance expenditures on bipolar disorder: clinical and parity implications. *Am J Psychiatry*. 2003;160:1286-90.

[2] Murray CJL, Lopez AD. Global mortality, disability, and the contribution of risk factors: Global Burden of Disease Study. *Lancet* 1997;349:1436-1342.

[3] Angst J, Gamma A, Benazzi F, Ajdacic V, Eich D, Rossler W. Toward a re-definition of subthreshold bipolarity: epidemiology and proposed criteria for bipolar-II, minor bipolar disorders and hypomania. *J Affect Disord*. 2003;73:133-46.

[4] Tohen M, Waternaux CM, Tsuang MT. Outcome in Mania. A 4-year prospective follow-up of 75 patients utilizing survival analysis. *Arch Gen Psychiatry* 1990; 47: 1106-1111.

[5] Judd LL, Akiskal HS, Schettler PJ, Coryell W, Maser J, Rice JA, Solomon DA, Keller MB. The comparative clinical phenotype and long term longitudinal episode course of bipolar I and II: a clinical spectrum or distinct disorders? *J Affect Disord* 2003; 73: 19-32

[6] Judd LL, Akiskal HS, Schettler PJ, Coryell W, Endicott J, Maser JD, Solomon DA, Leon AC, Keller MB. A prospective investigation of the natural history of the long-term weekly symptomatic status of bipolar II disorder. *Arch Gen Psychiatry* 2003; 60: 261-269.

[7] Müller-Oerlinghausen, Berghöfer A, Bauer M. Bipolar disorder. *Lancet* 2002; 359: 241-247.

[8] Akiskal HS, Bourgeois ML, Angst J, Post R, Moller H, Hirschfeld R. Re-evaluating the prevalence of and diagnostic composition within the broad clinical spectrum of bipolar disorders. *J Affect Disord* 2000; 59 (Suppl 1):5 –30.

[9] Hirschfeld RM. Bipolar spectrum disorder: improving its recognition and diagnosis. *J Clin Psychiatry* 2001; 62 (Suppl 14): 5-9.

[10] Frye MA, Ketter TA, Leverich GS, Huggins T, Lantz C, Denicoff KD, Post RM. The increasing use of polypharmacotherapy for refractory mood disorders: 22 years of study. *J Clin Psychiatry* 2000; 61: 9-15.

[11] Levine J, Chengappa KN, Brar JS, Gershon S, Yablonsky E, Stapf D, Kupfer DJ. Psychotropic drug prescription patterns among patients with bipolar I disorder. *Bipolar Disord* 2000; 2: 120-130.

[12] Angst J, Sellaro R. Historical perspectives and natural history of bipolar disorder. *Biol Psychiatr* 2000; 48: 445-457.

[13] Leverich GS, Nolen WA, Rush AJ, McElroy SL, Keck PE, Denicoff KD, Suppes T, Altshuler LL, Kupka R, Kramlinger KG, Post RM. The Stanley Foundation Bipolar Treatment Outcome Network. I. Longitudinal methodology. *J Affect Disord* 2001; 67: 33-44.

[14] Sachs, G Step-BP Blank Mood Chart, Available at *www.manicdepressive.org/images/samplechart.gif* Accessed on 6/1/2003.

[15] Bauer MS, Crits-Christoph P, Ball WA, Dewees E, McAllister T, Alahi P, Cacciola J, Whybrow PC. Independent assessment of manic and depressive symptoms by self-rating. Scale characteristics and implications for the study of mania. *Arch Gen Psychiatry* 1991; 48: 807-812.

[16] Kobak KA, Greist JH, Jefferson JW, Katzelnick DJ, Mundt JC. New technologies to improve clinical trials. *J Clin Psychopharmacol* 2001; 21: 255-256.

[17] Wothke, W. Longitudinal and multi-group modeling with missing data. In: Little TD, Schnabel KU, Baumert J ed. - *Modeling Longitudinal and Multiple Group Data: Practical Issues, Applied Approaches and Specific Examples.* Mahwah, NJ: Lawrence Erlbaum Associates, 2000: 1-24.

[18] MS Bauer (1991) *op cit.*

[19] Young RC, Biggs, JT, Ziegler VE, Meyer DA. A rating scale for mania: reliability, validity and sensitivity. *Br J Psychiat* 1978; 133: 429-435.

[20] Hamilton M: A rating scale for depression. *J Neurol Neurosurg Psychiatry* 1960; 23: 56-62.

[21] Sheehan DV, Lecrubier Y, Sheehan KH, Amorim P, Janavs J, Weiller E, Hergueta T, Baker R, Dunbar GC. The Mini-International Neuropsychiatric Interview (M.I.N.I.): the development and validation of a structured diagnostic psychiatric interview for DSM-IV and ICD-10. *J Clin Psychiatry* 1998; 59 (Suppl 20): 22-33.

[22] Bauer M, Grof P, Gyulai L, Rasgon N, Glenn T, Whybrow PC. *Using Technology to Improve Longitudinal Studies: Self-Reporting in Bipolar Disorder*. In press (Bipolar Disorders).

[23] Beck AT. Beck *Depression Inventory*. Harcourt Brace & Company, San Antonio 1996.

[24] Bauer M, Rasgon N, Grof P, Altshuler L, Gyulai L, Glenn T, Whybrow PC. *Mood changes related to antidepressants in patients with bipolar disorder*. Submitted manuscript.

[25] Judd LL, Akiskal HS, Schettler PJ, Endicott J, Maser J, Solomon DA, Leon AC, Rice JA, Keller MB. The long-term natural history of the weekly symptomatic status of bipolar I disorder. *Arch Gen Psychiatry* 2002; 59: 530-537.

[26] Benazzi F. Prevalence and clinical correlates of residual depressive symptoms in bipolar II disorder. *Psychother Psychosom* 2001; 70: 232-238.

[27] Keitner GI, Solomon DA, Ryan CE, Miller IW, Mallinger A, Kupfer DJ, Frank E. Prodromal and residual symptoms in bipolar I disorder. *Compr Psychiatry* 1996; 37: 362-267.

[28] Rasgon NL Bauer M, Grof P, Gyulai L, Elman S, Glenn T, Whybrow PC. *Gender-specific Mood Changes in Patients With Bipolar Disorder*. Submitted manuscript.

[29] Rasgon NL, Bauer M, Glenn T, Elman S, Whybrow PC: Menstrual Cycle Related Mood Changes In Women With Bipolar Disorder. *Bipolar Disord* 2003; 5: 48-52.

[30] Leibenluft E, Ashman SB, Feldman-Naim S, Yonkers, KA. Lack of relationship between menstrual cycle phase and mood in a sample of women with rapid cycling bipolar disorder. *Biol Psychiatr* 1999; 46: 577-580.

[31] Scharer LO, Hartweg V, Valerius G, Graf M, Hoern M, Biedermann C, Walser S, Boensch A, Dittmann S, Forsthoff A, Hummel B, Grunze H, Walden J. Life charts on a palmtop computer: first results of a feasibility study with an electronic diary for bipolar patients. *Bipolar Disord* 2002;4 (Suppl 1): 107-108.

[32] Kobak KA, Greist JH, Jefferson JW, Mundt JC, Katzelnick DJ. Computerized assessment of depression and anxiety over the telephone using interactive voice response. *MD Comput* 1999; 16: 64-68.

[33] Carr AC, Ancill RJ, Ghosh A, Margo A. Direct assessment of depression by microcomputer. A feasibility study. *Acta Psychiatr Scand* 1981; 64: 415-422.

[34] Statistisches Bundesamt Deutschland. Ausstattung privater Haushalte mit Informationstechnik – Duetschland. 2003. Available at: *www.destatis.de/basis/d/evs/budtab2.htm*. Accessed 6/22/2003.

[35] U.S. Department of Commerce, *Economics and Statistics Administration and National Telecommunications and Information Administration. A nation online: how Americans are expanding their use of the Internet*. February 2002.

[36] Woodhead B. Computer Reseller News; 1999; Nov 17. Available at: www.itnews.com.au/story.cfm?id=507. *Accessed* 10/28/2002.

[37] Cotterchio M, Kreiger N, Darlington G, Steingart A. Comparison of self-reported and physician-reported antidepressant medication use. *Ann Epidemiol* 1999; 9: 283-289.

[38] Goodman MT, Nomura AM, Wilkens LR, Kolonel LN. Agreement between interview information and physician records on history of menopausal estrogen use. *Am J Epidemiol* 1990; 131: 815-825.

[39] Jain MG, Rohan TE, Howe GR. Agreement of self-reported use of menopausal hormone replacement therapy with physician reports. *Epidemiology* 1999; 10: 260-263.

[40] Nischan P, Ebeling K, Thomas DB, Hirsch U. Comparison of recalled and validated oral contraceptive histories. *Am J Epidemiol* 1993; 138: 697-703.

[41] Gonder-Frederick LA, Julian DM, Cox DJ, Clarke WL, Carter WR. Self-measurement of blood glucose. Accuracy of self-reported data and adherence to recommended regimen. *Diabetes Care* 1988; 11: 579-585.

[42] Malo JL, L'Archeveque J, Trudeau C, d'Aquino C, Cartier A. Should we monitor peak expiratory flow rates or record symptoms with a simple diary in the management of asthma? *J Allergy Clin Immunol* 1993; 91: 702-709.

[43] Gong H Jr, Simmons MS, Clark VA, Tashkin DP. Metered-dose inhaler usage in subjects with asthma: comparison of Nebulizer Chronolog and daily diary recordings. *J Allergy Clin Immunol* 1988; 82: 5-10.

[44] Weiss RD, Najavits LM, Greenfield SF, Soto JA, Shaw SR, Wyner D. Validity of substance use self-reports in dually diagnosed outpatients. *Am J Psychiatr* 1998; 155: 127-128.

[45] van Berge Henegouwen MT, van Driel HF, Kasteleijn-Nolst Trenite DG. A patient diary as a tool to improve medicine compliance. *Pharm World Sci* 1999; 21: 21-24.

[46] Gehrman P, Matt GE, Turingan M, Dinh Q, Ancoli-Israel S. Towards an understanding of self-reports of sleep. *J Sleep Res* 2002; 11: 229-236.

[47] Petit L, Azad N, Byszewski A, Sarazan FF, Power B. Non-pharmacological management of primary and secondary insomnia among older people: review of assessment tools and treatments. *Age Ageing* 2003; 32: 19-25.

[48] Backhaus J, Junghanns K, Broocks A, Riemann D, Hohagen F. Test-retest reliability and validity of the Pittsburgh Sleep Quality Index in primary insomnia. *J Psychosom Res* 2002; 53: 737-740.

[49] Monk TH, Reynolds CF 3D, Kupfer DJ, Buysse DJ, Coble PA, Hayes AJ, Machen MA, Petrie SR, Ritenour AM. The Pittsburgh Sleep Diary. *J Sleep Res* 1994; 3: 111-120.

[50] Denicoff KD, Leverich GS, Nolen WA, Rush AJ, McElroy SL, Keck PE, Suppes T, Altshuler LL, Kupka R, Frye MA, Hatef J, Brotman MA, Post RM. Validation of the prospective NIMH-Life-Chart Method (NIMH-LCM-p) for longitudinal assessment of bipolar illness. *Psychol Med* 2000; 30: 1391-1397.

[51] Carroll BJ, Feinberg M, Smouse PE, Rawson SG, Greden JF. The Carroll rating scale for depression. I. Development, reliability and validation. *Br J Psychiatry* 1981; 138: 194-200.

[52] Rush AJ, Gullion CM, Basco MR, Jarrett RB, Trivedi MH. The Inventory of Depressive Symptomatology (IDS): psychometric properties. *Psychol Med* 1996; 26: 477-486.

[53] Dell'Osso L, Pini S, Cassano GB, Mastrocinque C, Seckinger RA, Saettoni M, Papasogli A, Yale SA, Amador XF. Insight into illness in patients with mania, mixed mania, bipolar depression and major depression with psychotic features. *Bipolar Disord* 2002; 4: 315-322.

[54] KD Denicoff (2000) *op cit.*

[55] Altman EG, Hedeker D, Peterson JL, Davis JM. The Altman Self-Rating Mania Scale. *Biol Psychiatr* 1997; 42: 948-955.

[56] Shugar G, Schertzer S, Toner BB, Di Gasbarro I. Development, use, and factor analysis of a self-report inventory for mania. *Compr Psychiatry* 1992; 33: 325-331.

[57] MS Bauer (1991) *op cit.*

[58] Bauer MS, Vojta C, Kinosian B, Altshuler L, Glick H. The Internal State Scale: replication of its discriminating abilities in a multisite, public sector sample. *Bipolar Disord* 2000; 2: 340-346.

[59] Cassidy F, Murry E, Forest K, Carroll BJ. Signs and symptoms of mania in pure and mixed episodes. *J Affect Disord* 1998; 50: 187-201.

[60] Akiskal HS, Hantouche EG, Bourgeois ML, Azorin JM, Sechter D, Allilaire JF, Chatenet-Duchene L, Lancrenon S. Toward a refined phenomenology of mania: combining clinician-assessment and self-report in the French EPIMAN study. *J Affect Disord* 2001; 67: 89-96.

[61] Bauer MS (1991) *op cit.*

[62] MT van Berge Henegouwen (1999) *op cit.*

[63] Kraag GR, Gordon DA, Menard HA, Russell AS, Kalish GH. Patient compliance with tenoxicam in family practice. *Clin Ther* 1994; 16: 581-593.

[64] Stone AA, Shiffman S, Schwartz JE, Broderick JE, Hufford MR. Patient compliance with paper and electronic diaries. *Control Clin Trials* 2003; 24: 182-199.

[65] Hyland ME, Kenyon CA, Allen R, Howarth P. Diary keeping in asthma: comparison of written and electronic methods. *BMJ* 1993; 306: 487-489.

[66] Jamison RN, Raymond SA, Levine JG, Slawsby EA, Nedeljkovic SS, Katz NP. Electronic diaries for monitoring chronic pain: 1-year validation study. *Pain.* 2001 Apr;91(3):277-85.

[67] Baer L, Brown-Beasley MW, Sorce J, Henriques AI. Computer-assisted telephone administration of a structured interview for obsessive-compulsive disorder. *Am J Psychiatry.* 1993 Nov;150(11):1737-8.

[68] Bendtsen P, Timpka T. Acceptability of computerized self-report of alcohol habits: a patient perspective. *Alcohol Alcohol* 1999;34:575-80.

[69] Burt T, IsHak WW. Use of technology in outcome measurement. In: IsHak, WW, Burt T, Sederer LI, (Eds). *Outcome measurememt in psychiatry. A critical review.* Washington, DC: APA; 2002: 383-391.

[70] DeMarco T. *Controlling Software Projects: Management, Measurements and Estimates,* New York: Prentice-Hall: 1982.

[71] Cnaan A, Laird NM, Slasor P. Using the general linear mixed model to analyse unbalanced repeated measures and longitudinal data. *Stat Med* 1997; 30: 2349-2380.

[72] Albert PS. Longitudinal data analysis (repeated measures) in clinical trials. *Stat Med* 1999; 18: 1707-1732.

[73] Edwards LJ. Modern statistical techniques for the analysis of longitudinal data in biomedical research. *Pediatr Pulmonol* 2000; 30: 330-344.

[74] Touloumi G, Pocock SJ, Babiker AG, Darbyshire JH. Impact of missing data due to selective dropouts in cohort studies and clinical trials. *Epidemiology.* 2002 May;13:347-55.

[75] Unnebrink K, Windeler J. Intention-to-treat: methods for dealing with missing values in clinical trials of progressively deteriorating diseases. *Stat Med.* 2001 30;20:3931-46.

[76] The International Conference on Harmonization (ICH) *[http://www.ifpma.org/ich1.html].* Accessed 11/25/2003.

[77] K Unnebrink (2001) *op cit.*

[78] T Burt (2002) *op cit.*

[79] T Burt (2002) *op cit.*

In: Focus on Bipolar Disorder Research
Editor: Malcomb R. Brown, pp.15-35
ISBN 1-59454-059-4

Chapter 2

THE RECENT STUDIES ON THE ELECTRO-BIOCHEMICAL ASPECTS OF BIPOLAR DISORDER

Alagu Thiruvengadam
University of Maryland

ABSTRACT

The role of cations such as sodium, potassium, calcium and lithium in bipolar disorder has been studied extensively in the past. Ionic gradients exert significant influence on the neurons by affecting the resting membrane potentials, action potentials, neurotransmitter release, signaling and signal transduction. Clinical measurements show that the membrane potentials of leucocytes in bipolar patients are significantly hyperpolarized whereas they are slightly depolarized in euthymic patients on lithium. Calculations using the Goldman-Hodgkin-Katz equation show that lithium would depolarize the membrane potential. Hodgkin's circuit representing the neuronal membrane potentials and the ionic gradients confirm these calculations. Experimental data supporting these calculations are also reviewed. Action potentials in neurons are generally analyzed with the help of equivalent electric circuits. These circuits belong to a class of antiresonant parallel circuits. The specific circuits used by Hodgkin-Huxley and Cole are analyzed along with the basic circuit in this class. Comparison of these results with currently available electroencephalographic measurements shows that the basic circuit is the most suitable circuit for human neurons. This analysis leads to a non-dimensional parameter called excitability. Excitability is very useful in comparing epilepsy, mania and depression. It also helps in understanding the role of anti-convulsants in both epilepsy and in mania. Available experimental evidence in support of these theoretical results is also presented. It is further shown that the rate of neurotransmitter release is related to excitability. According to this analysis lithium reduces the excitability by reducing the membrane resistance. Experimental evidence shows that the resistance is related to the Na, K-ATPase activity. This relationship between NaK pump activity and excitability is called *electro-biochemical coupling*. Further research is needed to understand this coupling and its role in bipolar disorder leading to better diagnostic techniques and to the discovery of drug targets.

INTRODUCTION

Ever since John Cade discovered the efficacy of lithium as a mood stabilizer, a great deal of interest was devoted to the role of cations in bipolar disorder [1, 2, and 3]. Detailed measurements of sodium and potassium gradients across the cell membranes from bipolar patients were made. The cell maintains the homeostasis of the membrane potentials by controlling the sodium and potassium gradients with the help of the Na, K-ATPase enzyme which is also called the sodium pump. This led to the suggestion that the sodium pump is involved in the pathogenesis of bipolar disorder [4, 5]. Cation gradients play a significant role in the resting membrane potentials, action potentials, signaling and transduction in neurons. An understanding of this role is of great interest in bipolar disorder. The first systematic measurements of membrane potentials in leukocytes taken from bipolar patients, normal controls and euthymic patients on lithium were made by El-Mallakh et al. [6] in 1996. Thiruvengadam [7] calculated the effect of lithium on membrane potentials using Goldman-Hodgkin-Katz equations showing that lithium would depolarize the membrane potentials. The experimental results of El-Mallakh et al. [6] confirmed this result. The direct current circuit used by Hodgkin and Huxley [8] was also used to further confirm this result. Graf et al. [9], Adam-Vizi et al. [10] and Yonemura and Sato [11] conducted various experiments confirming that lithium would depolarize the membrane potentials.

The effect of lithium on action potentials has also been the subject of study by various investigators including Graf et al. [9], Ulrich et al. [12] and Thiruvengadam [13]. Hodgkin and Huxley [8] and Cole [14] used alternating current circuits to analyze their action potential measurements in squid giant axons. These circuits belong to a class of circuits called antiresonant parallel circuits. Thiruvengadam [13] used these circuits as well as a circuit which is basic to this class of circuits and called it the basic circuit. This analysis led to a non-dimensional parameter called excitability. The excitability consists of three basic electrical properties of the membrane namely the resistance, the conductance and the inductance. It is shown that lithium reduces the resistance of the membrane thereby reducing the excitability which in turn reduces the action potentials. The earlier measurements by Graf et al. [9] and Ulrich et al. [12] confirm this result. Furthermore, this analysis explains how anticonvulsants are the only effective mood stabilizers since epilepsy and mania are connected by excitability. Katz [15] showed that the probability of the release of vesicles containing the neurotransmitters is related to the action potentials. Since excitability controls the action potentials, the release rate is dependant on excitability. Thus, lithium plays a role on the release of neurotransmitters by altering the excitability.

Bonting and Caravaggio [16] measured the cation conductance in various membranes ranging from human erythrocytes to electric eels. They found that the conductance was directly proportional to Na, K-ATPase activity. Since conductance is the reciprocal of resistance, it follows that the resistance is inversely proportional to the sodium pump activity. Therefore excitability is a function of sodium pump activity. This relationship between excitability and sodium pump activity is called *electro-biochemical coupling.* As early as 1970, Singh [4] suggested that the defects in the Na pump might be the cause of this illness. El-Mallakh and Wyatt [5] proposed a Na, K-ATPase hypothesis which was supported by nearly 135 references. Looney and El-Mallakh [17] performed a Meta analysis which showed again that the Na pump activity is involved in bipolar disorder. Wood et al. [18] measured the ouabain binding sites and found that their densities were significantly reduced in the lymphocytes of bipolar patients. Cherry and Swann [19] studied the potassium uptake in cultured lymphoblasts taken from bipolar patients and this uptake was significantly lower. All these studies indicate that the Na pumps are indeed affected in bipolar patients and emphasize the need for further research in understanding the relationship between the excitability of the membrane and the Na pump activity.

LITHIUM AND MEMBRANE POTENTIAL

The voltage difference across the cell membrane is called the membrane potential. This potential difference is caused by the ionic gradients across the membrane. The primary contribution for this potential comes from sodium and potassium gradients. The cell maintains the homeostasis of this potential by controlling these gradients by means of an enzyme called Na, K-ATPase which is also known by other names including NaK pump and simply Na pump. This enzyme transports three ions of Na to the exterior of the cell and two ions of potassium to the interior of the cell. Since this transport takes place against the higher concentration of the ions, this enzyme is known as a pump. The cell membrane is generally negatively charged and hence it is said to be polarized. When it is excessively polarized it is called hyperpolarized. When it is less polarized it is said to be depolarized.

The earliest attempt to study the effect of lithium on membrane potential was made by Yonemura and Sato [11] in 1967 using frog muscle fibers immersed in Li Ringer solution. They found that lithium would depolarize the membrane after a few hours ranging from two to four hours. The next study was performed by Graf et al. [9] in 1983 using the membrane of the frog spinal chord motor neurons. They found that 15 m mol Li would depolarize the membrane with in 10 minutes. They also found that the intra cellular potassium would decrease during that time. Adam-Vizi et al. [10] confirmed this result in 1987 using rat cortex slices. In 1996, El-Mallakh et al. [6] reported the results of their investigations on hospitalized manic patients, matched normals and euthymic patients on lithium. The membrane potentials of leukocytes from hospitalized manic patients were significantly hyperpolarized while those of euthymic patients were slightly depolarized when compared with that of controls. Thiruvengadam [7] calculated the membrane potential of mammalian neurons using the Goldman-Hodgkin-Katz (G-H-K) equation and found that the addition of lithium would depolarize the membranes. The modified G-H-K equation with the addition of lithium is given by (see ref.7 for its derivation)

$$V = 62\log_{10}\frac{4.7 + \dfrac{P_{Li}}{P_{Na}}\dfrac{Li_0^+}{Na_0^+}}{100} \quad [1]$$

Where V = the membrane potential
P_{Li} =Permeability of lithium
P_{Na}=Permeability of sodium
Li_0 = extra cellular concentration of lithium
Na_0 = extra cellular concentration of sodium.

From this equation it follows that the membrane potential would depolarize with the addition of lithium [7].

LITHIUM AND MEMBRANE RESISTANCE

Hodgkin and Huxley [8] showed that the total conductance of the membrane is the algebraic sum of the contributions from the conductance of potassium ions, sodium ions and chlorine ions [Koester, 20]. If we add lithium as another conductor in the direct current (DC) circuit as shown in figure 1, the total conductance will increase because the algebraic sum of the conductance will increase. Since the resistance is the inverse of conductance, the resistance will decrease by the addition of lithium. Cole [21], as early as 1941, measured the electrical resistance of squid giant axon membrane in seawater environment. Following Cole, Guttmann [22] found that the resistance of membranes in nerve and muscle fibers of frogs decreased during the action of narcotics and other chemicals such as $MgCl_2$, $CaCl_2$, and $BaCl_2$. In spite of the large amount of literature on lithium, there is no direct measurement of the resistance of excitable membranes with lithium. It would be useful to collect such data in the future. Again figure 1 demonstrates that an increase in resistance will hyperpolarize the membrane potential and a decrease will depolarize it according to Ohm's law. This confirms the prediction of the G-H-K equation. Furthermore the significant result of this analysis is that lithium would decrease the resistance of the membrane.

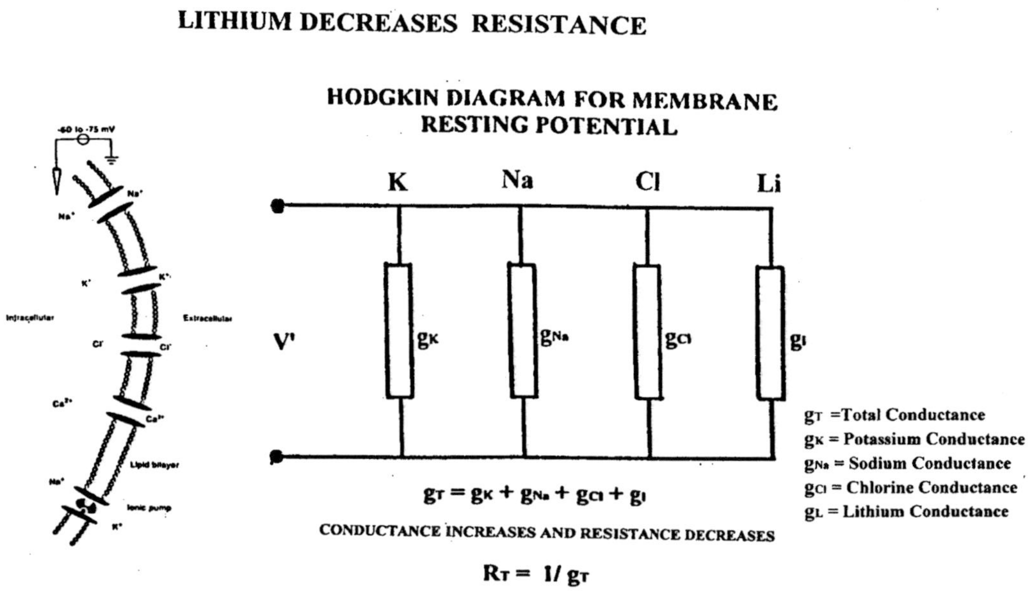

Figure 1. A direct current circuit is generally used to represent the membrane conductance. K, Na, Cl are the normal ions that give rise to the membrane resting potential. The total conductance is given by the algebraic sum of these three conductances. However, if lithium is added as an additional cation, then the total conductance will increase as shown in this figure. Since resistance is the reciprocal of conductance, the resistance will decrease by the addition of lithium.

Membrane Resistance and Excitability of Neurons

What role does the resistance of membranes play in bipolar disorder? In order to answer this question, let us analyze the electrical response of membranes. It is common practice in neuroscience to use equivalent electrical circuits for studying the currents in the membrane [23]. When the current and the voltage vary with time, as is the case with action potentials in excitable membranes, only alternating current (AC) circuits must be used. Hodgkin and Huxley [8] used the alternating current (AC) circuit shown in figure 2(a) in which the resistance and the capacitance are parallel to each other. Cole [3] used the AC circuit shown in figure 2(b) in which an inductance is added in series with the resistance. The capacitance is parallel to both of them. The reason for adding the inductance was that Cole consistently measured the inductance in all of his measurements and he could not ignore it. The above two AC circuits are special cases of a class of circuits known as parallel antiresonant AC circuits [24, 25]. The basic circuit among this class of circuits is shown in figure 2(c) in which the resistance, the inductance and the capacitance are all parallel to each other.

The response of these circuits to a train of input signals generated in the neuron can be analyzed using the electrical circuit theory as shown in the Appendix. From this analysis it can be shown that the excitability of the membrane is given by the following equation:

$$E_x = \frac{R^2 C}{L} \qquad [1]$$

Where E_x = Excitability
R = Resistance
ZC = Capacitance
And L = Inductance.

As shown in the Appendix, the available clinical data suggest that the basic circuit represents the human neurons.

Electrical signals produced in the neurons are amplified as action potentials and transmitted through the axon to its terminal called the synapse. These action potentials trigger the biochemical reactions responsible for the release of vesicles containing the neurotransmitters. An understanding of these reactions comes from the analysis of electrical circuits such as the basic circuit. The response of this circuit is shown in figure 3. According to this figure, the relative action potentials (y-axis) decrease with increasing relative frequencies (x-axis) up to a value of one and then increase with increasing relative frequencies. The relative action potential is a measure of how much the input signal is amplified. The relative frequency is the ratio of the frequency at which that particular action potential is transmitted to the resonant frequency of the neuron. Analyses of published clinical EEG data show that the resonant frequency is about 15 cycles per second in humans [26]. Most observed frequencies are less than this frequency. Frequencies above 30 cps are rare. Hence only the relative frequencies less than one are of great interest in this study. The relationship between the relative action potentials and the relative frequency depend upon the excitability of the neuron. The higher the excitability the higher is the relative action potential at a given relative frequency. This ability to magnify the action potentials decreases as the excitability decreases at the same frequency. For example the action potential may be amplified as much as 50 times at a relative frequency of 0.2 corresponding to an excitability of 100. On the other hand it would amplify only by a factor three at the same relative frequency corresponding to an excitability of one. This figure demonstrates how the relative action potentials depend significantly on the excitability which in turn is governed by the electrical properties of the membrane.

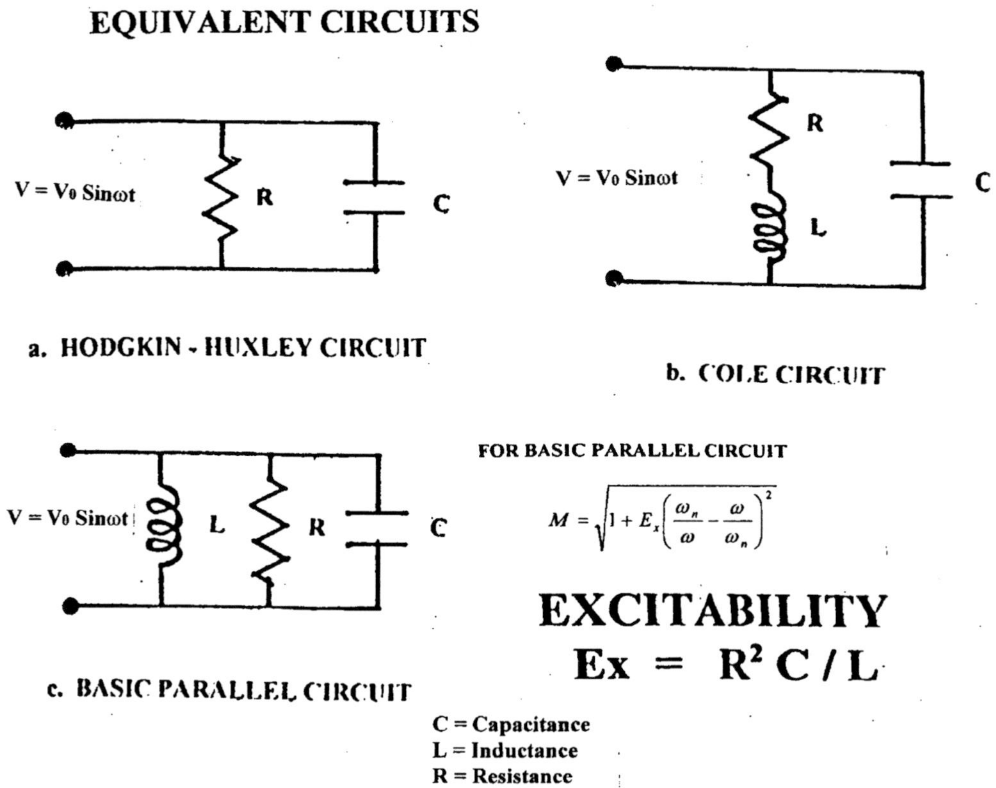

Figure 2. The alternating current (AC) circuits used in the analysis of the role of membrane resistance in the amplification of action potentials are shown in this figure. These circuits have been used by early pioneers in neuroscience such as Cole, Hodgkin and Huxley. 2(a) shows the AC circuit used by Hodgkin-Huxley to analyze their data obtained from giant axons of squids. The circuit in 2(b) was used by Kenneth Cole to calculate the inductance of the membranes of giant axons of squids. The basic parallel circuit, 2(c), is the fundamental circuit in this class of circuits known as antiresonant parallel circuits. The amplification of signals in the axon into action potentials is given by the equation for the basic circuit as shown in the inset. The excitability of the membrane controls the level of amplification at a specific frequency and is given by the square of the membrane resistance times the conductance divided by the inductance as shown in this figure.

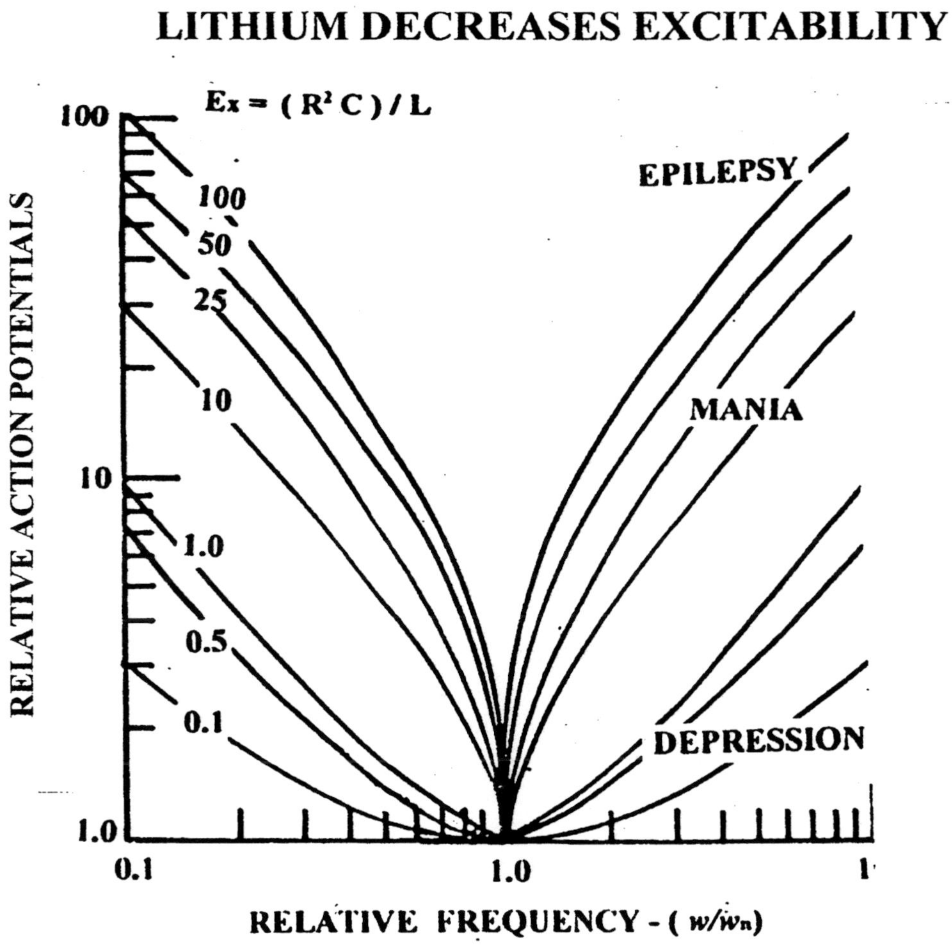

Figure 3. The relationship between the relative action potential and the relative frequency at various excitabilities is shown in this figure. (Refer the Appendix for the derivation). At a given excitability the relative action potentials decrease with increasing relative frequencies and then increase with increasing relative frequencies. This is the classic case of antiresonant response of this class of circuits. The excitability is the second parameter that controls the relative action potentials. As the excitability increases the relative action potentials also increase at a given relative frequency. The higher values of excitability represent epilepsy as evidenced by clinical EEG data. Excitabilities around one indicate normal controls. Mania and depression are on either side of normal controls. (Refer the Appendix for further discussion). Since resistance plays a large role in excitability, lithium also exerts a significant influence on the excitability through its effect on resistance. The efficacy of anticonvulsants in mood stabilization and epilepsy is also relevant to this figure.

The clinical EEG data from epileptic patients (Figure 8 in appendix) show that the excitabilities can be as high as 1000 in epileptic patients. The excitability would be in the range of one in babies (Figure 9 and ref.27). It is most likely that the excitability for normal adults would be in the same range. The evidence for mania comes from the fact that the addition of lithium decreases the membrane resistance as shown in figure 1. The decrease in resistance would decrease the excitability thereby decreasing the action potentials. Graf et al. [9] found that the action potentials in frog spinal chord neurons were reduced during lithium treatment. Ulrich et al. [12] noticed that the EEG amplitudes in normal volunteers decreased after ten days of lithium treatment. This is perhaps the mechanism by which lithium mediates the mania and stabilizes the mood. Goodwin and Jamison [1] as well as in several articles [2] summarize the vast majority of knowledge accumulated so far on the role of lithium in bipolar disorder. The additional evidence comes from the fact that some effective mood stabilizers are also anticonvulsants. Specifically Neaverson and Jefferson [28], Wood et al. [18] and Cherry and Swann [19] reported that the Na, K-ATPase activity was normalized during lithium therapy. Although these data indirectly support the present analysis, it would be useful to collect direct experimental evidence connecting excitability and lithium effects. The data that directly support the concept of excitability come from the electro encephalographic (EEG) data from epileptic patients as discussed in the appendix. The electrodes used in vagus nerve stimulation technique offer an opportunity to collect such data [29]. At lower excitabilities less than one the relative action potentials are less than one. This suggests that the reported efficacy of vagus nerve stimulation is due to the resetting of the excitabilities in depressive patients. It is also suggested that this is the mechanism of action of electro convulsive therapy in depressive patients. The next task is to show how the rate of release of vesicles containing the neurotransmitters is related to the excitability.

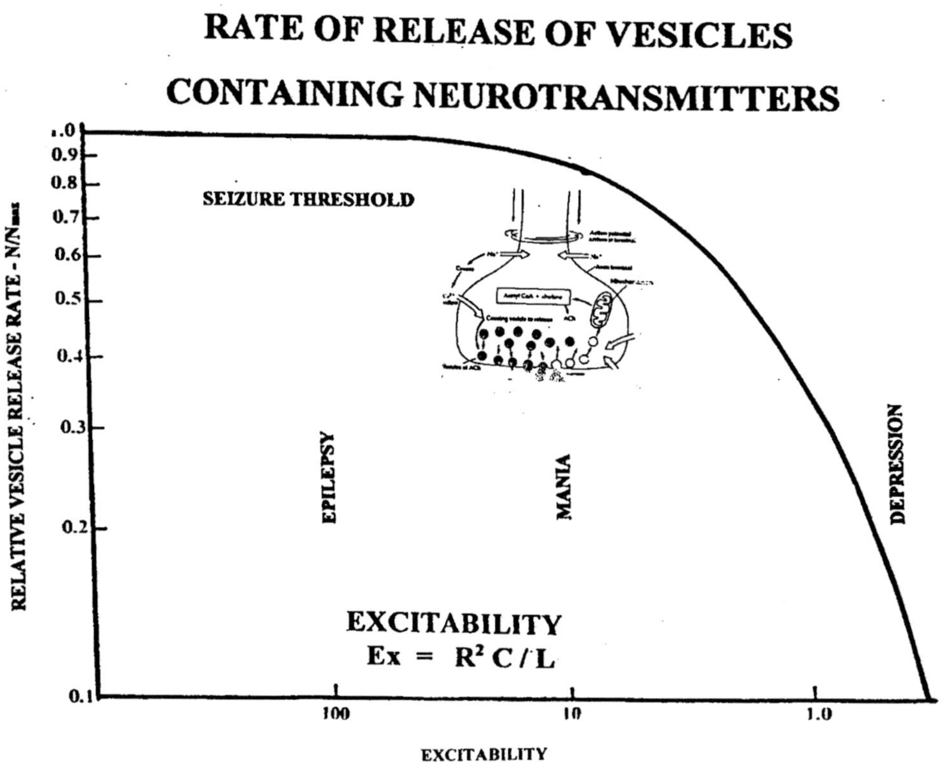

Figure 4. The relative rate release of vesicles as a function of excitability is shown in this figure. At higher excitabilities the relative rate of release is close to 100 percent. This would explain the seizures. At excitabilities less than ten, the release rate decreases rapidly. At excitabilities less than one, the release rates approach ten percent. Further clinical research is needed to determine the threshold excitabilities for seizures, mania and depression.

EXCITABILITY AND THE RATE OF RELEASE OF VESICLES

Katz [15] showed that the voltage pulses (action potentials) arriving at the axon terminal trigger the release of vesicles containing neurotransmitters. He used several statistical methods to calculate the probability of release of these vesicles (see also 30). Let us use a simple Poisson distribution to demonstrate how excitability is related to the rate of release of vesicles. Since the excitability controls the action potentials at a given frequency (Figure 3), let us use the excitability in the Poisson distribution as shown below:

$$N = N_{\max} e^{E_x} \qquad [2]$$

Where N = Number of vesicles released per unit time,
N_{max} = Maximum possible number released per unit time
And E_x = Excitability.

A plot of the relative rate of release as a function of the excitability is shown in figure 4. The relative rate decreases slowly with decreasing excitability and then decreases rapidly at excitabilities less than 10. This figure supports the prevailing view that the excessive release of neurotransmitters leads to seizures and the lack of sufficient release rates lead to depression. The threshold seizure values can be assigned either as threshold excitability or as threshold release rate. Clinical research is needed to determine these thresholds.

EXCITABILITY AND N, K-ATPASE ACTIVITY

It follows from these discussions that the membrane resistance plays a very important role in the excitability of neurons. Bonting and Caravaggio [16] measured the cation flux across six different biological membranes ranging from electric eels to human erythrocytes as a function of the Na, K-ATPase activity and presented their data in the form of a table. These data are shown in figure 5. As can be seen in this figure, the cation conductance is directly proportional to the enzyme activity over a 25000-fold range. This result can be stated as:

Conductance = m A

Where A is the Na, K-ATPase activity and m is the proportionality constant. Since conductance is the reciprocal of resistance:

$$\frac{1}{R} = mA \qquad (3)$$

Equations [1] and [3] show that the electrical excitability and the activity of the biochemical enzyme are coupled together. Changes in the Na, K-ATPase activity lead to changes in membrane resistance, which in turn affect the excitability of neurons. This is called the *electro-biochemical coupling*. As discussed earlier, Neaverson and Jefferson [28], Wood et al. [18], Cherry and Swann [19], and Looney and El-Mallakh [17] found that the Na,

K-ATPase activity is decreased during mania. According to equation [3], the decrease in activity would increase the resistance thereby increasing the excitability as the square of the resistance. (See equation [1]]. Graf et al. [9] measured the action potentials in frog spinal chord motor neurons before and after immersion in lithium chloride solution and showed that the lithium decreased the action potential. This experiment offers direct evidence that lithium reduces the excitability.

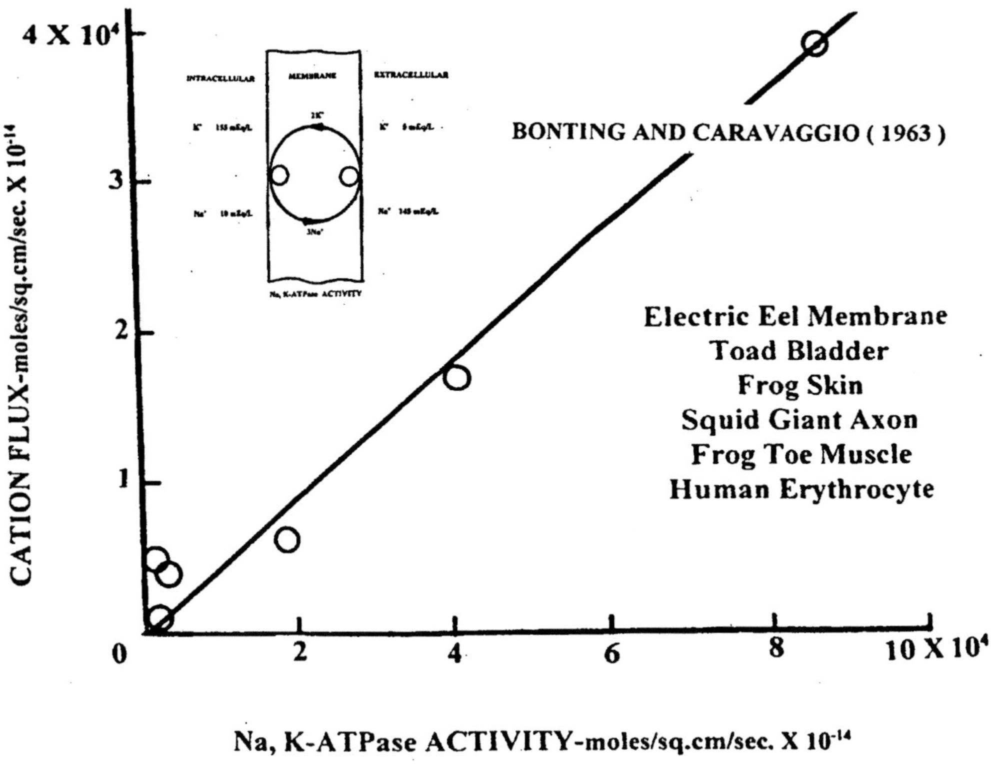

Figure 5. Bonting-Caravaggio data show a linear correlation between the cation conductance and the NA, K-ATPase activity over a 25,000 fold range. This relationship shows a quantitative link between biochemical activity and electrical excitability.

Further evidence comes from clinical EEG studies of patients with affective disorders. Kano et al. [31] studied 44 patients with affective disorders and 44 normal controls. They found that inter hemispheric and intra hemispheric relationships were disturbed with patients with affective disorders. Ulrich et al. [12] studied 11 healthy volunteers before and after ten days of lithium administration and two weeks after discontinuation. They found that the EEG amplitudes decreased after 10 days of lithium treatment. This is additional evidence that lithium indeed reduces the action potentials. Similar studies by Small et al. [32] found significant slowing of dominant background EEG frequencies occurring with lithium therapy, which did not entirely resolve in the latter two to five days after lithium withdrawal. Additional systematic research is needed to explore the coupling between the excitability and the biochemical enzyme activity.

Na, K-ATPase Activity and Bipolar Disorder

The importance of Na pump enzyme in bipolar disorder was suggested by Singh [4] as early as 1970. Since then many investigators studied this enzyme in bipolar patients. El-Mallakh and Wyatt [5] formulated a Na, K-ATPase activity hypothesis of bipolar disorder after reviewing well over 130 research papers. Looney and El-Mallakh [17] performed a Meta analysis of these results and concluded that the Na pump activity was significantly related to bipolar disorder. The sodium and potassium gradients, the membrane potential, the resistance of the membrane and the neurotransmitter release are all related to this enzyme activity. The Na, K-ATPase enzyme consists of two subunits called alpha and beta. Each of these subunits is composed of three isoforms ($\alpha1$, $\alpha2$, $\alpha3$ and $\beta1$, $\beta2$, $\beta3$]. These isoforms play important roles in the differences in the functional properties and activities of the enzyme in different tissues [Geering, 33] as reflected in various diseases including renal malfunction, hypertension and diabetes. Rose et al. [34] found a significant reduction in the abundance of alpha2 isoform in postmortem temporal cortex gray matter from individuals suffering from bipolar disorder. Vasarhelyi et al. [35] studied the erythrocyte Na pump subunit isoforms in preterm and term neonates and found that the alpha 1 and the beta 2 isoforms were developmentally regulated. It would be interesting to study these isoforms in bipolar patients to see if the isoform abundance is any different from that of controls.

Pedemonte et al. [36] studied the regulation of Na pump activity by protein kinase C (PKC) and found that the amino acid(s) located at the alpha subunit NH2 terminus participate in the regulation of the Na pump activity by PKC. The importance of PKC in bipolar patients has been investigated by Manji et al. [37] and Lenox et al. [38]. The sodium pump activity and associated regulatory mechanisms are directly reflected in the potential, the resistance and the excitability of the membrane. It is suggested that such measurements using erythrocytes and lymphocytes from bipolar patients would throw more light into the pathogenesis of bipolar disorder.

An attempt has been made to apply some of the basic neuroscience ideas to understand a complex illness such as bipolar disorder. Further research is needed to relate the effects of anticonvulsants such as sodium valproate, carbamazepine, lamotrigine, topiramate and gabapentin with the excitability of neurons. Direct measurement of membrane potentials and resistance with different levels of lithium would be useful using the methods of Ward et al. [39]. Direct measurement of excitability using vagus nerve stimulation electrodes would provide data from humans with the illness at different levels of mood stabilizers [29].

Conclusions

Calculations using the Goldman-Hodgkin-Katz equation indicate that the membrane potential would be depolarized by the addition of lithium. Similarly, an analysis of the direct current circuit for the membrane resting potential shows that the addition of lithium would reduce the electrical resistance of the membrane and thereby depolarizes the membrane if the lithium acts as a cation in addition to potassium and sodium. A non-dimensional parameter called the excitability is derived from the study of the alternating current circuits that are generally used as equivalent circuits representing the action potentials of the membranes. The excitability is given by the square of the resistance times the capacitance divided by the inductance of the membrane. The excitability governs the amplification of the potentials in the membrane at a given frequency. Since the addition of lithium would reduce the resistance, it would also reduce the excitability of the membrane thereby reducing the potentials. It is also shown that the rate of release of vesicles containing the neurotransmitters is related to the excitability. These results offer a possible explanation of how lithium mediates mania. Available experimental data indicate that the resistance is inversely proportional to the Na, K-ATPase activity. Thus it is shown that the enzyme inhibition would increase the excitability of the neurons. This would support the available clinical data. Several experimental studies reported in scientific literature support these results. Further research is needed to understand the mechanisms by which the Na pump activity is decreased in bipolar patients.

APPENDIX

Analysis of the Equivalent Electrical Circuits

The pioneers in neuroscience used equivalent electrical circuits to understand their measurements of membrane potentials and action potentials. The voltage response of the three AC circuits shown in figure 2 may be analyzed as follows. Since the Hodgkin-Huxley circuit and Cole circuit are special cases of the basic circuit we will start with this circuit. The equation for impedance is given by [See [24 and 25)]:

$$Z = \frac{1}{\sqrt{\frac{1}{R^2} + \left[\frac{1}{X_L} - \frac{1}{X_C}\right]^2}} \quad [1]$$

$$V = V_0 Sin\omega t \quad [2]$$

Where R = the membrane resistance,
Z = the membrane impedance
$X_L = \omega L$ = the inductive reactance,
ω = the angular frequency of voltage and current,
L = the inductance of the membrane,
C = the capacitance of the membrane,
$X_C = 1/\omega C$ = the capacitive reactance of the membrane,
V_0 = the maximum voltage at t=0 in $V=V_0 \sin\omega t$ and
t = time

The natural frequency of the circuit is given by:

$$\omega_n = \frac{1}{\sqrt{LC}} \quad [3]$$

Using equation [3] in [1] and rearranging, we get

$$Z = \frac{R}{\sqrt{1 + E_x \left(\frac{\omega_n}{\omega} - \frac{\omega}{\omega_n} \right)^2}} \qquad [4]$$

Where

$$E_x = \frac{R^2 C}{L} \qquad [5]$$

Let us call R/Z ratio as M. Then

$$M = \sqrt{1 + E_x \left(\frac{\omega_n}{\omega} - \frac{\omega}{\omega_n} \right)^2} \qquad [6]$$

E_x is called the *Excitability* of the membrane since it gives the combination of the electrical properties of the membrane indicating how excitable the membrane is. The amplification of the currents is larger at higher excitabilities at a given frequency. Cole [2) called the inverse of *excitability* “Damping”. M is the factor by which the input currents are magnified as a result of the impedance of the anti-resonant parallel circuits. Since the current is directly proportional to the voltage as per Ohm’s law, M also represents the amplification of action potentials and therefore it is called the *Relative Action Potential.* The relationship between the relative action potentials and the relative frequency ω/ω_n is plotted in figure 3 for various values of the excitability for the basic parallel circuit.

The Hodgkin-Huxley circuit (figure 2a) is a special case of the basic circuit in which there is no inductance. For this circuit, the impedance is given by [see ref.24]:

$$Z = \frac{1}{\sqrt{\frac{1}{R^2} + \frac{1}{X_C{}^2}}} = \frac{R}{\sqrt{1 + \left(\frac{R}{X_C} \right)^2}} \qquad [7]$$

For this case:

$$M = \sqrt{1 + (\omega RC)^2} \qquad [8]$$

Figure 6 shows a plot of this equation [8].

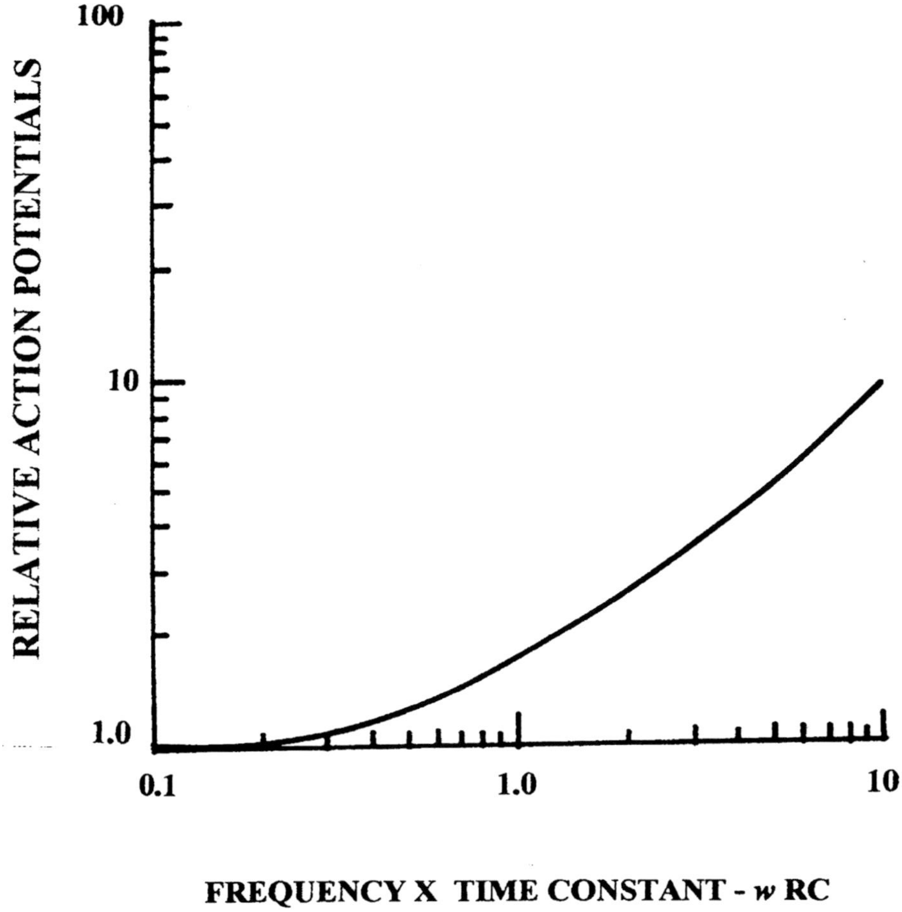

Figure 6. This figure shows the relative action potentials as a function of the relative frequency for the Hodgkin-Huxley circuit. The available clinical EEG data for humans do not agree with the response of this circuit. The clinical data show a decrease in relative voltages with increasing relative frequencies at relative frequencies below one whereas this circuit predicts an increase with relative frequencies.

The equation for the impedance, Z, for the Cole circuit shown in figure 2b is given by [see ref.25]:

$$Z = \frac{\sqrt{R^2 + (\omega L)^2}}{\sqrt{(1 - \omega^2 LC)^2 + (\omega RC)^2}} \quad [9]$$

Substituting equation [3] in [9], we get:

$$Z = \frac{R\sqrt{1+\frac{1}{E_x}\left(\frac{\omega}{\omega_n}\right)^2}}{\sqrt{\left[1-\left(\frac{\omega}{\omega_n}\right)^2\right]^2+E_x\left(\frac{\omega}{\omega_n}\right)^2}}$$ [10]

Again

$$M = \sqrt{\frac{\left[1-\left(\frac{\omega}{\omega_n}\right)^2\right]^2+E_x\left(\frac{\omega}{\omega_n}\right)^2}{1+\frac{1}{E_x}\left(\frac{\omega}{\omega_n}\right)^2}}$$ [11]

Figure 7 shows a plot of this equation [11].

Discussion of the Equations

Equations [6], [8] and [11] are shown plotted in figures 3, 6, and 7 respectively. They show that the Relative Action Potential decreases with decreasing excitabilities at a given relative frequency. It was shown in figure 1 that the addition of lithium would decrease the membrane resistance. From equation [5], a decrease in resistance would decrease the excitability. For example, if the resistance decreases by a factor of two, the excitability would decrease by a factor of four. Such a decrease in excitability would have a profound effect on the membrane potentials. In order to verify which circuit represents the human neurons, available clinical data from electroencephalographic (EEG) measurements were used as discussed below.

Comparison with Clinical Results

Barlow [26] analyzed the epileptic EEG data from the Goettingen Library of Clinical EEG data. He plotted the amplitudes of the voltages in decibel scale as a function of frequency for a large set of data. Figure 8 shows the re-plot of the data from figure 7-13 of Barlow's book [26]. The resonant frequency was assumed to occur at zero decibels (since log 1 = 0) and was determined to be about 15 cycles per second by extrapolation of the curve. The solid lines represent the equation [6] for excitabilities of 100 and 1000. The relative action potentials are presented in decibel scale to match the clinical data. The data points represented by squares, circles, +s, and xs are for different sets of EEGs smoothed out by Barlow over a range of frequencies. For a complete discussion of each set of data, reference [26] may be consulted. The data presented in figure 8 lend credence to the basic parallel circuit shown in figure 2c and the analysis shown in figure 3. The results of Hodgkin-Huxley circuit shown in figure 6 and of Cole circuit shown in figure 7 would not agree with these clinical data.

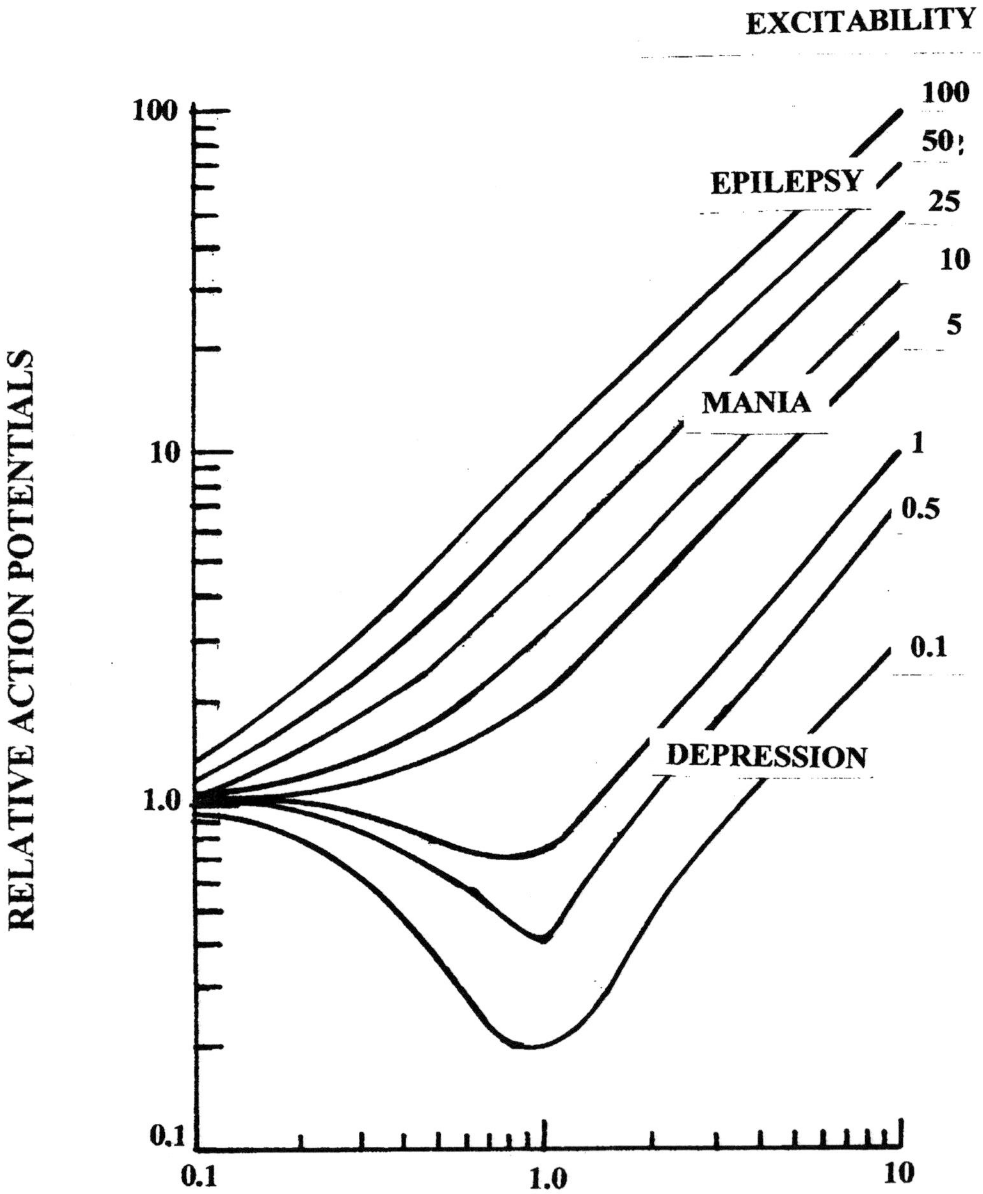

Figure 7. This figure shows the response of Cole circuit. Again the clinical EEG data from epileptic patients do not support the predictions of this circuit.

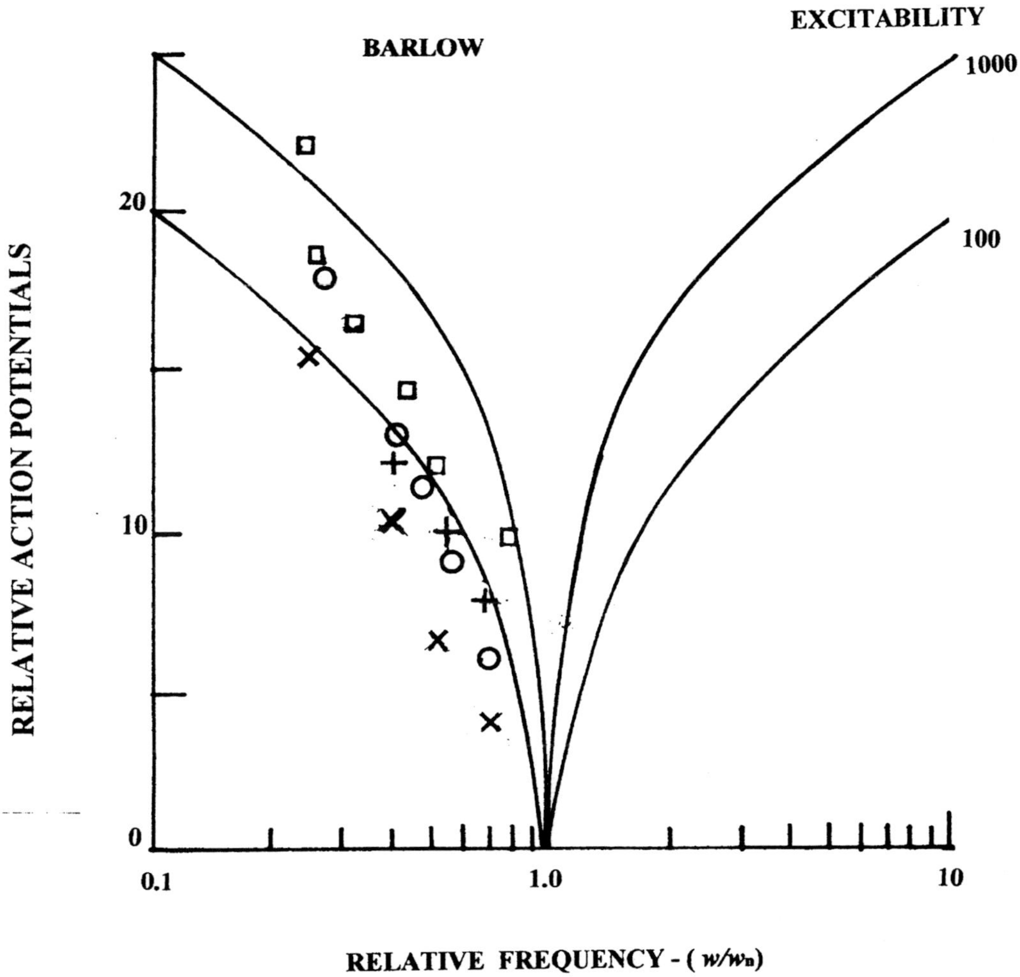

Figure 8. This figure compares the clinical EEG data from epileptic patients with the predictions of basic circuit. The squares, circles, +s and xs shown in this figure are taken from Barlow [26]. The voltages are shown in decibel scales for comparison. Only the basic circuit predicts the right relationship between the voltages and the frequencies. It is interesting to note that the excitabilities are in the range 100 to 1000 in epileptic patients. Refer to the text for further discussion of this figure.

Figure 9 shows a similar comparison of the data collected by Stroganova et al. [27] with the predictions of the basic circuit. Two sets of data (one for eight months old infant and the other for 11 months old infant) during visual attention at two electrode locations (AF3 and O1) are plotted against relative frequency. The solid lines represent the predictions of the basic circuit for two values of excitabilities, 1 and 0.5. Figure 10 shows the classification of EEG frequency ranges and their corresponding amplitude ranges in EEG technology. For example, the lowest frequency delta waves have the highest amplitudes whereas the highest frequency beta waves have the lowest amplitudes. Theta and alpha waves have the middle ranges of frequencies and amplitudes. This again lends support to the basic circuit.

The main purpose of the analysis is to understand the role of lithium in bipolar disorder. However, one cannot ignore the way the excitabilities line up in a sequence indicating epilepsy at higher excitabilities and "normal" at excitabilities around one. According to this analysis, excitabilities for mania fall in between the values for epilepsy and "normal"values and the values for depression would be below normal values. Clinical data from vagus nerve electrodes [29] would be useful in verifying these predictions. It is also interesting to note that several anticonvulsants are also effective mood stabilizers.

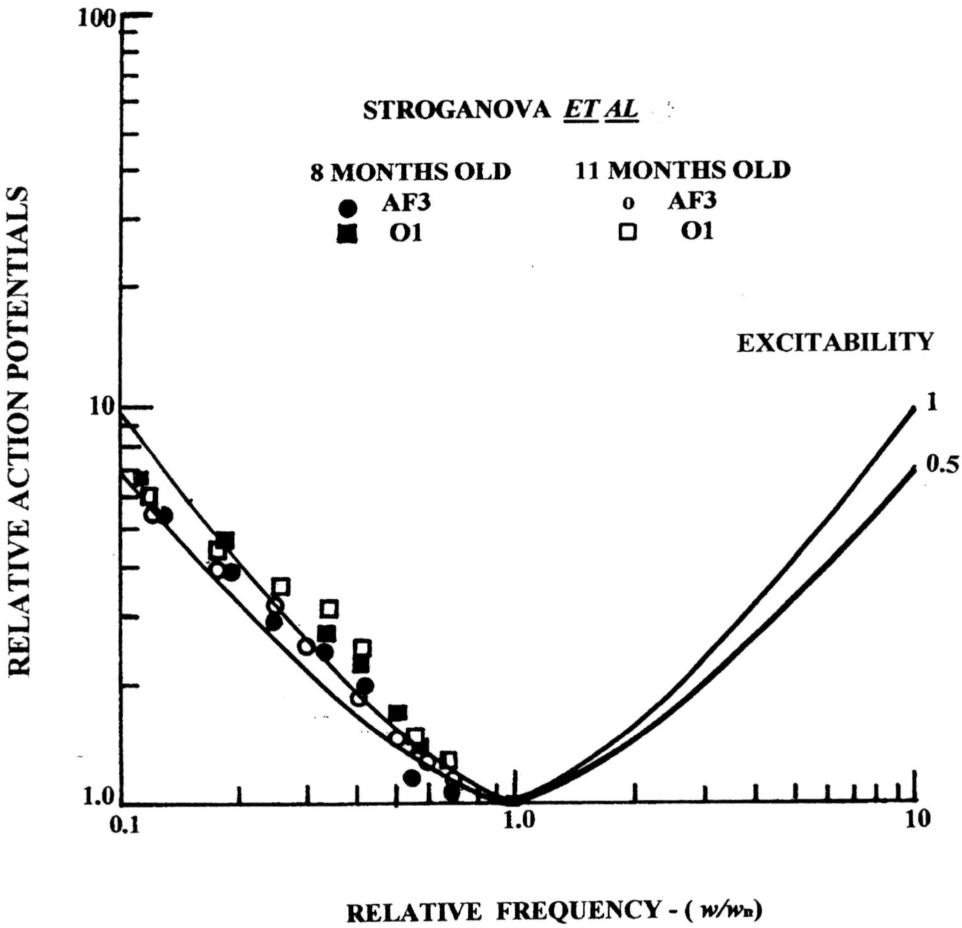

Figure 9. This figure shows a comparison of the relative action potentials predicted by the basic circuit with the clinical EEG data from eight month old infants and eleven month old infants by Stroganova et al. [27]. The filled circles and squares are for the eight month old infants and the open circles and squares are for the eleven month old infants at two scalp locations during visual attention. The excitabilities are in the range of 0.5 to 1.0.

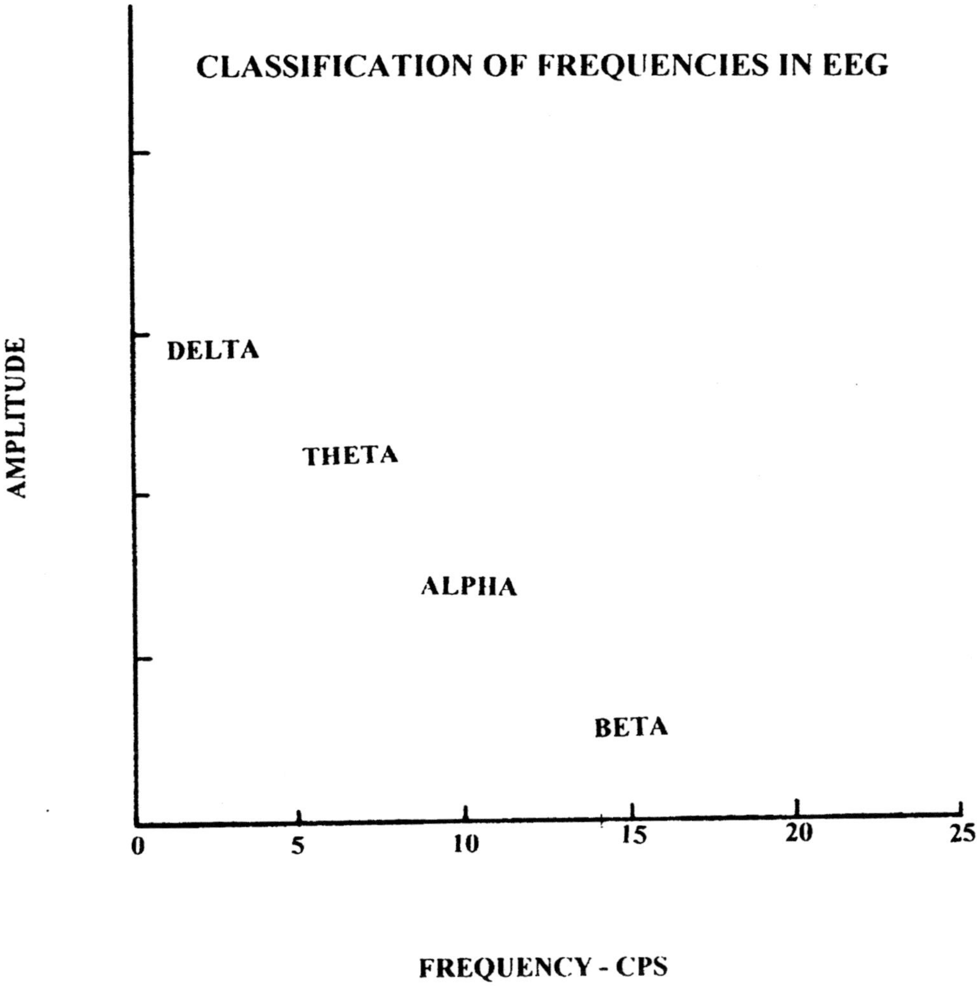

Figure 10. This figure shows the classification of EEG waves and their corresponding frequencies. The lowest frequency delta waves have the highest amplitudes (arbitrary scale) whereas the highest frequency beta waves have the lowest amplitudes. Theta and alpha waves have the middle range. The frequency dependency of these waves and their relative amplitudes are in qualitative agreement with the prediction of the basic circuit.

REFERENCES

[1] Goodwin, FK, and Jamison, KR, *Manic depressive illness*, Oxford university press, 1990.

[2] Soares, JC, and Gershon, S, (Eds.), *Bipolar disorders, Basic mechanisms and therapeutic implications*, Marcel Dekker, Inc. 2000.

[3] Manji, HK, Bowden, CL, and Belmaker, RH, (Eds.), *Bipolar medications: Mechanisms of action*, American Psychiatric Press, Inc. 2000.

[4] Singh, MM, A unifying hypothesis on the biochemical aspects of affective disorder, *Psychiat Q*, 1970; 44:706-724. .

[5] El-Mallakh, RS, and Wyatt, RJ, The Na, K-ATPase hypothesis for bipolar illness, *Biol. Psychiatry*, 1995; 37: 235-244.

[6] El-Mallakh, RS, Li, R, Worth, CA, Peiper, SC, Leukocyte transmembrane potential in bipolar illness, *J. Affective Disorders*, 1996; 41: 33-3.

[7] Thiruvengadam, A, Effect of lithium and sodium valproate ions on resting membrane potentials in neurons: an Hypothesis, *J. Affective Disorders*, 2001; 65: 95-99.

[8] Hodgkin, AL, and Huxley, AF, A quantitative description of membrane current and its application to conduction and excitation in nerve, *J. Physiology*, (London), 1952; 117: 500-544.

[9] Grafe, P, Reddy, MM, Emmert, H, and Tenbruggencate, G, Effects of lithium on electrical activity and potassium ion distribution in the vertebrate central nervous system, *Brain Research*, 1983; 279: 65-76.

[10] Adam-Vizi, V, Banay-Schwartz, M, Wajda, I, and Lajtha, A, Depolarization of brain cortex slices and synaptosomes by lithium. Determination of K+ equilibrium potential in cortex slices, *Brain Research*, 1987; 410(2): 257-63.

[11] Yonemura, K, and Sato, M, The resting membrane potential and cation movement in frog muscle fibers after exposure to lithium ions, *The Japanese Journal of Physiology*, 1967; 17: 678-97.

[12] Ulrich, G, Herrmann, WM, Hegerl, U, and Mueller-Oerlinghausen, B, Effect of lithium on the dynamics of encephalographic vigilance in healthy subjects, *J. Affect. Disord.* 1990; 20; 19-25.

[13] Thiruvengadam, A, Electro-biochemical coupling, excitability of neurons and bipolar disorder, *Fourth International Symposium on Bipolar Disorder, Bipolar Disorder Supplement 1*, 2001; 3: .

[14] Cole, KS, Equivalent electric circuits, *J. Gen. Physiology*, 1928; 12: 29.

[15] Katz, B, *The release of neural transmitter substances*, Thomas, Springfield, IL. 1969.

[16] Bonting, SL, and Caravaggio, LL, Studies on sodium potassium activated adenosine triphosphatase. V. Correlation of enzyme activity with cation flux in six tissues, *Archives of Biochemistry and Biophysics*, 1963; 101: 37-46.

[17] Looney, SW, and El-Mallakh, Meta-analysis of erythrocyte Na, K-ATPase activity in bipolar illness, *Depression and Anxiety*, 1997; 5: 53-65.

[18] Wood, AJ, Smith, CE, Clarke, EE, Cowen, PJ, Aronson, JK, and Graham-Smith, DG, Altered in vitro adaptive responses of lymphocyte Na, K-ATPase in patients with manic depressive psychosis, *J. Affective Disorders*, 1991; 21: 199-206 .

[19] Cherry, L, and Swann, AC, Cation transport mediated Na, K-ATPase in lymphoblastoma cells from patients with bipolar disorder, their relatives, and unrelated control subjects, *Psychiatry Research*, 1994; 53: 111-118 .

[20] Koester, J, Membrane potential, Ch.6, in *Principles of neuroscience*, 3rd ed. (Eds. Kandel, ER, Schwartz, J, and Jessel, TM,), New York, Elsevier, 1991; p.90 and p.1036.

[21] Cole, KS, Rectification and inductance in the squid giant axon, *J. Gen. Physiology*, 1941; 25: 29-51.

[22] Guttmann, R, The electrical impedance of muscle during the action of narcotics and other agents, *J. Gen. Physiology*, 1939; 40: 567-591.

[23] Shepherd, G, Electronic properties of axons and dendrites, Ch. 5, Fundamental neuroscience, (Zigmond, M, et al.) *Academic Press*, 1999.

[24] Dawes, CL, *A course in electrical engineering, Vol. II, Alternating current*, McGraw-Hill, New York, 1947.

[25] Kerchner, R, and Corcoran, G, *Alternating current circuits*, John Wiley & Sons, Inc. New York, 1962.

[26] Barlow, JS, *The electroencephalogram - its patterns and origins*, A Bradford book, MIT Press, Cambridge, MA. 1993; p.100.

[27] Stroganova, TA, Orekova, E, and Posikera, EEG alpha rhythm in infants, *Clinical Neurophysiology*, 1999; 110: 997-1012. .

[28] Neaverson, MH, and Jefferson, JW, Deficient Na, K-ATPase activity in different affective states in bipolar affective disorder and normalization by lithium therapy, *Neuropsychobiology*, 1989; 22: 18-25.

[29] George, MS, Sackeim, HA, Rush, JA, Marangell, LB, Nahas, Z, Husain, MM, Lisanby, S, Burt, T, Goldman, J, Ballenger, JC, Vagus nerve stimulation: A new tool for brain research and therapy, *Biological Psychiatry*, 2000; 47: 287-295. .

[30] Kandel, ER, Ch.13, Transmitter release, *Principles of neural science*, (Eds. Kandel et al.). Elsevier, New York, 1991.

[31] Kano, K, Nakamura, M, Matsuoka, T, Iida, H, Nakajima, T, The topographical features of EEG in patients with affective disorders, 1992; J. Electroenceph. *Clin. Neurophysio.*, 1992; 83: 124-129.

[32] Small, JG, Milstein, V, Perez, HC, Small, IF, Moore, DF, EEG and neurological studies of lithium in normal volunteers, *Biol. Psychiatry*, 1972; 5: 65-77.

[33] Geering, K, Na, K-ATPase, *Current Opinion in Nephrology and Hypertension*, 1997; 6: 434-39. .

[34] Rose, AM, Mellettt, BJ, Valdes, R JR, Kleinman, JE, Herman, MM, LI, R, El Mallakh, RS. Alpha2 isoform of the Na, K-Adenosine Triphosphatase is reduced in temporal cortex of bipolar individuals, *J. Gen. Physiol*, 1986; 87(4): 591-606 .

[35] Vasarhelyi, B, Tulassay, T, Ver, A, Dobos, M, Kocsis, I, and Seri, I. Developmental changes in erythrocyte Na, K-ATPase subunit abundance and enzyme activity in neonates, *Arch. Dis. Child Fetal Neonatal*, 2000; 83: F135-F138. .

[36] Pedemont, CH, and Bertorello, AM, Short-term regulation of the proximal tubule Na, K-ATPase; increased/decreased Na, K-ATPase activity mediated by protein kinase C isoforms, *J. Bioenerg. Biomembr.* 2001; 33(5): 439-47.

[37] Manji, HK, Chen, G, Hsiao, JK, Masana, MI, Moore, GJ, Potter, WZ, Regulation of signal transduction pathways by mood-stabilizing agents, in *Bipolar medications – Mechanisms of action*, Manji, HK, et al., (Eds) American Psychiatric Press, Inc. 2000; 129-177.

[38] Lenox, RH, McNamara, RK, and Watson, DG, A molecular target for the long-term action of lithium in the brain, in *Bipolar medications – Mechanisms of action*, Manji, HK, et al., (Eds) American Psychiatric Press, Inc. 2000; 197-218.

[39] Ward, MW, Rego, AC, Frenguelli, BG, and Nicholls, DG, Mitochondrial membrane potential and glutamate excitotoxicity in cultured cerebellar granule cells, *Journal of Neuroscience*, 2000; 20 (19): 7208-7219

In: Focus on Bipolar Disorder Research
Editor: Malcomb R. Brown, pp. 37-57
ISBN 1-59454-059-4

Chapter 3

NEUROPSYCHOLOGICAL FUNCTION IN BIPOLAR DISORDER: THE ONION GRADUALLY SHEDS ITS SKIN

Michael R. Basso
University of Tulsa, University of Oklahoma—Tulsa Campus

ABSTRACT

A growing body of literature indicates that bipolar disorder is associated with significant neurobehavioral dysfunction. This chapter reviews the literature concerning neuropsychological dysfunction in people with bipolar disorder. Relevant studies concerning structural and functional brain abnormalities associated with bipolar disorder are also summarized. Implications of these data for future research and clinical practice are considered.

INTRODUCTION

During the past twenty years, considerable research has demonstrated that neuropsychological dysfunction is a common correlate of bipolar disorder (cf. Martinez-Aran, Vieta, Colom, Reinares, Benabarre, Gasto, & Salamero, 2000). Yet, the nature and severity of these abnormalities, remains unsettled, and numerous conundrums exist. Moreover, the etiology and implications of neuropsychological anomalies in bipolar disorder is uncertain. As further research evolves, this empirical flux is becoming scientific steadiness. To elaborate upon these findings, present review will review relevant literature, delineate consensual findings, and discuss implications of these data for future research and clinical practice.

THE SCOPE OF NEUROPSYCHOLOGICAL FUNCTION IN BIPOLAR DISORDER

Early studies of neuropsychological function in bipolar disorder identified significant abnormalities involving non-verbal reasoning as measured by the Wechsler intelligence scales. In these investigations, acutely ill patients commonly manifested relative weaknesses in Performance IQ compared to Verbal IQ. Such findings led early theorists to assert that bipolar disorder principally reflected right hemisphere dysfunction (cf. Flor-Henry, 1983). Yet, although Performance IQ scores tend to be sensitive to right hemisphere dysfunction, they are also relatively non-specific. Specifically, diffuse cerebral dysfunction may result in relatively worse Performance than Verbal IQ scores (Kaufman & Lichtenberger, 2002). Indeed, later research involving the Wechsler intelligence scales has failed to conclusively demonstrate convincing weaknesses involving Performance relative to Verbal IQs in persons with bipolar disorder. Many studies reveal average Verbal and Performance IQ scores, with little difference occurring between the two IQ indices (Bearden, Hoffman, & Cannon, 2001). Such data suggest relatively little support for specific right hemisphere dysfunction in bipolar disorder. In contrast, there is evidence that the left hemisphere may be involved in bipolar symptoms. For example, Fenn and George (1999) report a case study of an elderly man who displayed manic symptoms secondary to ischemic lesions in the left basal ganglia, frontal cortex, and parietal lobe. This would suggest that left hemisphere dysfunction may also contribute to manic symptomatology.

In contrast to studies of intelligence, research examining executive function has revealed a more consistent pattern of abnormality. Executive function refers to capacity for abstract reasoning, idea generation, and self-regulation, and its neural substrate is presumed to be the frontal lobes (Lezak, 1995). Patients with bipolar disorder frequently demonstrate impairment in this domain. In particular, patients with bipolar disorder seem to display relative deficits on measures of verbal fluency, conceptual sequencing, planning and problem-solving, abstract reasoning, and cognitive flexibility (Borkowska & Rybakowki, 2001; Coffman, Bornstein, Olson, Schwarzkopf, & Nasrallah, 1990; Clark, Clayton, Andreasen, Lewis, Fawcett, & Scheftner, 1985; Flor-Henry, 1983; Goldberg, Gold, Greenberg, Griffin, Schulz, Pickar, Kleinman, & Weinberger, 1993; Martinez-Aran, Penades, Vieta, Colom, Reinares, Benabarrere, Salamero, & Gasto, 2002; McGrath, Scheldt, Welham, & Clair, 1997; Savard, Rey, & Post, 1980; Seidman, Kremen, Koren, Faraone, Goldstein, & Tsuang, 2002; Wolfe, Granholm, Butters, Saunders, & Janowsky, 1987). These data imply that executive dysfunction commonly occurs in bipolar disorder. Nonetheless, despite their reputed sensitivity to frontal lobe dysfunction, executive function measures are relatively non-specific indicators of cerebral abnormalities (cf. Lezak, 1995). Thus, in isolation, these findings should not be interpreted as evidence that bipolar disorder reflects a specific deficit involving the frontal lobes.

Similar to executive function, attention and concentration are commonly abnormal in bipolar disorder. In these investigations, various facets of attention have been studied. For instance, selective attention refers to the ability to focus upon one stimulus when confronted with multiple distracters. Sustained attention concerns the ability to maintain attention upon an activity over a lengthy time. Working memory involves the ability to hold information in attention while simultaneously manipulating the material or engaging in problem-solving. People with bipolar disorder have almost uniformly shown relative deficits in this domain (Coffman et al., 1990; Clark, Iversen, & Goodwin, 2002; Goldberg et al., 1993; McGrath et al., 1997; McGrath, Chapple, & Wright, 2001; Seidman, et al., 2001). Among others, Goldman-Rakic (1994) suggested that the neural substrate of working-memory resided in dorsal-lateral region of the frontal lobes, with contributions of subcortical regions occurring as well. Yet, measures of attention and working memory are relatively non-specific indicators of cerebral dysfunction. Thus, presuming a specific frontal lobe deficit in bipolar disorder based solely on neuropsychological test data would likely be premature.

In addition to attention and working memory, new-learning ability is commonly affected in bipolar disorder. In particular, people with bipolar disorder commonly show significantly lower performance than normal individuals without psychopathology and individuals with unipolar depression on measures of verbal and visual new-learning. These differences have been reported in numerous studies (Burt, Prudic, Peyser, Clark, & Sackeim, 2000; Cavanagh, Van Beck, Muir, & Blackwood, 2002; Clark, Iversen, & Goodwin, 2001; Coffman et al., 1990; Seidman et al., 2002; Sweeney, Kmiec, & Kupfer, 2000; van Gorp, Altshuler, Theberge, & Mintz, 1999). Notably, the bipolar patients tended to display performance that was classified as impaired relative to normative standards. Owing to this impairment, these data potentially imply dysfunction of temporal-limbic structures in bipolar disorder. Nonetheless, given that bipolar patients likewise demonstrate abnormal performance on a wide variety of neurobehavioral function, temporal-limbic dysfunction may not be their sole area of anomaly.

Other aspects of neuropsychological function that are often implicated in bipolar disorder include speed of information processing and visual spatial perception. Regarding the former, relatively few studies have thoroughly examined this ability (e.g., Fleck, Sax, & Strakowski, 2001). Regarding visual spatial perception, deficits are inconsistently demonstrated. Some studies have found no impairment (cf. Bearden et al., 2001), whereas others have reported significant deficit (El-Badri, Ashton, Moore, Marsh, & Ferrier, 2001). This inconsistency likely reflects differences in abilities assessed under the rubric of "visuospatial perception." Thus, conclusive statements concerning deficit in these areas of ability cannot be made presently.

Although neurobehavioral abnormality in bipolar disorder seems broad, its depth and severity is not entirely certain. For instance, early studies suggested that as few as 5% of bipolar patients manifest clinical deficit in neuropsychological function (Astrup, 1959). However, more recent studies imply that cognitive impairment may occur more commonly. For example, in a sample of nearly 90 bipolar inpatients, Basso and colleagues (Basso, Lowery, Neel, Purdie, & Bornstein, 2002) found that the majority displayed impaired scores on half of the tests comprising a neuropsychological battery. Moreover, several studies have compared neuropsychological function of bipolar patients to people diagnosed with schizophrenia. In the latter disorder, moderate to severe neuropsychological impairment is common, and it is recognized as a serious problem associated with the illness. Although there are some exceptions (Goldberg et al., 1993; Hawkins, Hoffman, Quinlan, Rakfeldt, Docherty, & Sledge, 1997; Martinez-Aran et al., 2002; Mojtabai, Bromet, Harvey, Carlson, Craig, & Fennig, 2000), several studies suggest that severity of impairment is comparable in schizophrenia and bipolar disorder (cf. Dickerson, Sommerville, Origoni, Ringel, & Parente, 2001; Hoff, Shukla, Aronson, Cook, Ollo, Baruch, Jandorf, & Schwartz, 1990; McGrath et al., 1997; Morice, 1990). Others have suggested that neuropsychological deficits in schizophrenia and bipolar disorder are roughly equivalent in general, with schizophrenics showing worse performance only on a subset of measures (Verdoux & Liraud, 2000; Zihl, Gron, & Brunnauer, 1998). Findings such as these suggest that far more than 5% of patients may show clinical impairment in neurobehavioral function. As such, neuropsychological impairment likely poses a meaningful problem for people with bipolar disorder.

PUTATIVE NEURAL SUBSTRATES OF NEUROPSYCHOLOGICAL DYSFUNCTION

Given that the range of neuropsychological deficit seems broad, it may be presumed that cerebral abnormalities are similarly diffuse. Indeed, investigations using brain imaging methodology imply that abnormalities are widely distributed throughout the brains of people with bipolar disorder. For example, a meta-analysis of imaging studies revealed that abnormalities involving the frontal lobes and basal ganglia are a reliable finding in bipolar disorder (Videbech, 1997). A more recent review concludes that scattered punctate lesions throughout deep white matter are among the most commonly reported anomalies in bipolar patients (Monkul, Malhi, & Soares, 2003). Occurrence of these lesions varies widely in frequency, with estimates ranging from 5-62% of bipolar patients showing them (Bearden et al. 2001).

Using structural imaging methods, small deep white matter hyperintensities are among the most distinct pathological changes in bipolar disorder. These are thought to reflect small pin-point or punctuate lesions. For instance, Silverstone, McPherson, Li, and Doyle (2003) found that people with bipolar disorder have twice as many lesions as a group of unipolar depressives. There are indications that bipolar patients have more deep white matter abnormalities than do schizophrenics. These lesions appear in young as well as older patients, and they are not explained by co-morbid medical illness (Bearden et al., 2001). They seem to have a relative affinity for periventricular white matter, and they also are common in basal ganglia structures (Dupont et al., 1990; 1995; McDonald et al., 1999). In some studies, these abnormalities have corresponded with worse neuropsychological test performance and greater clinical morbidity (poorer treatment outcomes, more hospitalizations etc.) (e.g., Dupont et al., 1995; Moore et al., 2001).

In addition to white matter lesions, gross brain abnormalities have been reported. In particular, increasing ventricle to brain ratios and sulcal widening have been reported in the literature. Yet, these data are inconsistently obtained across studies (cf. Beyer & Krishnan, 2002; Bearden et al., 2001), thereby raising doubts about their reliability.

Apart from diffuse structural abnormalities, broad functional anomalies have been reported. Yet, these data also tend to be contradictory. For example, Baxter, Phelps, Maziotta, Schwartz, Garner, Selin, and Sumida (1985) assessed resting brain activity of manic, depressed, and mixed-episode bipolar patients with positron emission tomography. The depressed and mixed-episode patients showed lower overall brain glucose metabolism than the manic and control patients, and the uptake rate increased as these patients entered euthymic or manic states. Other studies show that bipolar disorder is associated with diffuse hypermetabolism (Kennedy, Javanmard, & Vaccarino, 1997; Kishimoto, Takazu, Ohno, Yamaguchi, Fujita, Kuwahara, Ishii, Matsushita, Yokoi, & Iio, 1987; Soares & Mann, 1997).

Although studies such as these have examined cerebral volumes and metabolism diffusely, other investigations have focused upon specific regions of interest. In this regard, a substantial number of studies indicates that frontal lobe abnormalities occur commonly in bipolar disorder. For instance, in their thorough review of imaging studies, Monkul et al. (2003) summarize 9 studies that assessed volumes of frontal lobe structures in bipolar disorder. These investigations consistently revealed that people with bipolar disorder have smaller than normal cortical volumes, especially in the pre-frontal region. These findings have been replicated in research that was not included in the Monkul et al. review (Hirayasu et al., 2001). Notably, Sax and colleagues (Sax, Strakowski, Zimmerman, DelBello, Keck, & Hawkins, 1999) assessed prefrontal cortex in 17 inpatients with mania and 12 controls, and they found that the inpatients had significantly smaller prefrontal cortex volumes. Moreover, both groups were administered a continuous performance test, which is thought to measure vigilance, speed of information processing, and executive function (via self-regulation). The manic group performed worse than the control group, and poor performance correlated with decreased cerebral volume in prefrontal cortex and the hippocampus. Potentially underlying cerebral volume anomalies, some data indicate abnormal cytoarchitecture, with greater rates of cellular apoptosis and necrosis in the prefrontal cortex of bipolar patients (Uranova, Orlovskaya, Vikhreva, Zimina, Kolomeets, Vostrikov, & Rachmanova, 2001).

In addition to structural abnormalities, several studies report functional abnormalities in frontal lobe structures. In particular, Soares and Mann (1997) reviewed the literature concerning functional imaging studies of bipolar disorder, and they asserted that frontal lobe hypometabolism is one of the more reliable findings to emerge, especially in the orbital-frontal region. Such outcomes may occur regardless of presenting mood state. For example, in one of the early studies to address this issue, Buchsbaum et al. (1984) found that depressed bipolar patients manifest hypometabolism over the frontal lobes. In a subsequent study, Buchsbaum et al. (1986) examined glucose uptake in a heterogeneous group of manic and depressed bipolar patients, and the patients displayed lower activation than control subjects in the frontal lobes and adjoining basal-ganglia structures.

In some studies, frontal lobe hypometabolism has been assessed during performance on measures of executive function. Specifically, Blumberg et al. (1999) employed positron emission tomography to study cerebral activation at rest and during a word generation task. Participants included manic and euthymic bipolar patients. The manic patients showed relative hypometabolism bilaterally at rest and over the right orbital-frontal region during the word generation test. In a study of cerebral activation during a decision-making task, Rubinsztein et al. (2001) found that manic patients displayed bilateral frontal hypoactivation compared to control subjects. Recently, however, Blumberg et al. (2003) examined cerebral metabolism in manic, depressed, and euthymic bipolar patients as well as a control group. Activation was assessed at rest and during performance of a selective attention test. Remarkably, the pattern of hypometabolism varied according to mood state. Similar to Rubinsztein et al. (2001), manic patients manifested bilateral orbital-frontal hypoactivation, whereas depressed patients showed relative activation bilaterally. When activation levels were summed across mood states, the bipolar group as a whole manifested significantly lower left orbital-frontal activation than the control group. In contrast to these data, Koek, Yerevanian, Tachiki, Smith, Alcock, and Kopelowicz (1999) measured electroencephalographic activity twice in a group of 13 patients with bipolar disorder over a two year period. Patients were assessed once during a manic episode and again during a depressive episode. The investigators found that depression was associated with greater fronto-temporal activation in the right than left hemisphere, whereas mania corresponded with a converse pattern of arousal.

Collectively, these findings imply that bipolar disorder corresponds with frontal lobe abnormality, with a certain pattern of abnormality found wanting. To some extent, the structural abnormalities suggest that this is a chronic feature of the disorder, as cerebral volumes are presumed to be relatively stable. Yet, in people with unipolar depression,

Shelline (2000; 2003) has demonstrated that cerebral structures, such as the hippocampus, may undergo atrophy during acute depression. Upon remission, hippocampal volumes tend to increase, but not to an entirely normal volume. Perhaps cerebral abnormality in bipolar disorder may vary in kind. Functional imaging studies support this hypothesis to some degree. In particular, Blumberg et al.'s (2003) finding that hypoactivation may vary in the right hemisphere according to mood state, but left frontal hypoactivation seems to be a chronic marker of bipolar disorder, even in a euthymic state. Yet, too few studies exist in this regard to form a confident consensus.

In addition to frontal lobe structures, other regions of interest have been examined. In particular, investigations using structural and functional imaging methods have identified the basal ganglia, amygdala, hippocampus, thalamus, cerebellum, and temporal lobe cortex as abnormal in bipolar disorder (Ali et al., 2000; Baumann & Bogerts, 2001; Bearden et al., 2001; Monkul et al., 2003; Soares & Mann, 1997). Yet, these findings have been inconsistently replicated in the literature (e.g., Beyer, & Krishnan, 2002; Brambilla et al., 2001; Caetano et al., 2001; Hauser et al., 2000), and generalized assertions regarding their presence or meaning cannot be confidently made.

Collectively, the existing literature implies that a broad pattern of cerebral abnormality may be expected in bipolar disorder. Perhaps the most consistent anomalies involve white matter punctate lesions and frontal lobe abnormalities. Yet, the empirical literature remains relatively nascent, and increasingly consistent findings may emerge as further research is published. Regardless, the data suggest that neuropsychological impairment in bipolar disorder likely corresponds with genuine structural and functional cerebral abnormalities.

Mitigating Factors

Despite the apparent preponderancy of data implicating neuropsychological impairment in bipolar disorder, only some people display such impairment. Nonetheless, the empirical literature has not clarified what factors contribute to neuropsychological dysfunction, as investigations have tended to examine heterogeneous samples of bipolar patients (cf. Bearden et al., 2001; Cassens, Wolfe, & Zola, 1990).

Some studies have attempted to examine neuropsychological function in a more refined manner, and have assessed neuropsychological function among individuals in a specific episode of mood disturbance, either manic or depressed. For example, Sax et al. (1999) compared sustained attention and reaction time speed of manic inpatients to a control group. The patients manifested significantly worse performance than the control group. Clark et al. (2001) likewise compared neuropsychological function of manic inpatients to a control group. Similar to Sax et al. (1999), Clark et al. found that the manic inpatients performed significantly worse than the control group on a measure of sustained visual attention and reaction time. Moreover, their verbal learning ability was impaired relative to the control group. Others (McGrath et al., 2001; Murphy, Sahakian, Rubinsztein, Michael, Rogers, Robbins, & Paykel, 1999) have similarly reported relative deficits involving new-learning, working memory, and executive function in mania. These findings indicate that mania corresponds with significant neurobehavioral impairment. Yet, this may be expected; mania is defined by loosening of associations and disorganized behavior. It would seem likely that individuals would be less able to attend to information, learn new material, or generate problem solutions during a manic rather than euthymic state.

Although mania is the defining syndrome of bipolar disorder, a large proportion of those diagnosed with it will also manifest major depression some time during their lives. Because depression often corresponds with complaints of forgetfulness, inattention, indecision, apathy, and anergia, some deficits in neuropsychological function might be expected. Indeed, a relatively large body of data indicates that unipolar depression corresponds with significant neurocognitive difficulties, typically involving executive function, new-learning, working memory, attention, new-learning, and speed of information processing (cf., Basso & Bornstein, 1999a; 1999b; Burt, Zembar, & Niederehe, 1995;Christensen, Griffiths, Mackinnon, & Jacomb, 1997; Fleck, Shear, Zimmerman, Getz, Corey, Jak, Lebowitz, & Strakowski, 2003; Franke, Maier, Hardt, Frieboes, Lichtermann, & Hain, 1993; Kindermann & Brown, 1997; Martin, Oren, & Boone, 1991; Sackeim, Freeman, McElhiney, Coleman, Prudic, & Devanand, 1992; Veiel, 1997). Given that such anomalies occur in unipolar depression, significant neuropsychological dysfunction might also be expected during bipolar depressive states.

In this regard, relatively few studies have compared depressed bipolar patients to a normal control group. Among those that do, available data suggest that depressed bipolar patients manifest worse neuropsychological function than psychiatrically normal individuals. Other studies contrast neurobehavioral function of depressed people with bipolar disorder to those with unipolar depression. Some of these studies reveal few significant differences between the two disorders. For instance, Neu and colleagues (Neu, Kiesslinger, Schlattman, & Reischies, 2001) compared inpatients with either unipolar or bipolar depression, and found no differences between patient groups on a broad battery of neuropsychological measures. Furthermore, in a recent review of the literature, Quraishi and Frangou (2002) suggest that neurobehavioral dysfunction in bipolar and unipolar depression is relatively similar, and no major differences exist. Yet, a number of studies contradict this assertion. For example, Wolfe et al. (1987) compared patients with bipolar depression, unipolar depression, or Huntington's disease to a control group. Individuals with bipolar depression performed significantly worse than the unipolar depressives and a control group, but they performed comparably to the patients with Huntington's disease. Borkowska and Rybakowski (2001) administered a battery of neuropsychological tests to two groups of depressed inpatients. The bipolar group consisted of 15 patients, whereas the unipolar group was comprised of 30 patients. The bipolar group performed worse than the unipolar group on measures of non-verbal intelligence, selective attention, and executive attention. Similar findings have also been reported (Savard et al., 1980).

Taken together, these findings suggest that neuropsychological impairment occurs during depressive states in bipolar disorder. Yet, they fail to clarify whether severity of neuropsychological impairment in bipolar depression is equivalent to that demonstrated in unipolar depression. The available studies are limited by small sample sizes and test batteries that vary in their sensitivity to cerebral dysfunction. Thus, no clear assertions can be made concerning relative deficit in bipolar versus unipolar depression.

Further contributing to a sense of uncertainty, the level of relative impairment present in individuals who present with mixed features of mania and depression has not been well defined. Moreover, there are few studies that compare neuropsychological function across manic, depressed, and mixed episodes of bipolar disorder. Consequently, it is uncertain whether depression yields neurocognitive dysfunction to the same degree as mania or mixed features of mania and depression. These issues are important to address, because in doing so, we may better understand the relationship between mood state and mental status. Yet, to date, there has been only a single study to compare neurobehavioral function across these different episodes.

Basso et al. (2002) administered a relatively broad battery of neuropsychological tests to 37 manic, 25 depressed, and 24 mixed-feature bipolar inpatients as well as a group of 31 control subjects. The three inpatient groups performed significantly worse than the control group on all indices, including measures of verbal learning, executive function, speed of information processing, and psychomotor speed. Yet, the three patient groups performed comparably to one another, and there were no significant differences between them. Furthermore, an impairment index was computed in which test scores that fell 1.0 standard deviations below the mean of the control group were summed. On average, the three bipolar groups achieved impaired scores on half of the neuropsychological tests.

These data provide no compelling evidence of significant differences among patients with manic, depressed, or mixed-features. The three groups of bipolar patients displayed no statistically significant differences in performance across the neuropsychological test battery, they showed equivalent numbers of impaired test scores, and estimated effects sizes for differences between the three bipolar groups were minimal. In the context of existing research, there seems to be little evidence that manic, mixed-feature, and depressed episodes yield differential neuropsychological dysfunction in bipolar disorder. Rather, bipolar disorder may exert significant and commensurate impairment regardless of presenting mood episode.

To some extent, these findings may be expected. As previously noted, earlier investigations demonstrated that acute mania and bipolar depression correspond with significant neuropsychological deficit (Hoff et al., 1990; McGrath et al., 1997; Wolfe et al., 1987). Prior to the Basso et al. (2002) study, there had been no direct comparison of manic, depressed, and mixed-feature patients. Thus, the relative degree of impairment associated with each type of mood disturbance was uncertain. Yet, to some extent, concluding that no significant neurobehavioral differences exist between bipolar mood states may seem counterintuitive. The presenting symptoms of depression and mania are markedly different, and patterns of cerebral dysfunction may vary across manic, depressed, and mixed-feature episodes. Perhaps the underlying neural substrate of depression and mania may vary, but their summary effect on mental status may be equally severe.

Apart from presenting mood symptoms, bipolar disorder may also vary according to presence of psychotic features. As previously noted, a number of studies have compared bipolar patients to those with schizophrenia (Dickerson et al., 2001; Goldberg et al., 1993; Hawkins, et al., 1997; Hoff et al., 1990; Martinez-Aran et al., 2002; McGrath et al., 1997; Mojtabai et al., 2000; Morice, 1990; Verdoux & Liraud, 2000; Zihl et al., 1998). These investigations yielded varying outcomes. In particular, one study examined patients who were in the midst of their first psychiatric hospitalization. Groups of participants included bipolar patients with psychotic features, unipolar patients with psychotic features, and schizophrenics, and they were administered a broad battery of neuropsychological tests (Mojtabai et al., 2000). The schizophrenic group performed worse than the two psychotic mood disordered groups, with no difference observed between the bipolar and unipolar groups. In contrast, Coffman et al. (1990) compared a heterogeneous (manic, depressed, or mixed) group of bipolar patients with psychotic features to a control group on a series of neuropsychological tests. The psychotic bipolar patients performed significantly worse than the control group on nearly all measures included in the battery. Moreover, their mean scores were generally impaired compared to normative standards. Similarly, Albus and colleagues (Albus, Hubmann, Wahlheim, Sobizack, Franz, & Mohr, 1996) examined neuropsychological function in groups of first episode schizophrenic, unipolar depressed, and heteregenous bipolar patients. They found that the schizophrenic patients and the unipolar and bipolar patients with psychotic features performed significantly worse than a control group. The non-psychotic mood disorder groups performed commensurate with the control group. This suggests that presence of psychotic features corresponds with greater neuropsychological impairment. Taken together, the findings of Albus et al. (1996) and Coffman et al. (1990) suggest that presence of psychotic features in bipolar disorder contributes to a significant worsening of neurobehavioral status, equivalent to schizophrenia. Yet, these studies have not compared psychotic and non-psychotic bipolar patients. In a study involving unipolar depressives, Basso & Bornstein (1999b) found that psychotic unipolar depression yielded significant and broad cognitive impairment compared to the non-psychotic variant. Possibly, bipolar patients would demonstrate a similar outcome, but such a study, to our knowledge, has not been reported yet. Thus, no firm conclusions regarding the effect of psychotic features in bipolar disorder can be made.

A notable uncertainty raised by the studies reviewed thus far concerns the durability of neuropsychological deficits in bipolar disorder. In particular, they show that neuropsychological abnormalities occur during acute mood disturbance. Such mood disturbance is relatively common in bipolar disorder. In particular, the illness is characterized by episodic mood events, and rates of relapse and recurrence are estimated between 80-90% (Hilty, Brady, & Hales, 1999). Between episodes, patients tend to experience residual deficits in activities of daily living and social and occupational functioning. Perhaps cognitive impairment similarly remains during relatively euthymic periods.

A surprisingly sizable number of studies has addressed neuropsychological function during euthymic periods. Most of these studies indicate that some residual neuropsychological impairment remains during euthymic intervals, but the severity and extent of such impairment varies across studies. For example, Clark et al. (2002) compared executive function, verbal memory, working memory, speed of information processing, and sustained attention in euthymic bipolar patients and a control group. The bipolar patients were classified as euthymic based on scores of 8 or lower on both the Young Mania Rating Scale and the Hamilton Rating Scale for Depression. The two groups were essentially equal on most measures, except on a measure of sustained visual attention. On that measure, the euthymic bipolar group performed significantly worse than the control group. In a separate study, Rubinsztein, Michael, Paykel, and Sahakian (2000) administered a wide variety of neuropsychological tests to a group of 18 bipolar patients who had sustained a relative remission for four months. Visual-spatial memory function and speed of information processing was impaired relative to a control group, but executive function performance was normal. In contrast, other studies have found that euthymic bipolar patients are uniformly impaired across multiple areas of ability, including executive function, new-learning, working memory, speed of information processing, visual-spatial perception, and dexterity (Cavanagh et al., 2002; Denicoff, Ali, Mirsky, Smith-Jackson, Leverich, Duncan, Connell, & Post, 1999; El-Badri et al., 2001; Ferrier, Stanton, Kelly, & Scott, 1999; Fleck et al., 2003; Harmer,

Clark, Grayson, & Goodwin, 2002; van Gorp, Altshuler, Theberge, Wilkins, & Dixon, 1998; van Gorp et al., 1999; Wilder-Willis, Sax, Rosenberg, Fleck, Shear, & Strakowski, 2001).

To some extent, inconsistencies between studies may be attributable to different definitions of euthymia. Patients with bipolar disorder commonly manifest residual symptoms between distinct manic or depressive episodes (cf. Post et al. 2003). In some studies, the degree to which patients are well-characterized as euthymic varies, with some investigations clearly indicating that participants have few if any symptoms (cf. Clark et al., 2002), whereas other studies do not include sufficient detail to evaluate symptom severity. In studies that reveal more severe neurobehavioral impairment, participants may have been more symptomatic. Yet, owing to vagaries of patient descriptions, such an assertion cannot be evaluated with great certainty.

Some studies have not only compared euthymic bipolar patients to control groups but also to schizophrenic patients with mild residual symptoms. Similar to the aforementioned research involving euthymic bipolar groups, these studies have uniformly found that the euthymic patients display impaired performance compared to control subjects (Martinez-Aran et al., 2002; Krabbendam, Honig, Wiersma, Vuurman, Hofman, Derix, Nolen, & Jolles, 2000; Rossi, Arduini, Daneluzzo, Bustini, Prosperini, & Stratta, 2000). In one of these studies, Martinez-Aran et al. (2002) compared a group of bipolar patients who had sustained a symptom remission of at least 6-months to a schizophrenic group that had no exacerbation and no negative symptoms in 12-months. The two groups displayed a similar pattern of neuropsychological deficits across a broad battery of neuropsychological tests, with severity of impairment being more pronounced in the schizophrenic group. Although these patients were relatively symptom-free, they continued to demonstrate significant cognitive impairment.

Because bipolar patients typically maintain some degree of social or occupational impairment despite a remission of mood symptoms (cf. MacQueen, Young, & Joffe, 2001), residual cognitive deficits might contribute to poor outcomes. In this regard, Zubieta and colleagues (Zubieta, Huguelet, O'Neil, & Giordani, 2001) examined euthymic patients who had all sustained psychotic features during a manic episode. These individuals were compared to a control group on a broad battery of tests. The euthymic patients showed deficits in executive function, verbal learning, and dexterity. Despite the relative absence of mood symptoms, the euthymic patients manifested residual deficits in social and occupational function, and these deficits corresponded with poor performance on measures of executive function and memory. Accordingly, neuropsychological impairment may contribute to worsening functional outcomes in bipolar disorder.

Although these cross-sectional studies suggest that cognitive impairment remains during euthymic states, they may be confounded because patients have not been followed over time. Regrettably, there have been few longitudinal studies of bipolar patients across mood episodes. Yet, consistent with the cross-sectional studies, these investigations reveal that cognitive function decreases during depressed episodes and improves during euthymic intervals (Donnelly, Murphy, Goodwin, & Waldman, 1982; Henry, Weingartner, & Murphy, 1973). It seems likely that impairment would likely exacerbate during manic and mixed episodes as well.

Collectively, these data imply that some degree of residual impairment is present in euthymic bipolar patients. Because some relative deficit remains between manic or depressive episodes, neuropsychological abnormality may be a chronic characteristic of bipolar disorder.

Notably, bipolar disorder seems to correspond with cytoarchitecture abnormalities in frontal and temporal lobe cortex (cf. Nasrallah, 1991; Rajkowska, 2002). For instance, there is evidence of abnormal layering of glial cells in frontal cortex (Rajkowska, Halaris, & Selemon, 2001) among other cellular anomalies (cf. Rajkowska, 2002). Some investigators have hypothesized that these findings reflect a process in which pre-natal neuronal migration and early cerebral development goes astray (Nasrallah, 1991). As such, a pathological diathesis may exist prior to bipolar symptom onset. The cause of such cerebral anomalies is uncertain, and believed due to genetic influences or pre-natal trauma. As summarized by Bearden et al. (2001), there is some support for this neurodevelopmental hypothesis. Specifically, those patients who develop bipolar disorder in adolescence seem to have delayed language and motor development that was present prior to symptom onset. Furthermore, there are indications that patients demonstrate cerebral anomalies as early as their first manic episodes. For example, patients sustaining their first manic episode have been shown to have basal-ganglia, cingulate, thalamic, and lateral ventricle volumes that are significantly different from normal (cf. Hirayasu et al., 1999; Sigurdsson et al. 1999; Strakowski et al., 2002). Accordingly, neuropsychological function and cerebral structures may be abnormal prior to symptom onset.

Alternatively, Post (1992) has asserted that successive episodes of mood disturbance contribute to increasing cerebral dysfunction. With successive manic or depressive episodes, brain dysfunction increases, and some residual abnormality may occur, even during asymptomatic intervals. This would correspond with a greater likelihood of neurobehavioral abnormality during euthymic episodes. In this perspective, some pre-morbid cognitive abnormality may have existed prior to onset of mood disorder, but neuropsychological deficit would be expected to worsen with successive mood episodes.

Consistent with this latter hypothesis, several studies have found relationships between worsening neuropsychological function and chronicity of illness. For example, Tham and colleagues (Tham, Engelbrektson, Mathe, Johnson, Olsson, & Aberg-Wistedt, 1997) examined a heterogeneous group of euthymic bipolar and euthymic unipolar depressives on portions of the Halstead-Reitan Neuropsychological Test Battery. Similar to other studies of euthymic patients, performance was relatively abnormal. Furthermore, worsening function corresponded with increasing number of hospitalization for mood episodes. In a homogenous group of euthymic bipolar patients, van Gorp et al. (1998) found that worsening executive function and verbal memory corresponded with lifetime months of mania and depression. In contrast to duration of illness in months, other investigators have focused upon discrete episodes of mood disturbance as a predictor of cognitive impairment. For example, Lebowitz, Shear, Steed, and Strakowski (2001) compared neuropsychological function of bipolar patients who were in the midst of either a first or recurrent episode of mania. They found that verbal fluency was impaired compared to control subjects in the recurrent mania group, whereas the patients sustaining a first episode of mania performed commensurate with the control group. In studies of euthymic bipolar patients, neuropsychological deficits are more common as patients have sustained higher frequencies of prior manic episodes. In a unique investigation, Denicoff et al. (1999) utilized the NIMH Life Chart Method to document lifetime number of depressive and manic episodes as well as lifetime duration of illness. Their euthymic patients were administered measures of executive function, attention, and memory, and neuropsychological test scores were regressed upon number of episodes and duration of illness. The results indicated that increasing number of hospitalizations and mood episodes corresponded with worse performance on measures of executive function and verbal learning. Duration of illness predicted poor performance on measures of attention and concentration. Thus, consistent with Post's (1992) hypothesis, increasing number of mood episodes and longer illness duration correspond with worsening neuropsychological function. Yet, it should be recognized that these relationships are not entirely longitudinal, and, consequently, a causative relationship between illness variables and cognitive impairment cannot be concluded. Nonetheless, these data provide a viable and provocative explanation of how neuropsychological dysfunction may evolve in bipolar disorder.

Some studies utilizing imaging methodology reported findings consistent with Post's (1992) hypothesis. In particular, DelBello et al. (1999) compared cerebral volumes of people sustaining either their first or a recurrent episode of mania. Those experiencing a recurrent episode showed abnormally small cerebellar vermis, and there were indications that this decreased volume corresponded with number of prior depressive episodes. Similarly, Strakowski et al. (2002) compared cerebral volumes of a control group to groups of first-episode and recurrent episode bipolar patients. Lateral ventricles were significantly larger in the recurrent bipolar patients than first episode and control groups, and increasing ventricle volume corresponded with greater numbers of past manic episodes. Additionally, Brambilla et al. (2001) found that lateral ventricle volume in the right hemisphere increased in relation to number of prior mood episodes (both manic and depressed). Yet, other studies have failed to find relationships between morbidity characteristics and cerebral structures. Nonetheless, these collective data generally support the assertion that increasing illness duration or mood exacerbations correspond with worsening brain and neuropsychological abnormality.

Whether these deficits were present prior to onset of the bipolar symptoms or are a consequence of mood episodes is uncertain. Possibly a diathesis stress model exists. Specifically, some individuals may begin life with subtle cerebral and associated neuropsychological anomalies. As stressful circumstances occur, an episode of mania or clinical depression may result (Tsuchiya, Byrne, & Mortensen, 2003). The effects of mood disturbance may exacerbate pathological cerebral and cognitive function, as there are indications that depressive episodes can contribute to cell loss in the hippocampus (cf. Lee, Ogle, & Sapolsky, 2002) and increasing neuropsychological impairment (cf. Basso & Bornstein, 1999a; Lebowitz et al., 2001). Such an assertion is highly speculative, and further research is necessary to clarify its merit.

What Can Be Concluded?

The data herein reviewed is broad but nascent and somewhat prone to flux. Yet, with the publication of each study, the opaque onion of scientific uncertainty gradually sheds its skin, and some facts emerge. Collectively, the existing literature suggests that neuropsychological impairment is a common correlate of bipolar disorder. Yet, underlying this statement, uncertainty remains concerning the pattern and severity of neurobehavioral dysfunction. In particular, inconsistent findings exist across studies, and a relatively small number of papers have addressed many of the relevant issues. To some extent, contradictory findings across studies likely reflect differences in abilities measured, tests administered, and patient characteristics. For example, some studies examine broad ranges of neuropsychological function, whereas others tend to address circumscribed abilities. Investigations that employ wide-ranging measures of function may be better able to characterize which neuropsychological abilities are affected and which are not. Furthermore, neuropsychological measures vary in their sensitivity in detecting cognitive impairment and associated brain dysfunction. Possibly, studies with null findings employed measures that were less sensitive than those which identified significant neurobehavioral deficit. Additionally, it seems likely that some patients will more likely demonstrate abnormal cognitive function, and studies have only begun to evaluate patient factors that correspond with pronounced cognitive deficits. For instance, available research suggests that mania and depression tend to be marked by significant impairment relative to normal controls. Yet, it seems likely that other characteristics correlate with greater cognitive impairment. For example, because no study has directly evaluated whether patients with and without psychotic features differ in their neurobehavioral status, we do not know whether psychotic features in bipolar disorder contributes to more pronounced deficit than an absence of such features. Another salient factor that has not been addressed is inpatient versus outpatient status. Meta-analyses of neuropsychological function in unipolar depression indicates that inpatients display cognitive impairment more commonly than outpatients (Burt et al., 1995; Christensen et al., 1997; Kindermann & Brown, 1997; Veiel, 1997). Perhaps bipolar inpatients will likewise manifest greater impairment than their outpatient counterparts. Failure to address such issues in previous research may also have contributed to contradictory outcomes across studies.

These factors notwithstanding, tentative conclusions regarding types and severity of neuropsychological deficits can be made. In particular, much of the existing research demonstrates that people with bipolar disorder display abnormal performance on measures of executive function, working memory, speed of information processing, and new-learning. Owing to the number of studies reporting these effects, they seem relatively reliable. There are some studies suggesting that visual-perceptual deficits and psychomotor slowing are also present, but these anomalies have been reported with less frequency. Thus, they seem less reliable. Investigations involving intellectual function have yielded inconsistent outcomes, with some studies identifying below average IQs, and others finding normal intelligence. Few investigations have identified deficits involving language function. The paucity of such findings may reflect the fact that measures of language function are infrequently administered, and few investigations seem to have addressed that area of function.

The aforementioned neurobehavioral difficulties seem to be present to a greater extent during acute mood episodes than during euthymic periods. Greater severity notwithstanding, a compelling body of research implies that neuropsychological impairment remains present during euthymic intervals. The breadth and severity of such deficit has been inconsistently reported across studies. In studies conducted with patients whose euthymia is well-documented, the breadth of residual impairment seems limited to new-learning, attention, and speed of information processing, and the severity of deficit appears less severe than in patients who are acutely ill. Collectively, these findings imply that neuropsychological deficit is chronic for many people with bipolar disorder. Nonetheless, it remains uncertain which patients will continue to display impairment during euthymic intervals.

Neurobehavioral difficulties appear to correspond with a variety of cerebral anomalies in acute and euthymic bipolar disorder. Among the most frequently reported are an elevated number of deep white matter hyperintensities. Volumetric and functional abnormalities involving pre-frontal cortex and temporal lobe structures are also found with some consistency across several studies. Other anomalies are sufficiently contradicted across studies that little certainty exists concerning their reliable occurrence. The etiology and significance of such cerebral abnormalities remains open to conjecture. In particular, it is uncertain whether cerebral anomalies precede or result from episodes of mania and depression. In a relatively small number of these studies, degree of structural and functional deficit appears to correspond with severity of neuropsychological deficit. Regardless, the presence of these irregularities in brain volume and function implies that cerebral dysfunction is a common correlate of bipolar disorder.

IMPLICATIONS

To better clarify the nature of neuropsychological function in bipolar disorder, future research should endeavor to define patient groups in an explicit manner. Research in which patients with manic, mixed, or depressed features are combined into a single comparison group permits insufficient specificity of findings. Accordingly, it may further our knowledge if homogenous groups of manic, mixed, or depressed features are examined. Investigations of euthymic patients should attempt to define euthymia in an explicit and consensual manner. Granted, there is considerable disagreement concerning what constitutes euthymia (cf. MacQueen et al. (2001). Nonetheless, inasmuch as comparisons can be made between different groups of euthymic samples, we may gain a better understanding of what contributes to residual neurobehavioral impairment. Furthermore, future research may yield more informative results if researchers focus upon individual differences between bipolar patients. For instance, our understanding of the relationship between mood and cognition may be refined if investigators discern what clinical characteristics (e.g., presence of psychotic features, recurrent versus initial episode, presence of melancholic depression, etc.) correspond with neuropsychological deficit.

For clinical purposes, it would be helpful to identify the implications of neuropsychological impairment in bipolar disorder. In schizophrenia, ample evidence suggests that cognitive deficits predict poor treatment response, impaired social function, and decreased capacity for self-care (Zarate, Tohen, Land, & Cavanagh, 2000). Preliminary data indicate that such neuropsychological dysfunction similarly predicts unemployment and disability status, poor ability to manage daily affairs, and inability to provide competent consent to treatment in bipolar disorder (Basso et al. 2001; Ghormley & Basso, 2004; Zarate et al., 2000; Zubieta et al., 2001). As such, presence of neuropsychological deficit in bipolar disorder appears to be a meaningful target of treatment, and it should pose a salient concern to treatment providers.

REFERENCES

Albus, M., Hubmann, W., Wahlheim, C., Sobizack, N., Franz, U., & Mohr, F. (1996). Contrasts in neuropsychological test profile between patients with first-episode schizophrenia and first-episode affective disorders. *Acta Psychiatrica Scandinavica, 94*, 87-93.

Ali, S., Denicoff, K., Altshuler, L., Hauser, P.,Li, X., Conrad, A., Mirsky, A., Smith-Jackson, E., & Post, R.(2000). A preliminary study of the relation of neuropsychological performance to neuroanatomic structures in bipolar disorder. *Neuropsychiatry, Neuropsychology, and Behavioral Neurology, 3*, 20-28.

Astrup, C., Fossum, A., & Holmbee, R. (1959). A follow-up study of 270 patients with acute affective psychoses. *Acta Psychiatrica et Neurologica, 34(Supp 135)*, 1-65.

Basso, M. R., & Bornstein, R. A. (1999a). Relative memory deficits in recurrent versus first-episode major depression on a word-list learning task. *Neuropsychology, 13*, 557-563.

_____ . (1999b). Neuropsychological deficits in psychotic vs. non-psychotic unipolar depression. *Neuropsychology, 13,* 69-75.

Basso, M. R., Lowery, N., Purdic, R., & Neel, J. (2001). *Neuropsychological Impairment Predicts Functional Outcomes in Bipolar Disorder*. Paper presented at the 41st annual convention of the New Clinical Drug Evaluation Unit-National Institute of Mental Health, Phoenix, Arizona.

Basso, M, Lowery, N., Neel, J., Purdie, R., & Bornstein, R. (2002). Neuropsychological Impairment Among Manic, Depressed, and Mixed-Episode Inpatients With Bipolar Disorder. *Neuropsychology, 16*, 84-91.

Baumann, B., & Bogerts, B. (2001). Neuroanatomical studies on bipolar disorder. *British Journal of Psychiatry, 178(Supp l41)*, 142-147.

Baxter, L. Jr, Phelps, M., Mazziotta, J., Schwartz, J., Garner, R., Selin, C., & Sumida, R. (1985). Cerebral metabolic rates for glucose in mood disorders. Studies with positron emission tomography and fluorodeoxyglucose F 18. *Archives of General Psychiatry, 42*, 441-447.

Bearden, C., Hoffman, K., & Cannon, T. The neuropsychology and neuroanatomy of bipolar affective disorder: a critical review. (2001*). Bipolar Disorders, 3*, 106-153.

Beyer, J., & Krishnan, K. (2002). Volumetric brain imaging findings in mood disorders. *Bipolar Disorders, 4*, 89-104.

Blumberg, H., Leung, H., *Skudlarski, P., Lacadie, C., Fredericks, C., Harris, B., Charney, D., Gor, J., Krystal, J., & Peterson, B* (2003). A functional magnetic resonance imaging study of bipolar disorder: state- and trait-related dysfunction in ventral prefrontal cortices. *Archives of General Psychiatry, 60*, 601-609.

Blumberg, H., & Stern, H. (1999). Rostral and orbital prefrontal cortex dysfunction in the manic state of bipolar disorder. *American Journal of Psychiatry, 156*, 1986-1988.

Borkowska, A., & Rybakowski, J. (2001). Neuropsychological frontal lobe tests indicate that bipolar depressed patients are more impaired than unipolar. *Bipolar disorders, 3*, 88-94.

Brambilla, P., *Harenski,* K., *Nicoletti, M., Mallinger, A., Frank, E., Kupfer, D., Keshavan, M.*, and *Soares, J.* (2001). Anatomical MRI study of basal ganglia in bipolar disorder patients. *Psychiatry Research,* 106, 65-80.

Buchsbaum, M., DeLisi, L., Holcomb, H., Cappelletti, J., King, A., Johnson, J., Hazlett, E., *Dowling-Zimmerman, S., Post, R., Morihisa, J., et al.* (1984). Anteroposterior gradients in cerebral glucose use in schizophrenia and affective disorders. *Archives of General Psychiatry, 41*, 159-166.

Buchsbaum, M., Wu, J., DeLisi, L., Holcomb, H., Kessler, R., Johnson, J., King, A., Hazlett, E., Langston, K., & Post, R. (1986). Frontal cortex and basal ganglia metabolic rates assessed by positron emission tomography with [18F]2-deoxyglucose in affective illness. *Journal of Affective Disorders, 10*, 137-152.

Burt, T., Prudic, J., Peyser, S., Clark, J., & Sackeim, H. (2000). Learning and memory in bipolar and unipolar major depression: effects of aging. *Neuropsychiatry, Neuropsychology, and Behavioral Neurology, 13*, 246-253.

Burt, D., Zembar, M., & Niederehe, G. (1995). Depression and Memory Impairment: A Meta-Analysis of the Association, Its Pattern, and Specificity. *Psychological Bulletin, 117*, 285-305.

Caetano, S., *Sassi R*; *Brambilla,* P., *Harenski, K.*, *Nicoletti, M.*, *Mallinger., A.*, *Frank, E.*, *Kupfer, D.*, *Keshavan, M.*, and *Soares, J.* (2001. MRI study of thalamic volumes in bipolar and unipolar patients and healthy individuals. *Psychiatry Research,* 108, 161-168.

Cavanagh, J., Van Beck, M., Muir, W., & Blackwood, D. (2002). Case-control study of neurocognitive function in euthymic patients with bipolar disorder: An association with mania. *British Journal of Psychiatry, 180*, 320-326.

Cassens, G., Wolfe, L., & Zola, M. (1990). The neuropsychology of depressions. *Journal of Neuropsychiatry and Clinical Neurosciences, 2*, 202-213.

Christensen, H., Griffiths, K., Mackinnon, A., & Jacomb, P. (1997). A quantitative review of cognitive deficits in depression and Alzheimer-type dementia. *Journal of the International Neuropsychological Society: JINS, 3*, 631-651.

Clark, D., Clayton, P., Andreasen, N., Lewis, C., Fawcett, J., & Scheftner, W. (1985). Intellectual functioning and abstraction ability in major affective disorders. *Comprehensive Psychiatry, 26*, 313-325.

Clark, L., Iversen, S., & Goodwin, G. (2001.) A Neuropsychological Investigation of Prefrontal Cortex Involvement in Acute Mania. *American Journal of Psychiatry, 158*, 1605-1611.

Clark, L., Iversen, S., & Goodwin, G. (2002). Sustained attention deficit in bipolar disorder. *British Journal of Psychiatry*, *180*, 313-319.

Coffman, A., Bornstein, A., Olson, C., Schwarzkopf, B., & Nasrallah, H. (1990). Cognitive impairment and cerebral structure by MRI in bipolar disorder. *Biological Psychiatry, 27*, 1188-1196.

DelBello, M., *Strakowski, S., Zimmerman, M., Hawkins, J., & Sax, K.* (1999). MRI analysis of the cerebellum in bipolar disorder: a pilot study. *Neuropsychopharmacology*, 21, 63-68.

Denicoff, K., Ali,S., Mirsky, A., Smith-Jackson, E., Leverich, G., Duncan, C., Connell, E., & Post, R. (1999). Relationship between prior course of illness and neuropsychological functioning in patients with bipolar disorder. *Journal of Affective Disorders,* 56, 67-73.

Dickerson, F., Sommerville, J., Origoni, A., Ringel, N., & Parente, F. (2001). Outpatients with schizophrenia and bipolar I disorder: Do they differ in their cognitive and social functioning? *Psychiatry Research, 102*, 21-27.

Donnelly, E., Murphy, D., Goodwin, F., & Waldman, I. (1982). Intellectual function in primary affective disorder. *British Journal of Psychiatry, 140*, 633-636.

Dupont, R., Jernigan, T., & Butters, N. (1990). Subcortical abnormalities detected in bipolar affective disorder using magnetic resonance imaging: Clinical and neuropsychological significance. *Archives of General Psychiatry*, *47*, 55-59.

Dupont, R., Jernigan, T., Heindel, W., Butters, N., Shafer, K., Wilson, T., Hesselink, J., & Gillin, J. (1995). Magnetic resonance imaging and mood disorders. Localization of white matter and other subcortical abnormalities. *Archives of General Psychiatry, 52*, 747-755.

El-Badri, S., Ashton, C., Moore, P., March, V., & Ferrier, I. (2001). Electrophysiological and cognitive function in young euthymic patients with bipolar affective disorder. *Bipolar Disorders, 3*, 79-87.

Fenn, D., & George, K. (1999). Post-stroke mania late in life involving the left hemisphere. *Australian & New Zealand Journal of Psychiatry, 33*, 598-600.

Ferrier, I., Stanton, B., Kelly, T., & Scott, J. (1999). Neuropsychological function in euthymic patients with bipolar disorder. *British Journal of Psychiatry, 175*, 246-251.

Fleck, D., Sax, K., & Strakowski, S. (2001). Reaction time measures of sustained attention differentiate bipolar disorder from schizophrenia. *Schizophrenia Research, 52*, 251-259.

Fleck, Shear, Zimmerman, Getz, Corey, Jak, Lebowitz, & Strakowski. (2003). Verbal memory in mania: effects of clinical state and task requirements. *Bipolar Disorders, 5*, 375-380.

Flor-Henry, P. Functional hemispheric asymmetry and psychopathology. (1983). *Integrative Psychiatry, 1*, 46-52.

Franke, P., Maier, W., Hardt, J., Frieboes, R., Lichtermann, & Hain. (1993). Assessment of frontal lobe functioning in schizophrenia and unipolar major depression. *Psychopathology, 26*, 76-84.

Ghormley, C., & Basso, M. R. (2004). *Neuropsychological Impairment Diminishes Capacity to Provide Informed Consent in Depressed Inpatients*. Paper presented at 32nd annual convention of the International Neuropsychological Society, Baltimore, MD.

Goldberg, T., Gold, J., Greenberg, R., Griffen, S., Schulz, S., Pickar, D., Kleinman, J., & Weinberger, D. (1993). Contrasts between patients with affective disorders and patients with schizophrenia on a neuropsychological test battery. *American Journal of Psychiatry, 150*, 1355-132.

Goldman-Rakic. P. (1994). Working memory dysfunction in schizophrenia. *Journal of Neuropsychiatry and Clinical Neurosciences, 6*, 348-357.

Harmer, C., Clark, L., Grayson, L., & Goodwin, G. (2002). Sustained attention deficit in bipolar disorder is not a working memory impairment in disguise. *Neuropsychologia,* 40, 1586-1590.

Hauser, P., *Matochik, J., Altshuler, L., Denicoff, K., Conrad, A., Li, X.*, and *Post, R.* (2000). MRI-based measurements of temporal lobe and ventricular structures in patients with bipolar I and bipolar II disorders. *Journal of Affective Disorders, 60*, 25-32.

Hawkins, K., Hoffman, R., Quinlan, D., Rakfeldt, J., Docherty, N., & Sledge, W. (1997). Cognition, negative symptoms, and diagnosis: a comparison of schizophrenic, bipolar, and control samples. *Journal of Neuropsychiatry and Clinical Neurosciences, 9*, 81-89.

Henry, G., Weingartner, H., & Murphy, D. (1973). Influence of affective states and psychoactive drugs on verbal learning and memory. *American Journal of Psychiatry, 130*, 966-971.

Hilty, D., Brady, K., & Hales, R. (1999). A review of bipolar disorder among adults. *Psychiatric Services, 50*, 201-213.

Hirayasu, Y., Shenton, M., Salisbury, D., Kwon, J., Wible, C., Fischer, I., *Yurgelun-Todd, D.*, Zarate, C., Kikinis, R., Jolescz, F., & McCarley, R. (1999). Subgenual cingulate cortex volume in first-episode psychosis. *American Journal of Psychiatry, 156*, 1091-1093.

Hoff, A., Shukla, S., Aronson, T., Cook, B., Ollo, C., Baruch, S., Jandorf, L., & Schwartz, J. (1990). Failure to differentiate bipolar disorder from schizophrenia on measures of neuropsychological function. *Schizophrenia Research, 3*, 253-260.

Kaufman, A. S. & Lichtenberger, E. O. (2002). *Assessing adolescent and adult intelligence (2nd ed.)*. Boston, MA.: Allyn & Bacon.

Kennedy, S., Javanmard, M., & Vaccarino, F. (1997). A review of functional neuroimaging in mood disorders: positron emission tomography and depression. *Canadian Journal of Psychiatry, 42*, 467-45.

Kindermann, S., & Brown, G. (1997). Depression and memory in the elderly: A meta-analysis. *Journal of Clinical & Experimental Neuropsychology, 19*, 625-642.

Kishimoto, H., Takazu, O., Ohno, S., Yamaguchi, T., Fujita, Kuwahara, Ishii, Matsushita, Yokoi, & Iio. (1987). -1-1C-glucose metabolism in manic and depressed patients. *Psychiatry Research, 22*, 81-88.

Koek, R., Yerevanian, B., Tachiki, K., Smith, J., Alcock, J., & Kopelowicz, K. (1999). Hemispheric asymmetry in depression and mania. A longitudinal QEEG study in bipolar disorder. *Journal of Affective Disorders,* 53, 109-122.

Krabbendam,L., Honig, A., Wiersma, J., Vuurman, E., Hofman, P., Derix, M., Nolen, W., & Jolles, J. (2000). Cognitive dysfunctions and white matter lesions in patients with bipolar disorder in remission. *Acta Psychiatrica Scandinavica, 101*, 274-280.

Lebowitz, B., Shear, P., Steed, M., & Strakowski, S. (July-September, 2001). Verbal fluency in mania: relationship to number of manic episodes. *Neuropsychiatry, Neuropsychology, and Behavioral Neurology, 14*, 177-182.

Lee, A., Ogle, W., & Sapolsky, R. (2002). Stress and depression: possible links to neuron death in the hippocampus. *Bipolar Disorders, 4*, 117-128.

Lezak, M. (1995). *Neuropsychological assessment* (3rd ed.). London: Oxford University Press.

MacQueen, G., Young, L., & Joffe, R. (2001). A review of psychosocial outcome in patients with bipolar disorder. *Acta Psychiatrica Scandinavica, 103*, 163-170.

Martin, D., Oren, Z., & Boone, K. (1991). Major depressives' and dysthmics' performance on the Wisconsin Card Sorting Test. *Journal of Clinical Psychology, 47*, 684-690.

Martinez-Aran, A., Penades, R., Vieta, E., Colom, F., Reinares, M., Benabarrere, A., Salamero, M., & Gasto, C. (2002). Executive function in patients with remitted bipolar disorder and schizophrenia and its relationship with functional outcome. *Psychotherapy & Psychosomatics, 71*, 39-46.

Martinez-Aran, A., Vieta, E., Colom, F., Reinares, M., Benabarre, A., Gasto, C., & Salamero, M. (2000). Cognitive dysfunctions in bipolar disorder: evidence of neuropsychological disturbances. *Psychotherapy and psychosomatics,* 69(1), 2-18.

McDonald, W., Tupler, L., Marsteller, F., Figie, G., DiSouza, S., Nemeroff, C., & Krishnan, K. (1999). Hyperintense lesions on magnetic resonance images in bipolar disorder. *Biological Psychiatry, 45*, 965-971.

McGrath, J., Chapple, B., & Wright, M. (2001). Working memory in schizophrenia and mania: correlation with symptoms during the acute and subacute phases. *Acta Psychiatrica Scandinavica, 103*, 181-188.

McGrath, J., Scheldt, S., Welham, J., & Clair, A. (1997). Performance on tests sensitive to impaired executive ability in schizophrenia, mania and well controls: acute and subacute phases. *Schizophrenia research, 26(2-3)*, 127-137.

Mojtabai, R., Bromet, E., Harvey, P., Carlson, G., Craig, T., & Fennig, S. (2000). Neuropsychological differences between first-admission schizophrenia and psychotic affective disorders. *American Journal of Psychiatry, 157*, 1453-1460.

Monkul, E. S., Malhi, G. S., & Soares, J. C. (2003). Mood disorders-Review of structural MRI studies. *Acta Neuropsyciatrica, 15*, 368-380.

Moore, P., Shepherd, D., Eccleston, D., Macmillan, I., Goswami, U., McAllister, V., & Ferrier, I. (2001) Cerebral white matter lesions in bipolar affective disorder: relationship to outcome. *British Journal of Psychiatry, 178*, 172-176.

Morice, R. (1990). Cognitive inflexibility and pre-frontal dysfunction in schizophrenia and mania. *British Journal of Psychiatry, 157*, 50-54.

Murphy, F., Sahakian, B., Rubinsztein, J., Michael, A., Rogers, R., Robbins, T., & Paykel, E. (1999). Emotional bias and inhibitory control processes in mania and depression. *Psychological Medicine, 29*, 1307-1321.

Nasrallah, H. (1991). Neurodevelopmental aspects of bipolar affective disorder. *Biological Psychiatry, 29*, 1-2.

Neu, P., Kiesslinger, U., Schlattmann, P., & Reischies, F. (2001). Time-related cognitive deficiency in four different types of depression. *Psychiatry Research*, 103, 237-247.

Post, R. M., Leverich, G. S., Altshuler, L. L., Frye, M. A., Suppes, T. M., Keck, P. E., McElroy, S. L., Kupka, R., Nolen, W. A., Grunze, H., & Walden, J. (2003). An overview of recent findings of the Stanley Foundation Bipolar Network (Part I). *Bipolar Disorders, 5*, 310-319.

Post, R. M., (1992). Transduction of psychosocial stress into the neurobiology of recurrent affective disorder. *American Journal of Psychiatry, 149*, 999-1010.

Quraishi, S., & Frangou, S. (2002). Neuropsychology of bipolar disorder: a review. *Journal of Affective Disorders, 72*, 209-226.

Rajkowska, G. (2002). Cell pathology in bipolar disorder. *Bipolar Disorder,* 4, 105-116.

Rajkowska, G., Halaris, A., & Selemon, L. (2001). Reductions in neuronal and glial density characterize the dorsolateral prefrontal cortex in bipolar disorder. *Biological Psychiatry, 49*, 741-752.

Rossi, A., Arduini, L., Daneluzzo, E., Bustini, M., Prosperini, P., & Stratta, P. (2000). Cognitive function in euthymic bipolar patients, stabilized schizophrenic patients, and healthy controls. *Journal of Psychiatric Research*, 34, 333-339.

Rubinsztein, J., Fletcher, P., Rogers, R., Ho, L., Aigbrihio, F., Paykel, E., Robbins, T., & Sahakian, B. (2001). Decision-making in mania: A PET study. *Brain, 124*, 2550-2563.

Rubinsztein, J., Michael, A., Paykel, E., & Sahakian, B. (2000). Cognitive impairment in remission in bipolar affective disorder. *Psychological Medicine, 30*, 1025-1036.

Sackeim, H., Freeman, J., McElhiney, M., Coleman, E., Prudie, & Devanand. (1992). Effects of major depression estimates of intelligence. *Journal of Clinical & Experimental Neuropsychology, 14*, 268-288.

Savard, R., Rey, A., & Post., R. (1980). Halstead-Reitan Category Test in bipolar and unipolar affective disorders. Relationship to age and phase of illness. *Journal of nervous and mental disease, 168*, 297-304.

Sax, K., Strakowski, S., Zimmerman, M., DelBello, M., Keck, P., & Hawkins, J. (1999). Frontosubcortical neuroanatomy and the continuous performance test in mania. *American Journal of Psychiatry, 156*, 139-141.

Seidman, L., Kremen, W., Koren, D.,Faraone, S., Goldstein, J., & Tsuang, M. (2002.) A comparative profile analysis of neuropsychological functioning in patients with schizophrenia and bipolar psychoses. *Schizophrenia Research, 53*, 31-44.

Sheline, Y. (2000). 3D MRI studies of neuroanatomic changes in unipolar major depression: the role of stress and medical comorbidity. *Biological Psychiatry,* 48, 791-800.

Sheline, Y. (2003) Neuroimaging studies of mood disorder effects on the brain. *Biological Psychiatry,* 54, 338-352.

Sigurdsson, E., Fombonne, E., Sayal, K., & Checkley, S. (1999). Neurodevelopmental antecedents of early-onset bipolar affective disorder. *British Journal of Psychiatry, 174*, 121-127.

Silverstone, T., McPherson, H., Li, Q., & Doyle, T. (2003). Deep white matter hyperintensities in patients with bipolar depression, unipolar depression and age-matched control subjects. *Bipolar Disorders, 5*, 53-57.

Soares, J., & Mann, J. (1997). The functional neuroanatomy of mood disorders. *Journal of Psychiatric Research, 31*, 393-432.

Strakowski, S., Del Bello, M., Zimmerman, M., Getz, G., Mills, N., Ret, J., Shear, P., & Adler, C. (2002). Ventricular and Periventricular Structural Volumes in First- Versus Multiple-Episode Bipolar Disorder. *American Journal of Psychiatry, 159*, 1841-1847.

Sweeney, J., Kmiec, J., & Kupfer, D. (2000). Neuropsychologic impairments in bipolar and unipolar mood disorders on the CANTAB neurocognitive battery. *Biological psychiatry, 48*, 674-684.

Tham, A., Engelbrektson, K., Mathe, A., Johnson, L., Olsson, E., & Aberg-Wistedt, L. (1997). Impaired neuropsychological performance in euthymic patients with recurring mood disorders. *Journal of Clinical Psychiatry,* 58, 26-29.

Tsuchiya, K., Byrne, M., & Mortensen, P. (2003). Risk factors in relation to an emergence of bipolar disorder: a systematic review. *Bipolar Disorder, 5*, 231-242.

Uranova, N., Orlovskaya, D., Vikhreva, O., Zimina, I., Kolomeets, N., Vostrikov, V., & Rachmanova, V. (2001). Electron microscopy of oligodendroglia in severe mental illness. *Brain Research Bulletin, 55*, 597-610.

Van Gorp, W., Altshuler, L., Theberge, D., & Mintz, J. (1999). Declarative and procedural memory in bipolar disorder. *Biological psychiatry, 46*, 525-531.

Van Gorp, W., Altshuler, L., Theberge, D., Wilkins, J., & Dixon, W. (1998). Cognitive impairment in euthymic bipolar patients with and without prior alcohol dependence. A preliminary study. *Archives of General Psychiatry, 55*, 41-46.

Veiel, H. (1997). A preliminary profile of neuropsychological deficits associated with major depression. *Journal of Clinical & Experimental Neuropsychology, 19*, 587-603.

Verdoux, H., & Liraud, F. (2000). Neuropsychological function in subjects with psychotic and affective disorders. Relationship to diagnostic category and duration of illness. *European Psychiatry, 15*, 236-243.

Videbech, P. (1997). MRI findings in patients with affective disorder: a meta-analysis. *Acta Psychiatrica Scandinavica, 96*, 157-168.

Wilder-Willis, K., Sax, K., Rosenberg, H., Fleck, D., Shear, P., & Strakowski, S. (2001). Persistent attentional dysfunction in remitted bipolar disorder. *Bipolar Disorders,* 3, 58-62.

Wolfe, J., Granholm, E., Butters, N., Saunders, E., & Janowsky, D. (1987). Verbal memory deficits associated with major affective disorders: a comparison of unipolar and bipolar patients. *Journal of Affective Disorders, 13*, 83-92.

Zarate, C., Tohen, M., Land, M., & Cavanagh, S. (2000). Functional impairment and cognition in bipolar disorder. *Psychiatric Quarterly, 71*, 309-329.

Zihl, J., Gron, G., & Brunnauer, A. (1998). Cognitive deficits in schizophrenia and affective disorders: evidence for a final common pathway disorder. *Acta Psychiatrica Scandinavica, 97*, 351-357.

Zubieta, J., Huguelet, P., O'Neil, R., & Giordani, B. (2001) Cognitive function in euthymic bipolar I disorder. *Psychiatry Research, 102*, 9-20.

In: Focus on Bipolar Disorder Research
Editor: Malcomb R. Brown, pp. 59-74 ISBN 1-59454-059-4

Chapter 4

Co-Morbidity of Migraine and Affective Disorders

Ole Bernt Fasmer and Ketil Joachim Oedegaard
Department of Psychiatry, University of Bergen, Bergen, Norway

Abstract

Context

Migraine and depression are both common disorders in the general population, and epidemiological studies have shown a substantial co-morbidity between them.

Objective

The present investigation was undertaken to examine the prevalence of migraine in patients presenting with major affective disorders and to study the clinical characteristics of these patients.

Design

A total of 201 patients with an index episode of either major depression or mania were interviewed with a semi-structured interview based partly on DSM-IV criteria and partly on Akiskals criteria for affective temperaments. One hundred and nineteen of the patients were consecutively admitted to an open psychiatric ward, and an additional 82 patients were recruited from other wards or were outpatients.

Results

Symptoms of migraine were found to be common. In the sample of 119 consecutively admitted inpatients there was a 45 % prevalence of migraine in the patients with unipolar depressive disorder and 58 % in patients with bipolar disorders. Among the bipolar patients there was, however, a striking difference between the two diagnostic subgroups, with a prevalence of 74 % in bipolar II and 33 % in bipolar I disorder. In the whole sample of 201 patients we looked at the clinical characteristics of the patients with migraine (n = 117) compared to those without (n = 84). The patients with co-morbid migraine had a higher frequency of affective temperaments (49 % vs. 31 %), more depressive episodes (5.2 vs. 3.4), a greater number of anxiety disorders (2.6 vs. 1.9), and a higher frequency of panic disorder (50 % vs. 29 %) and agoraphobia (44 % vs. 24 %). They also more often had prominent irritability during depressive episodes (71 % vs. 51 %).

Conclusions

The present results support the contention that bipolar I and II are biologically separate disorders. Furthermore, it is possible that the presence of migraine may be used to delineate a distinct subgroup of the major affective disorders. These findings also point to the possibility of using the association of major affective disorders with migraine to study both the pathophysiology and the genetics of the major affective disorders.

Introduction

Both migraine and depression are common disorders in the general population, with a comparable prevalence, around 10 %, and with a similar gender distribution, females being more often affected than men [1, 2]. Both disorders have a genetic background, but for none of them has it been possible to pinpoint a single genetic locus [3, 4]. Prodromal and accompanying symptoms of migraine attacks often are psychiatric in nature, such as depression, elation, irritabiliy, anxiety, overactivity, difficulty thinking, anorexia or increased appetite. In some patients an organic mental syndrome can be part of a migraine attack [5]. In other patients an acute psychotic condition is the dominating clinical feature. This presentation, with paranoid delusions, hallucinations and anxiety, has been described in families with hemiplegic migraine [6]. Case series and uncontrolled studies have shown a strong association between migraine and affective disorders and this has been confirmed in epidemiological studies [7, 8, 9]. In a study from Detroit [7] the risk of experiencing episodes of major depression was found to be increased three times among migraine sufferers, and they also have an increased frequency of both bipolar I and II disorders. Furthermore, there is also a strong association between migraine and anxiety disorders [7, 8, 10]. Family studies have suggested that there is a syndromal relationship between migraine, depression and anxiety disorders [11].

There are few studies of migraine in patients presenting primarily with psychiatric disorders. Endicott found in a study from private specialist practice in New York [12] that between 20 and 50 % of patients with major affective disorders also had migraine and Mahmood and co-workers found a 26 % prevalence of migraine in patients with bipolar disorders [13]. There is however little information concerning the characteristics of the affective disorders in patients with co-morbid migraine. Merikangas and Stevens [11] have stated that the depressive episodes often have an atypical symptom pattern. We have previously reported that in patients hospitalized for major affective disorders approximately one half had co-morbid migraine, and among the migraine patients there was an equal prevalence of unipolar depressive and bipolar disorders. Most of the bipolar patients had bipolar II disorder [14]. We have also, in a sample of 102 patients, described the clinical characteristics of the patients with major affective disorders and co-morbid migraine [15]. The present study is an extension of these previous reports in a larger sample of patients.

METHODS

The study group (n= 201) comprised 177 psychiatric patients at one of the University hospitals of Bergen and 24 psychiatric patients from private practice in the county of Fusa outside Bergen. One hundred and nineteen subjects were consecutively admitted patients to a 12 bed open psychiatric ward. The patients were recruited during two separate time periods (62 and 57 patients). This ward is open 5 days a week. Most of the patients have initially been admitted to one of the closed wards of the hospital, and have subsequently been transferred to this open ward, when they are in the process of recovering. Criteria for admission to the ward are the need for further inpatient treatment, combined with the ability to function at home with their families during weekends. The length of the inpatient treatment is usually 1-3 months. Most of the patients admitted to this ward have affective disorders. The remaining patients from the hospital were either inpatients at other wards (n = 19), or were recruited from the outpatient department or the day care unit (n = 39). Patients were included if they presented with a major affective syndrome (major depression or mania), which was not clearly secondary to an organic or substance abuse disorder, were between 18 and 65 years old, and gave informed consent to participate. Patients that did not speak Norwegian with sufficient fluency to be interviewed without interpreter were excluded. The patients that were psychotic at intake were not psychotic when interviewed. The local ethics committee has approved the study protocol.

We used a semi-structured interview based on DSM-IV criteria [16] for affective disorders (major depressive episode, mania, hypomania), anxiety disorders (panic disorder, agoraphobia, specific phobia, social phobia, generalized anxiety disorder, obsessive compulsive disorder) and eating disorders (anorexia nervosa and bulimia nervosa). Hyperthymic, irritable and depressive temperaments were diagnosed according to the criteria of Akiskal and Mallya [17], and cyclothymic temperament according to Akiskal and Akiskal [18]. Criteria for the cyclothymic temperament requires at least three of five attributes of each of the following two sets, with an indeterminate early onset (<21 years). First group: 1. Hypersomnia versus decreased need for sleep. 2. Introverted self-absorption versus uninhibited people-seeking. 3. Taciturn versus talkative. 4. Unexplained tearfulness versus buoyant jocularity. 5. Psychomotor inertia versus restless pursuit of activities. Second group: 1. Lethargy and somatic discomfort versus eutonia. 2. Dulling of senses versus keen perceptions. 3. Slow-witted versus sharpened thinking. 4. Shaky self-esteem alternating between low self-confidence and overconfidence. 5. Pessimistic brooding versus optimism and carefree attitudes. The hyperthymic temperament requires at least five of the following characteristics, with an indeterminate early onset (<21 years): 1. Irritable, cheerful, overoptimistic, or exuberant. 2. Naive, overconfident, self-assured, boastful, bombastic, or grandiose. 3. Vigorous, full of plans, improvident, and rushing off with restless impulse. 4. Overtalkative. 5. Warm, people-seeking, or extroverted. 6. Overinvolved and meddlesome. 7. Uninhibited, stimulus-seeking, or promiscuous. The irritable temperament requires at least five of the following characteristics, with an indeterminate early onset (<21 years): 1. Habitually moody, irritable and choleric, with infrequent euthymia. 2. Tendency to brood. 3. Hypercritical and complaining. 4. Ill-humoured joking. 5. Obtrusiveness. 6. Dysphoric restlessness. 7. Impulsive. The depressive requires at least five of the following characteristics, with an indeterminate early onset (<21 years): 1. Gloomy, pessimistic, humourless, or incapable of fun. 2. Quiet, passive, and indecisive. 3. Sceptical, hypercritical, or complaining. 4. Brooding and given to worry. 5. Conscientious or self-disciplining. 6. Self-critical, self-reproaching, and self-derogatory. 7. Preoccupied with inadequacy, failure, and negative events to the point of morbid enjoyment of ones failures.

Unipolar depressive (major depressive disorder) and bipolar I disorders were diagnosed according to DSM-IV criteria. Bipolar II disorder was in this study defined to include patients fulfilling either DSM-IV criteria for the disorder or the criteria for a cyclothymic or hyperthymic temperament as described above, in addition to one or more major depressive episodes.

In addition the following information was recorded: age of onset of the first major affective episode and the first depressive episode, the number of depressive episodes, the presence of melancholic or atypical symptoms (DSM-IV criteria) in the present or in previous episodes, seasonal variability of depressive episodes, current or previous suicide attempt, psychotic symptoms, and the presence of prominent irritability or suspiciousness in the current or previous major depressive episodes.

Symptoms of the following psychiatric disorders were also recorded (DSM-IV criteria): attention-deficit/hyperactive disorder, learning disorders and abuse of alcohol and drugs. Use of tobacco currently or previously was noted. History of characteristic symptoms of the following somatic symptoms were asked for: allergic rhinitis or other allergic disorders, asthma or atopic eczema; Raynaud syndrome [19] and thyroid disorders.

The criteria of the Headache Classification Committee of the International Headache Society [20] were used to establish the diagnosis of migraine. In addition to migraine with and without aura the occurrence of migraine auras without headache was specifically recorded. Age of onset of migraine and the frequency of attacks (>1/week, >1/month, <1/month, no attacks last year) were also recorded.

Information about serious psychiatric disorders (major depression, bipolar disorder, psychosis, suicide) or migraine in first degree family members was obtained from interviews of patients or from hospital records.

The first 102 patients, 62 from the open ward, were interviewed by the first (OBF), and the last 99 patients, 57 from the open ward, by the second author (KJO). To assure an identical diagnostic approach both authors interviewed ten patients together.

Chi-square test or t-test (two-tailed) was used to calculate differences between groups, with a significance level of 0.05. SPSS version 11.0 was used for the statistical analyses.

Results

The mean age of the group of consecutively admitted inpatients (n = 119) was 36.5 ± 9.7 years. Eighty-six (72 %) patients were female. The index episode was depression in 89% of the patients and mania in 11 %. Sixty-one (51 %) had migraine (57%); 25 patients (21 %) had migraine with aura, 23 (19 %) had migraine without aura and 13 (11 %) had migraine aura without headache. In males the frequency of migraine was 42 % (14/33), and in females 55 % (47/86). A majority of the patients had suffered from migraine within the last 12 months (82%). Most of them did not present migraine headaches as a prominent complaint when interviewed and often a history of migraine was not noted in the hospital records. The age of onset of migraine was 22.4 ± 9.9 years (mean ± SD, range 5 - 51). In this sample there was an almost equal number of patients with bipolar disorder (n = 59) and unipolar depressive disorder (n = 60). Twenty % (n = 24) had a bipolar I disorder and 29 % (n = 35) a bipolar II disorder. Fifty-one % (44/86) of the women and 45 % (15/33) of the men had a bipolar disorder. In the bipolar II group 17 had a cyclothymic, one a hyperthymic, two an irritable, and one a depressive temperament. Seven of the cyclothymic patients were diagnosed as bipolar II without having had discrete hypomanic episodes. Among the bipolar I patients 9 had a cyclothymic, one an irritable and 3 a depressive temperament. In the unipolar depressive group 8 had a depressive temperament. Looking at the whole group of bipolar patients 58 % (n = 34) had migraine, compared to 45 % (n = 27) in the unipolar depressive group. When comparing the patients with bipolar I and bipolar II disorders there was a substantial difference: 33% (8/24) of the bipolar I patients and 74 % (26/35) of the bipolar II patients had a diagnosis of migraine (Figure 1). When looking separately at patients having migraine with aura (Figure 2) and migraine without aura (Figure 3) the tendencies are the same – there are more patients with each migraine type in the bipolar II group compared to bipolar I.

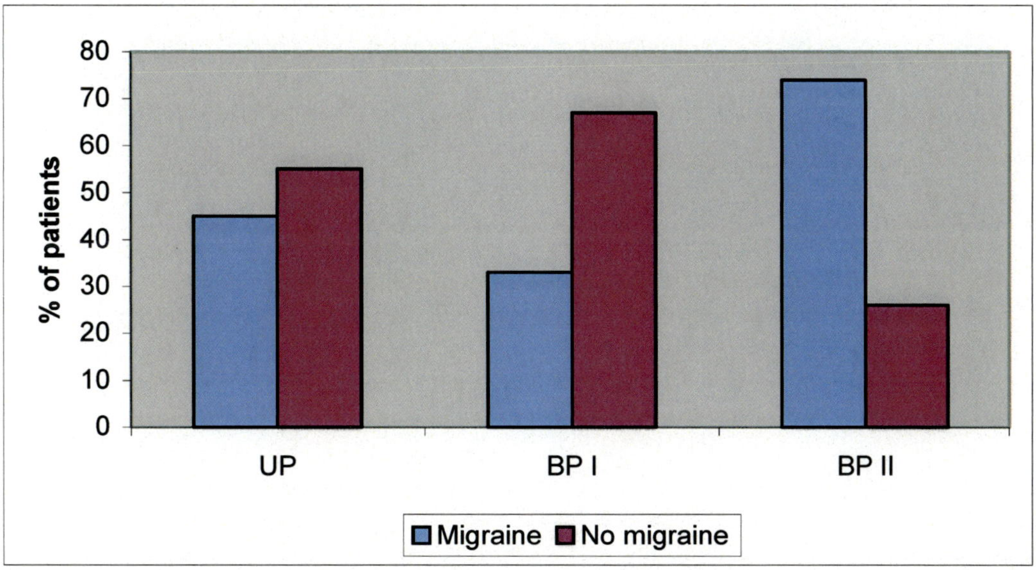

Figure 1 Percent of patients with and without migraine in unipolar depressive (UP, n = 60), bipolar II (BP II, n = 35) and bipolar I (BP I, n = 24) disorders (p = 0.003, Chi-square test).

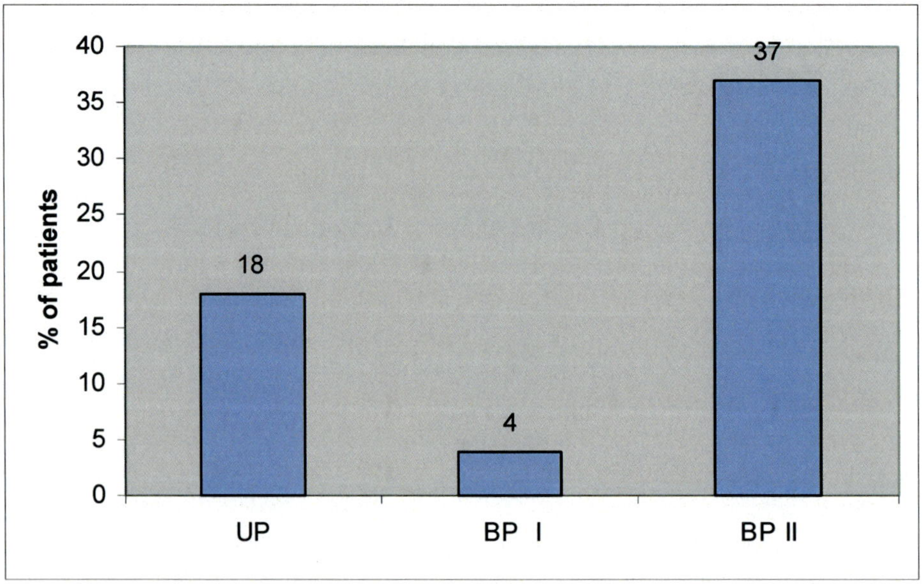

Figure 2 Percent of patients having migraine with aura in unipolar depressive (UP, n = 60), bipolar II (BP II, n = 35) and bipolar I (BP I, n = 24) disorders.

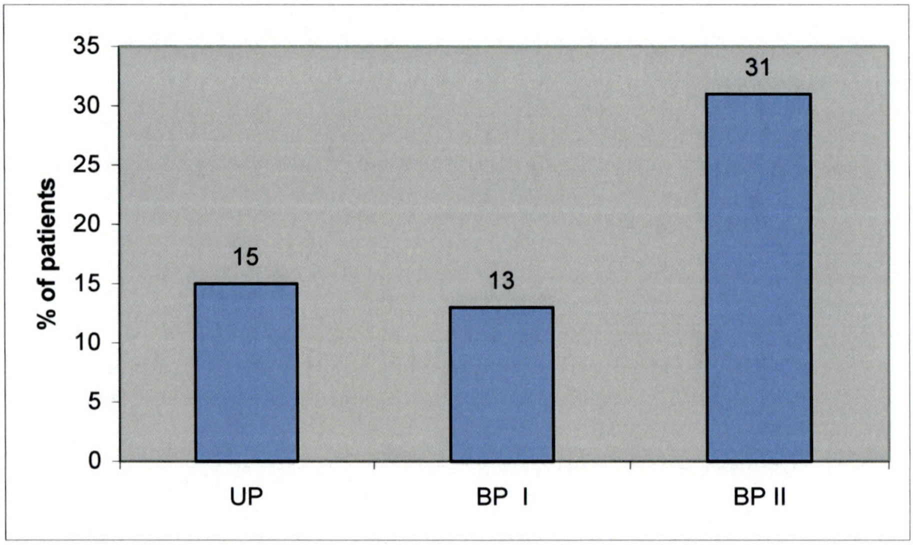

Figure 3 Percent of patients having migraine without aura in unipolar depressive (UP, n = 60), bipolar II (BP II, n = 35) and bipolar I (BP I, n = 24) disorders.

The frequency of migraine attacks was not significantly different in patients with bipolar II disorder compared to patients with unipolar depressive disorder: in the bipolar II group 8/25 patients had attacks more than once a week, 8 had more than once a month, 9 less than once a month and one did not have any migraine attacks the last year; while in the unipolar depressive group 4/24 patients had attacks more than once a week, 8 had more than once a month, 12 less than once a month and three did not have any migraine attacks the last year.

The mean age of the whole group of patients (n = 201) was 36.9± 10.2 years. One hundred and thirty-nine (69 %) patients were female and 138 (69 %) were inpatients. One hundred and seventeen patients had migraine (57%), and among these 57 (28%) patients had migraine with aura, 41 (20%) had migraine without aura and 18 (9%) patients had migraine aura without headache. The age of onset of migraine was 21.5 ± 10.0 years (mean ± SD, range 5 - 51). Characteristics of the whole sample, grouped accorded to the presence or absence of migraine, are detailed in table 1. There were no significant differences in age, age of onset of the first major affective episode, marital status, work activity, alcohol or substance abuse or family history of serious psychiatric illness. There were more inpatients in the no migraine group (80 % vs. 61 %) and more females in the migraine group (76 % vs. 60 %). As expected there were more patients in the migraine group with a family history of migraine (59 % vs. 27 %).

Table 1.

Characteristics of the sample (n = 201)	Migraine (n = 117)	No migraine (n = 84)	P
Age (years, mean ± SD)	37.4 ± 9.9	36.3 ± 10.5	NS*
First affective episode (years, mean ± SD)	25.6 ± 12.0	25.3 ± 10.0	NS*
	% (n)	% (n)	
Inpatient	61 (71)	80 (67)	0.04†
Gender (females)	76 (89)	60 (50)	0.01
Married or cohabiting	45 (53)	36 (30)	NS†
Use of tobacco (current)	68 (80)	58 (49)	NS†
Alcohol or substance abuse	32 (37)	26 (22)	NS†
Serious psychiatric illness in family	66 (77)	58 (49)	NS†
Migraine in family	59 (69)	27 (23)	<0.001†

* T-test (two-tailed).
† Chi-square test.
NS: Not significant

In table 2 the distribution of affective disorders and affective temperaments are shown. The number of patients with unipolar depressive disorder was similar in the migraine and no migraine groups. In the migraine group most of the bipolar patients had bipolar II disorder, while in the group without migraine most of the bipolar patients had bipolar I disorder. These results are similar to those presented in figure 1 for the inpatient sample of 119 patients. Fifty-one of 71 bipolar II patients filled the DSM-IV criteria for the disorder and 20 were diagnosed on the basis of a cyclothymic (n = 16) or a hyperthymic (n = 4) temperament without having had discrete hypomanic episodes. There was a significantly higher frequency of affective temperaments in the migraine group (49 % vs. 31 %). Among the migraine patients 27 % had a cyclothymic, 6 % a hyperthymic, 3 % an irritable and 12 % a depressive temperament, while in the group without migraine 18 % had a cyclothymic, 2 % a hyperthymic, none an irritable and 11 % a depressive temperament.

Table 2.

Affective disorders	Migraine(n = 117) % (n)	No migraine (n = 84) % (n)	P
Unipolar depressive disorder	40 (47)	56 (47)	NS
Bipolar II disorder	48 (56)	18 (15)	<0.001
Bipolar I disorder	12 (14)	26 (22)	0.009
Affective temperament	49 (57)	31 (26)	0.012

Chi-square test.
NS: Not significant.

The frequencies of anxiety and eating disorders are shown in table 3. In the whole sample the frequency of anxiety disorders was high in both groups, but still the migraine patients had significantly more often an anxiety disorder than patients without migraine (88 % vs. 77 %). When counting the number of anxiety disorders for each patient the migraine patients also had a significantly greater number of anxiety disorders. The age of onset of the first anxiety disorder was 16.0 ± 11.1 (mean ± SD) for the patients with migraine and co-morbid anxiety disorder (n = 101). This was earlier than the onset of migraine, which again was earlier than the onset of the first depressive episode. This is shown in figure 4. For 65 % of the patients with migraine and anxiety disorders the first anxiety disorder started before the migraine and in 62 % of the cases the first episode of major depression occurred after the onset of migraine. The first anxiety disorder was most often a specific phobia. In 39 patients the specific phobia occurred before and in 16 after the onset of migraine. The similar figures for panic disorder were 23 before and 30 after the onset of migraine and for agoraphobia 20 and 26. The age of onset of the different anxiety disorders were not significantly different between patients with and without migraine (data not shown).

Table 3.

Anxiety and eating disorders	Migraine (n = 117)	No migraine (n = 84)	P
Number of anxiety disorders	2.6 ± 1.7	1.9 ± 1.5	0.003*
	% (n)	% (n)	
Any anxiety disorder	88 (103)	77 (65)	0.04†
Panic disorder	50 (59)	29 (24)	0.002†
Agoraphobia	44 (52)	24 (20)	0.003†
Social phobia	44 (51)	32 (27)	NS†
Generalized anxiety disorder	50 (58)	46 (39)	NS†
Specific phobia	50 (59)	45 (38)	NS†
Obsessive compulsive disorder	19 (22)	18 (15)	NS†
Anorexia nervosa	16 (19)	4 (3)	0.005†
Bulimia nervosa	13 (15)	7 (6)	NS†

* T-test (two-tailed).
† Chi-square test.
NS: Not significant.

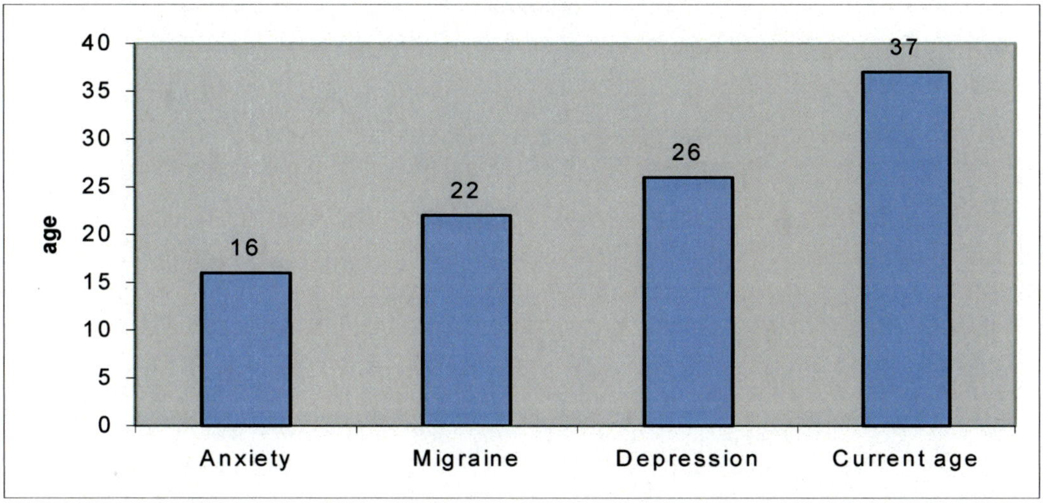

Figure 4 Age of onset of the first anxiety disorder, migraine and the first depressive episode in patients with migraine (n = 117).

In table 4 the characteristics of the depressive episodes are shown. The only difference that emerges between the groups is that the frequency of irritability is higher in the migraine group. There were no difference in the frequency of psychotic symptoms and when separating these symptoms into mood congruent and incongruent there were again no differences (data not shown). The frequencies of melancholic and atypical features of the depressive episodes also were very similar.

Table 4.

Characteristics of major depressive episodes	**Migraine (n = 115)***	**No migraine (n = 78)***	**P**
Onset first depressive episode (years ± SD)	25.9±11.4	25.9±9.8	NS*
Number of depressive episodes	5.2±5.7	3.4±3.6	0.014*
	% (n)	% (n)	
Seasonal variability	27 (32)	17 (14)	NS†
Psychotic symptoms	27 (32)	36 (30)	NS†
Melancholic features	34 (40)	32 (27)	NS†
Atypical features	25 (29)	27 (23)	NS†
Suicide attempt	44 (52)	37 (31)	NS†
Irritability	71 (83)	51 (43)	0.004†
Suspiciousness	60 (70)	56 (47)	NS†

* T-test (two-tailed).
† Chi-square test.
NS: Not significant.
Two patients in the migraine group and six in the no migraine group did not have depressive episodes.

There were no significant differences in the frequencies of attention-deficit hyperactive disorder, learning disorders, Raynaud`s syndrome, allergic rhinitis or thyroid disorders among the two groups. However there was a significantly higher frequency of asthma in the migraine group (23 % vs. 7 %).

COMMENT

The present findings indicate that major affective disorders associated with migraine for the most part represent unipolar depressive and bipolar II disorders. Few of the migraine patients had bipolar I disorder. In the sample with consecutively admitted inpatients the prevalence of migraine was highest among patients with bipolar II disorder (74 %), and this was significantly different from the prevalence among the bipolar I patients (33 %). The unipolar group had a prevalence in between (45 %). We also found that in the whole sample of patients (n = 201) almost half of the migraine patients (49 %) had an affective temperament. This was significantly different from that seen in patients without migraine (31 %). Furthermore, the migraine patients more often had an anxiety disorder, they had an increased number of anxiety disorders, especially panic disorder and agoraphobia and they had a greater number of depressive episodes. Other characteristics such as age, age of onset of the first major affective episode, marital status, and frequency of alcohol or substance abuse were not significantly different.

The symptoms of the depressive episodes were similar to those of patients without migraine, with equal frequencies of melancholic, atypical and psychotic symptoms. The only difference that emerged was an increased frequency of irritability during depressive episodes among the patients with migraine. One previous study on the personality of migraine sufferers found higher scores among women on the psychoticism scale of the Eysenck Personality Questionnaire [21], but other studies have been negative and have only reported increased levels of neuroticism [22]. Irritability may both be a part of the prodrome that often precedes migraine headaches [5] and a prominent symptom during hypomanic/manic or mixed depressive episodes [17, 23, 24, 25, 26]. Depressive mixed states (major depressive episodes with some hypomanic symptoms) have been found to be more prevalent in atypical depressions than in non-atypical depressions [27], and are associated with bipolar disorders [28, 29. Thus, the increased frequency of irritability among the migraine patients in the present study may reflect a linkage to bipolar disorders. We have, however, not asked specifically for symptoms of mixed depressive episodes in our patients, but we think it is probable that they have an increased frequency of such episodes compared to patients without migraine.

The high frequency of migraine among the men in this study (42 %, compared to 55 % among the women in the inpatient sample) is different from what is usually found in population studies. Rasmussen and Olesen [30] found in an epidemiological study from Denmark a male: female ratio of 1: 2 for migraine with aura and 1: 7 for migraine without aura. In a large group (n = 327) of patients with bipolar I disorder 27 % of the women and 14 % of the men had a history of migraine headaches [31]. However, the present findings are in agreement with those of Low and co-workers [32] who found migraine in 31 % of male and 44 % of female bipolar patients. Similarly, in a sample of bipolar patients, Mahmood, Romans and Silverstone [13] found an equal proportion of male (25 %) and female (27 %) migraine sufferers. The present study thus indicates that major affective disorders in males and females may be associated with an approximately equal frequency of migraine.

It has been suggested that bipolar disorder associated with migraine might represent a more severe variant of bipolar disorder, based on an earlier onset of the bipolar disorder and greater social impairment [13]. In the present study we found an increased number of depressive episodes among the migraine patients, but age of onset and frequency of psychotic symptoms ere not different. Therefore, the present data do not indicate that patients with major affective disorders and co-morbid migraine have a more serious affective disorder than patients without migraine.

In an epidemiological study from Detroit persons with migraine (n = 128) had a 26.6 % lifetime prevalence of major depression and a 9.4 % prevalence of dysthymia, compared to 4.7 % for manic episodes and 3.9 % for bipolar II disorder [7]. This relationship between unipolar and bipolar disorders is clearly in contrast to findings of the present study. One possible explanation for this difference may be selection bias in the present sample. The present definition of bipolar II disorder is also broader than the DSM-IV criteria. However with regard to the difficulty of diagnosing hypomania it is not unlikely that a diagnostic assessment of a community sample in line with the present investigation would have yielded a higher frequency of bipolar II disorders [28]. In an epidemiological study, from Zurich [33], persons with migraine (n = 61) had a threefold increased prevalence of mania or hypomania (8.8 %) and a twofold increased prevalence of major depression (14.7 %). These results are in accordance with our findings. Similarly, among patients attending a headache clinic the lifetime prevalence of bipolar spectrum disorders was found to be 8.6 % [34]. In a study of patients from a private psychiatric practice [12] the highest frequency of migraine (51 %) was found in patients with characteristics similar to bipolar II patients as defined in the present study. Patients with bipolar I disorder in that study had a migraine frequency of 22 % and strictly unipolar depressive patients a frequency of 27 %. A recent study from Canada [32] also found quite comparable results, a 35 % prevalence of migraine in bipolar I patients compared to 65 % in bipolar II patients.

Both suicidal ideation and suicide attempts have been reported to be increased in patients having migraine with aura and major depression compared to patients having major depression without migraine [35]. In the present study the number of patients with suicide attempts was not significantly different between the groups with and without migraine. The most probable explanation is the high baseline frequency of suicide attempts in the whole sample, obscuring any preferential association with migraine.

The present findings are similar to other studies with regard to the association between migraine and anxiety disorders [10, 36]. Patients with migraine and major depression most often have a co-morbid anxiety disorder [11 and this was also evident among the migraine patients in this study. Breslau and Davis [37] found in a community study a doubled frequency of anxiety disorders among migraine patients, and the association was especially strong for panic disorder, with a six-fold increase. The temporal association between the onset of the different anxiety disorders, migraine and major depression is also similar to previous findings from Zurich [33]. There seems to be a constellation with an early onset of an anxiety disorder (most often a specific phobia), 16.0 years in the present study, followed by migraine (21.5 years) and major depression (25.9 years).

These results confirm the findings from our previous and smaller studies [14, 15], and indicate that there may be a preferential association between migraine and bipolar II disorder. There is substantial evidence that bipolar I and bipolar II disorders represent two different nosological conditions [38]. It is however not always easy to separate hypomania from mania and patients with unipolar depressive disorder may on closer scrutiny show signs of bipolarity or develop mania or hypomania during follow up [28]. We therefore suggest that major affective disorders combined with migraine might represent a separate and distinct symptom cluster. As a group these patients may not simply be classified as belonging to either a unipolar or a bipolar disorder, at least not as defined according to DSM-IV. The present classification systems in psychiatry group patients with affective disorders into diagnostic categories on the basis of characteristic constellations of affective symptoms. However, it seems reasonable to envisage that different pathophysiological mechanisms may cause similar constellations of clinical psychiatric symptoms. At the present stage of our knowledge, significant co-morbid patterns may be the most promising way of creating new and more useful classification schemes. This has been suggested with regard to panic disorder in patients with bipolar disorder [39, 40, 41]. Use of a non-psychiatric disorder such as migraine may perhaps also be employed to define subgroups among the affective disorders.

Migraine is an organic disorder with a genetic background, even if environmental factors also are important both etiologically and in the precipitation of individual attacks [5. Vascular symptoms are prominent, but it is now fairly well established that the primary pathophysiological disturbance is neuronal [5]. Neurophysiological investigations into migraine have produced substantial information concerning the pathophysiology of this disorder [42]. It seems not unreasonable to suppose that there must be a basic neurophysiological derangement responsible both for the short-lasting, episodic phenomena seen in these patients (migraine, panic attacks, hypomania) and for the longer-lasting disturbances (major depression, affective temperaments). This may possibly be linked to disturbances in either the serotonergic [43, 44] or the dopaminergic system [45].

With regard to disturbance of 5-HT neurotransmission van Praag [46 has suggested that altered 5-HT neurotransmission is central to the pathophysiology of affective disorders, and that there is a subtype of depression characterized by 5-HT disturbance accompanied by anxiety and/or aggression. The increased number of anxiety disorders and prominent irritability as found in the present study among patients with major affective disorders and co-morbid migraine suggest that migraine could well be fitted into such a pattern. We also found a significantly increased frequency of anorexia (16 % vs. 4 %) in this study, and there is evidence for disturbances in 5-HT neurotransmission in patients with eating disorders [47]. Other links may be the increased frequency of suicidal thoughts and suicide attempts found among patients with migraine [35], and the high frequency of migraine among patients with impulse-control disorders [48].

We found a high frequency of asthma (30 %) among the migraine patients in this study. This was not surprising, since there is a well known association of asthma and migraine [49]. However we did not find any association between migraine and Raynaud`s syndrome.

The major limitation of the present study is the difficulty of knowing if the results may be generalised to patients with major affective disorders in the general population. The patients that were interviewed in this study clearly represented a selected group. However the findings probably give an indication concerning the frequency of migraine in patients attending psychiatric hospitals and underscore the importance of including questions on migraine when taking the history of these patients. Relatives were not systematically interviewed. If this had been done it might have given a better separation of bipolar II disorder from unipolar depressive disorder and this could perhaps also have allowed a better delineation of the affective temperaments. Concerning the statistics we have chosen to present P-values without trying to correct for multiple comparisons. We found an increased number of depressive episodes among the migraine patients, but with regard to the characteristics of depressive episodes the most noteworthy is probably the lack of significant differences. The finding of increased irritability will require confirmation in a larger clinical sample. Concerning the differences between bipolar I and bipolar II disorders, these results seem robust, and are in agreement with findings from other clinical samples [12, 32]. It will, however, be important to see if these findings can be confirmed in a community sample.

Results from epidemiological studies indicate that migraine with aura may have a stronger association to psychiatric disorders than migraine without aura [7]. This is in agreement with our finding that more patients have migraine with aura than migraine without aura, but it is in contrast to the findings of Endicott [12], who reported a larger number of patients with "common" compared to "classical" migraine among patients with major affective disorders. For both migraine with aura and migraine without aura we find approximately the same difference in prevalence between bipolar I and bipolar II disorders. It would be interesting to look for biological differences between the two groups of unipolar depressive patients, those with and those without migraine. If the hypothesis presented in this paper is correct, that the presence of migraine separates a distinct subgroup of affective disorders, there ought to be differences between these groups, perhaps most likely in measures reflecting altered serotonergic or dopaminergic neurotransmission.

The present findings underscore the importance of including questions concerning migraine when taking the history of patients with affective disorders. Decisions concerning pharmacotherapy of a patient with a major affective disorder should take into consideration such a common co-morbid condition as migraine, which is often not reported spontaneously by the patient because he or she does not think this is relevant during a psychiatric consultation. To our knowledge there are no studies that specifically have examined responses to drug treatment in patients with major affective disorders and co-morbid migraine. Guidelines for pharmacological treatment must therefore be based on data from the neurological literature combined with data from the treatment of major depressive disorder, bipolar II disorder and panic disorder. Concerning antidepressants, amitriptyline is the drug that has been best studied in the prophylactic treatment of migraine and has been shown to reduce the frequency of attacks by 40 % [50]. SSRIs are less effective than either amitriptyline or propanolol [51]. Results with lithium are variable [52, 53], and carbamazepine does not seem to have any effect in migraine [54].

Acknowledgments

This research has been supported financially by the legacy of Gerda Meyer Nyquist Gulbrandson & Gerdt Meyer Nyquist.

References

[1] Thase ME, Kupfer DJ. Recent developments in the pharmacotherapy of mood disorders. *J Consult Clin Psychology*. 1996; 64: 646-659.

[2] Silberstein SD, Lipton RB. Epidemiology of migraine. *Neuroepidemiology.* 1993; 12: 179-194.

[3] Gelernter J. Genetics of bipolar affective disorder: time for another reinvention ? *Am J Hum Genet.* 1995; 56: 1262-1266.

[4] Gardner K. The genetic basis of migraine: how much do we know ? *Can J Neurol Sci.* 1999; (Suppl 3): S37-S43.

[5] Davidoff RA. *Migraine: manifestations, pathogenesis, and management.* Philadelphia: F. A. Davis Company; 1995.

[6] Spranger M, Schwab S, Benninger C, Dichgans M. Familial hemiplegic migraine with cerebellar ataxia and paroxysmal psychosis. *Eur Neurol.* 1999; 41: 150 – 152.

[7] Breslau N, Merikangas K, Bowden CL. Comorbidity of migraine and major affective disorders. *Neurology.* 1994; 44 (Suppl 7): S17 – S22.

[8] Swartz KL, Pratt LA, Armenian HK, Lee LC, Eaton WW. Mental disorders and the incidence of migraine headaches in a community sample. *Arch Gen Psychiatry.* 2000; 57: 945-950.

[9] Kececi H, Dener S, Analan. Co-morbidity of migraine and major depression in the Turkish population. *Cephalalgia.* 2003; 23: 271 – 275.

[10] Marazziti D, Toni C, Pedri S et al. Prevalence of headache syndromes in panic disorder. *Int Clin Psychopharmacol.* 1999; 14: 247-251.

[11] Merikangas KR, Stevens DE. Comorbidity of migraine and psychiatric disorders. *Neurologic Clinics.* 1997; 15: 115-123.

[12] Endicott NA. Psychophysiological correlates of "bipolarity". *J Affect Disord.* 1989; 17: 47–56.

[13] Mahmood T, Romans S, Silverstone T. Prevalence of migraine in bipolar disorder. *J Affect Disord.* 1999; 52: 239-241.

[14] Fasmer OB. The prevalence of migraine in patients with bipolar and unipolar depressive disorders. *Cephalalgia.* 2001; 21: 894-899.

[15] Fasmer OB, Oedegaard KJ. Clinical characteristics of patients with major affective disorders and comorbid migraine. *World J Biol Psychiatry.* 2001; 2: 149-155.

[16] American Psychiatric Association. *Diagnostic and Statistical Manual of Mental Disorders, 4th ed. (DSM IV).* Washington DC, American Psychiatric Press; 1994.

[17] Akiskal HS, Mallya G. Criteria for the "soft" bipolar spectrum: treatment implications. *Psychopharmacol Bull.* 1987; 23: 68-73.

[18] Akiskal HS, Akiskal K. Cyclothymic, hyperthymic and depressive temperaments as subaffective variants of mood disorders. In: Tasman A, Riba MB, eds. *Annual Review of Psychiatry.* Vol. 11. Washington DC: American Psychiatric Press; 1992: 43-62.

[19] Miller D, Waters DD, Warnica W, Szlachcic J, Kreeft J, Theroux P. Is variant angina the coronary manifestation of a generalized vasospastic disorder ? *N Engl J Med.* 1981; 304: 763-766.

[20] Headache Classification Committee of the International Headache Society. Classification and diagnostic criteria for headache disorders, cranial neuralgias and facial pain. *Cephalalgia.* 1988; 8 (Suppl.7): 1-96.

[21] Brandt J, Celentano D, Stewart W, Linet M, Folstein M. Personality and emotional disorder in a community sample of migraine headache sufferers. *Am J Psychiatry.* 1990; 147: 303-308.

[22] Merikangas KR. Psychopathology and headache syndromes in the community. *Headache*. 1994; 34: S17-S26.

[23] Goodwin FK, Jamison KR. *Manic-Depressive illness*. New York: Oxford University Press; 1990.

[24] Akiskal HS. The distinctive mixed states of bipolar I, II, and III. *Clin Neuropharm*. 1992; 15 (Suppl. 1): 632 A-633 A.

[25] Koukopoulos A, Faedda G, Proietti R, D`Amico S, de Pisa E, Simonetto C. Mixed depressive syndrome. *Encephale*. 1992; 18 Spec No 1: 19-21.

[26] Perugi G, Akiskal HS, Micheli C et al. Clinical subtypes of bipolar mixed states: validating a broader European definition in 143 cases. *J Affect Disord.* 1997; 43: 169-180.

[27] Benazzi F. Atypical depression with hypomanic symptoms. *J Affect Disord*. 2001; 65: 179-183.

[28] Akiskal HS. The prevalent clinical spectrum of bipolar disorders: beyond DSM-IV. *J Clin Psychopharmacol*. 1996; 16 (Suppl 1): 4S-14S.

[29] Akiskal HS, Hantouche EG, Bourgeois ML et al. Gender, temperament, and the clinical picture in dysphoric mixed mania: findings from a French national study (EPIMAN). *J Affect Disord.* 1998; 50: 175-186.

[30] Rasmussen BK, Olesen J. Migraine with aura and migraine without aura: an epidemiological study. *Cephalalgia*. 1992; 12: 221-228.

[31] Blehar MC, De Paulo JR, Gershon ES, Reich T, Simpson SG, Nurnberger JI. Women with bipolar disorder: findings from the NIMH genetics initiative sample. *Psychopharmacol Bull*. 1998; 34:239-243.

[32] Low NCP, Galbaud du Fort G, Cervantes P. Prevalence, clinical correlates, and treatment of migraine in bipolar disorder. *Headache*. 2003; 43: 940 – 949.

[33] Merikangas KR, Angst J, Isler H. Migraine and psychopathology. *Arch Gen Psychiatry*. 1990; 47: 849-853.

[34] Robbins L, Ludmer C. The bipolar spectrum in migraine patients. *Am J Pain Management*. 2000; 10: 167-170.

[35] Breslau N. Migraine, suicidal ideation, and suicide attempts. *Neurology*. 1992; 42: 392-395.

[36] Marazziti D, Toni C, Pedri S et al. Headache, panic disorder and depression: comorbidity or a spectrum ? *Neuropsychobiology*. 1999; 31: 125-129.

[37] Breslau N, Davis GC. Migraine, major depression and panic disorder: a prospective epidemiological study of young adults. *Cephalalgia*. 1992; 12: 85-90.

[38] Coryell W. Bipolar II disorder: a progress report. *J Affect Disord*. 1996; 41: 159-162.

[39] MacKinnon DF, Xu J, McMahon FJ et al. Bipolar disorder and panic disorder in families: an analysis of chromosome 18 data. *Am J Psychiatry*. 1998; 155: 829–831.

[40] MacKinnon DF, Zandi PP, Cooper J et al. Comorbid bipolar disorder and panic disorder in families with a high prevalence of bipolar disorder. *Am J Psychiatry*. 2002; 159: 30-35.

[41] MacKinnon DF, Zandi PP, Gershon ES, Nurnberger JI, Depaulo JR. Association of rapid mood switching with panic disorder and familial panic risk in familial bipolar disorder. *Am J Psychiatry*. 2003; 160: 1696-1698.

[42] Hargreaves RJ, Shepheard SL. Pathophysiology of migraine – new insights. *Can J Neurol Sci*. 1999; 26 (Suppl 3): S12–S19.

[43] Wang W, Timsit-Berthier M, Schoenen J. Intensity dependence of auditory evoked potentials is pronounced in migraine: an indication of cortical potentiation and low serotonergic neurotransmission? *Neurology*. 1996; 46: 1404-1409.

[44] Chugani DC, Niimura K, Chaturvedi S et al. Increased brain serotonin synthesis in migraine. *Neurology*. 1999; 53: 1473-1479.

[45] Peroutka SJ. Dopamine and migraine. *Neurology*. 1997; 49: 650-656.

[46] VanPraag HM. 5-HT-related, anxiety- and/or aggression-driven depression. *Int Clin Psychopharmacol*. 1994; 9 (Suppl 1): 5-6.

[47] Kaye WH, Gwirtsman HE, George DT, Ebert MH. Altered serotonin activity in anorexia nervosa after long-term weight restoration. *Arch Gen Psychiatry*. 1991; 48: 556-562.

[48] McElroy SL, Soutullo CA, Beckman D, Taylor P, Keck PE. DSM-IV intermittent explosive disorder: a report of 27 cases. *J Clin Psychiatry*. 1998; 59: 203-210.

[49] Chen TC, Leviton A. Asthma and eczema in children born to women with migraine. *Arch Neurol*. 1990; 47: 1227-1230.

[50] Ramadan NM, Schultz LL, Gilkey SJ. Migraine prophylactic drugs: proof of efficacy, utilization and cost. *Cephalalgia*. 1997; 17: 73-80.

[51] Silberstein SD. Comprehensive menagement of headache and depression. *Cephalalgia*. 1998; 18 (Suppl 21): 50 – 55.

[52] Medina JL, Diamond S. Cyclical migraine. *Arch Neurol*. 1981; 38: 343 - 344.

[53] Peatfield RC, Clifford Rose F. Exacerbation of migraine by treatment with lithium. *Headache*. 1981; 21: 140 - 142.

[54] Post RM, Silberstein SD. Shared mechanisms in affective illness, epilepsy, and migraine. *Neurology*. 1994; 44 (Suppl 7): S37 – 47.

In: Focus on Bipolar Disorder Research
Editor: Malcomb R. Brown, pp. 75-112
ISBN 1-59454-059-4

Chapter 5

TRANSMEMBRANE SIGNAL TRANSDUCTION VIA G PROTEINS IMPLICATED IN AFFECTIVE DISORDERS

Yuji Odagaki
Department of Psychiatry, Saitama Medical School

ABSTRACT

Despite vast research from multifaceted points of view, the biochemical abnormalities underlying the predisposition to, and the pathophysiology of, affective disorders have not yet been fully understood. Recent explosive progress in technology and knowledge in neurobiology as well as molecular neurochemistry has directed our attention as to the plausible molecular mechanisms underlying the pathophysiology and treatment of affective disorders, from conventional hypotheses centering on the alterations in neurotransmitter concentration in synaptic cleft and/or sensitivity changes at monoamine receptor levels, to downstream intracellular signaling cascades via second, third, and fourth messengers finally leading to gene expression and neural plasticity. Since almost all receptors for neurotransmitters supposed to be relevant to the disorders, i.e., norepinephrine and serotonin, are known as metabotropic, G protein-coupled ones, except for few receptors such as 5-HT_3 subtype, it appears plausible to focus on the G protein-coupled intracellular signaling cascades such as cyclic AMP signaling and phosphoinositide (PI) pathways. However, theses pathways are controlled, not in a simply sequential and independent way, but in a complex fashion through crosstalk between them as well as feedback mechanisms at multiple levels. Furthermore, recent research unmasked some hitherto unrecognized and unexpected intracellular molecular components such as glycogen synthase kinase 3 (GSK-3) as a novel therapeutic target of mood stabilizers like lithium, making the surroundings of neurochemical research on pathogenesis and treatment of affective disorders more and more complex. In this chapter, the author critically reviews and appraises the exciting recent progress in research work concerning intracellular signal transduction systems implicated in the pathophysiology of affective disorders as well as in the therapeutic mechanisms of mood stabilizers and/or antidepressants. After briefly summarizing the G protein-coupled signaling cascades and their complex regulation, the effects of psychotropic drugs utilized to treat affective disorders on each components of these signaling pathways will be mentioned. Therewithal, clinical investigations aimed at elucidating possible molecular pathogenetic mechanisms underlying affective disorders utilizing postmortem brains and peripheral blood samples will be described. Although it appears difficult to interpret universally numerous results from different laboratories, often controversial and sometimes even contrasting, continuous research efforts aiming at elucidating the intracellular molecular mechanisms related to affective disorders and already established mood stabilizing agents will lead to our newer conceptualization of biological aspects of affective disorders as well as to development of novel therapeutic drugs for these disorders.

INTRODUCTION

Affective disorders are highly prevalent, usually chronic, and often life-threatening illnesses. Despite vast research from multifaceted points of view, the biological abnormalities underlying the predisposition to, and the pathophysiology of, these disorders have not yet been fully understood. Biochemical study using postmortem brains from patients with affective disorders is one of the most promising methods to have access more directly to the underlying pathophysiological alterations implicated in these "functional" disorders. Another widely utilized method is to investigate the abnormalities in peripheral tissues such as platelets and lymphocytes, assuming that these cells from patients suffering from affective disorders could serve as models of neural cells in the brains of those patients. It has been well recognized that these disorders are heterogeneous, and it is the most usual dichotomy to divide the disorders into unipolar and bipolar affective disorders based on the existence of manic or hypomanic state. Although even the bipolar affective disorders may be still heterogeneous with a high variation in symptomatology and course [1-3], it appears preferable in clinical studies to limit the subjects to bipolar (in particular, bipolar I type) affective disorders to address possible common abnormalities underlying pathophysiology of these disorders. It is, nevertheless, often difficult to include enough number of patients with definite clinical diagnosis of bipolar affective disorders in studies using postmortem brains and even peripheral tissues.

Therapeutic intervention to psychiatric disorders was revolutionized several decades ago by the development and introduction of psychotropic agents including lithium, antipsychotics, tricyclic antidepressants, monoamine oxidase inhibitors, and bezodiazepine anxiolytics. Parallel progress in neurobiological and psychopharmacological techniques and knowledge formulated the primary hypotheses of etiological basis of psychiatric illnesses such as schizophrenia and depression as well as mechanisms of action explaining how such psychotropic drugs exhibit their therapeutic efficacy and adverse effects. In the case of affective disorders, it has been shown that almost all antidepressants inhibit monoamine (norepinephrine and/or serotonin) transporters or their metabolic enzymes, and most antidepressants induce subsensitivity of β-adrenoceptor-coupled cyclic AMP (cAMP) production after long-term administration. These observations led to the classical hypothesis for affective disorders, where it was assumed that major depression and dysphoric symptoms arise from a dysfunction of monoamine-based neurotransmission, predominantly norepinephrine and/or serotonin, and that increased concentrations of extracellular neurotransmitters by administration of antidepressants would re-establish a normal tuning of neurotransmission via cell-surface receptors [4-8]. Although this theoretical framework has still been a useful model to facilitate our understanding of the concept of affective disorders and development of new antidepressants such as selective serotonin reuptake inhibitors, it became clearer that alterations in the availability of monoamine neurotransmitters and/or in the sensitivity of monoamine receptor function are not the only factors involved in the action of antidepressants or in the pathophysiology of affective disorders. Even if it is true that these alterations in neurotransmitter concentration in synaptic cleft or sensitivity changes at monoamine receptor levels are firstling of the effects of antidepressant treatment, serial postreceptor cascades via second, third, and fourth messengers, and finally leading to gene expression and neural plasticity, should play important roles in the long-term efficiency of antidepressant treatment.

Another evidence that directs our attention to the postreceptor intracellular signaling comes from many studies as to the effects of mood stabilizers such as lithium. Although numerous biochemical actions of lithium at presynaptic processes and receptor levels have been reported so far, no single effect seems sufficient to explain its bimodal therapeutic efficacy. As depicted below, lots of postreceptor events have been reported as molecular targets of therapeutic effect of lithium [9-19]. Furthermore, recent studies from several laboratories have identified hitherto unrecognized and unexpected intracellular molecular targets of lithium therapy involved in neuroplasticity as well as neurogenesis.

In this chapter, the author critically reviews and appraises the exciting recent progress in research work concerning intracellular signal transduction systems implicated in the pathophysiology and treatment of affective disorders. As almost all receptors for neurotransmitters supposed to be relevant to affective disorders, i.e., norepinephrine and serotonin, are metabotropic ones with common features that they convey external messages to intracellular signaling cascade through G proteins, G protein-coupled signaling systems are the main focus of this overview. After briefly summarizing the G protein-coupled signaling cascades, the effects of psychotropic drugs utilized to treat affective disorder patients on each components of these signaling pathways will be mentioned. Therewithal, clinical investigations aimed at elucidating possible molecular pathogenetic mechanisms underlying affective (in particular, bipolar) disorders utilizing postmortem brains and peripheral blood samples will be reviewed.

TRANSMEMBRANE SIGNALING VIA G PROTEINS IN NEURONAL NETWORKS

The most well known transmembrane signaling pathways in nerve cells are cAMP and phosphoinositide (PI) signaling pathways, both of which are mediated by heterotrimeric G proteins. These systems are of great interest in biological psychiatry, because all neurotransmitters implicated in the pathogenesis of psychiatric disorders, i.e., norepinephrine, serotonin, and dopamine, activate the cell-surface specific receptors, which utilize these types of intracellular signaling cascades to convey their message to the final cellular response via G proteins, with few exceptions such as 5-HT_3 receptors. There have been many excellent reviews dealing with the implications of these intracellular signaling pathways in pathophysiology and treatment of affective disorders [20-25]. Some other reviews also argue the biochemical pathogenesis of affective disorders, with special reference to cAMP pathway [26, 27], PI signaling cascades [28, 29], and G proteins [30-35].

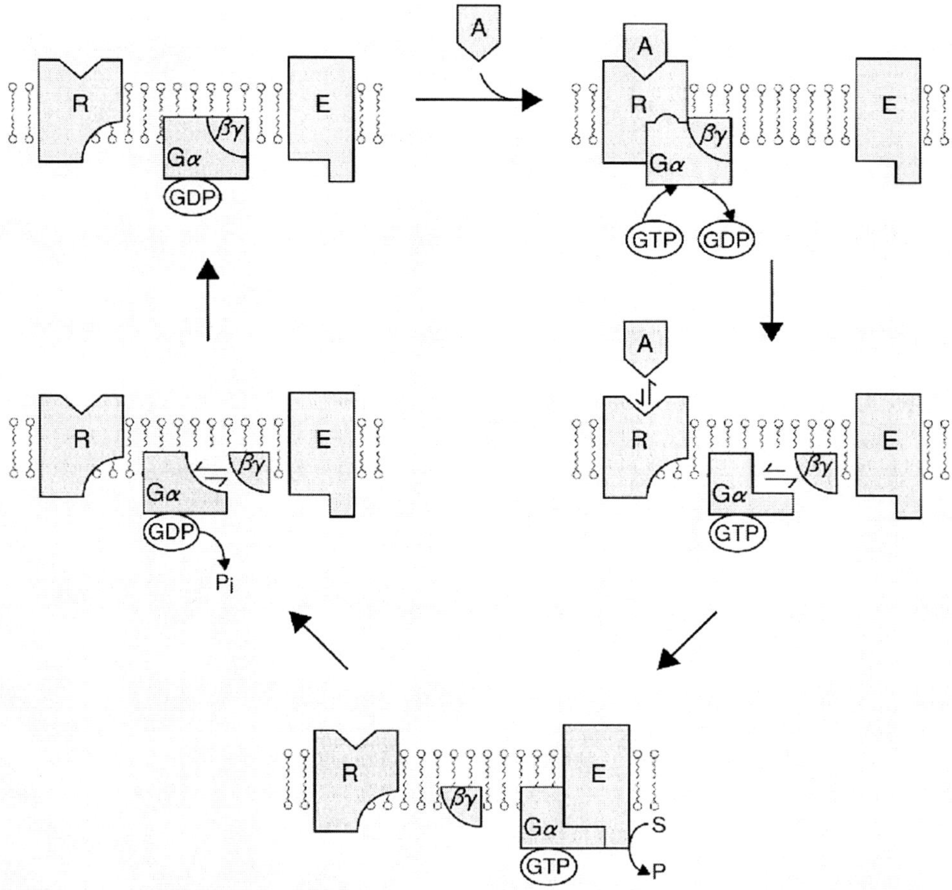

Figure 1. Schematic representation of cAMP signaling pathway. The binding of an agonist (A) to the specific receptor (R_s or R_i) leads to activation of G proteins, resulting in the modulation of adenylate cyclase (AC) activity. R_s and R_i represent stimulatory and inhibitory receptors, respectively, and the former is coupled with stimulatory G proteins (G_s) to stimulate AC, while the latter is coupled with inhibitory G proteins (G_i) to inhibit AC. AC is the enzyme catalyzing the production of cAMP from ATP, and newly synthesized cAMP binds to the regulatory subunits (R) of PKA, which causes a conformational modification of the enzyme that leads to the dissociation of the two catalytic (C) subunits from the R dimer. Once released from the holoenzyme, free C subunits are able to phosphorylate many substrate proteins such as CREB. Following activation, CREB binds to a CRE in various target genes to regulate their expression.

Cyclic AMP Signaling

The cAMP generating system [36] is regulated in bimodal directions, i.e., stimulatory and inhibitory, through G_s and G_i proteins, respectively (**Figure 1**). The second messenger cAMP is generated from ATP by a catalytic enzyme, adenylate cyclase (also referred to as adenylyl cyclase), and rapidly degraded by phosphodiesterase, of which at least seven different gene families are currently known to exist [37]. Adenylate cyclase also consists of at least nine isoforms, ranging in size from 110 to 200 kDa, which share several key topological and functional features [38, 39]. All of the isoforms of adenylate cyclase are activated by both forskolin and the GTP-bound α subunit of the G_s, whereas regulatory patterns by $\beta\gamma$ subunits, other G protein α subunits ($G_{\alpha i}$, $G_{\alpha o}$, and $G_{\alpha z}$), Ca^{2+}/calmodulin, and protein kinase C (PKC) are various, depending on the isoforms and experimental conditions [38]. Modulation of adenylate cyclase activity by Ca^{2+}/calmodulin and/or PKC should be one of the mechanisms explaining the so-called crosstalk between this system and the PI signaling pathway. The key enzyme of this signaling cascade is named cAMP-dependent protein kinase (PKA), which is a tetrameric holoenzyme complex consisting of two catalytic (C) subunits plus a dimer of regulatory (R) subunits (RI or RII) [40, 41]. Newly synthesized cAMP molecules bind to R subunits of PKA holoenzymes, causing them to release their C subunits. These free C subunits then phosphorylate a broad spectrum of proteins in both the cytoplasm and nucleus, depending on the type of cell, its state of differentiation, and the hormonal milieux. A major nuclear target for free C subunits is the cAMP response element binding (CREB) family of nuclear proteins, which bind to cAMP response elements (CREs) in the promoter regions of cAMP-responsive genes. Phosphorylation of CREB proteins alters their ability to form dimers and to interact with CREs, leading to the transcription of genes in response to elevated levels of cAMP [42, 43]. Many CREB proteins can be phosphorylated by other kinases like PKC, calcium/calmodulin-dependent protein kinase, and casein kinase II, as well, thus providing again a chance of interaction between cAMP signaling cascade and other non-cAMP-mediated intracellular signaling pathways.

PI Signaling

Another well-characterized G protein-coupled intracellular signal transduction pathway is referred to as PI pathway (**Figure 2**), in which a cell membrane component, phosphatidylinositol 4,5-bisphosphate (PIP_2), is hydrolyzed by the enzyme phosphoinositide-specific phospholipase C (PLC) [44-50]. Multiple forms of PLC are now known to exist, and five isozymes, designated as α, β, γ, δ, and ε, have been thus far identified [49]. Of these five isozymes, PLC-β is apparently the primary subtype that participates in receptor-coupled, G protein-mediated PI signaling [48]. When a variety of neurotransmitter receptor subtypes like muscarinic M_1 and M_3, α_1-adrenergic, serotonin 5-HT_{2A} and 5-HT_{2C} receptors, are activated by the respective agonists, stimulation of the enzyme PLC-β takes place through activated G proteins, especially $G_{q/11}$ [50], resulting in formation of two intracellular second messengers, 1,2-diacylglycerol (DAG) and inositol 1,4,5-trisphosphate (IP_3). DAG is an endogenous activator of Ca^{2+}-activated, phospholipid-dependent protein kinase (PKC), whereas IP_3 binds to the IP_3 receptors leading to the release of intracellular-stored Ca^{2+} from the smooth endoplasmic reticulum. It has been shown that the IP_3 receptor is selectively phosphorylated by PKA resulting in decreased potency of IP_3 to release Ca^{2+} [51], which serves another plausible mechanism for crosstalk between the cAMP and the PI signaling systems. Although metabolism of IP_3 is complex, it is generally accepted that IP_3 can be metabolized both by dephosphorylation to form inositol 1,4-bisphosphate [I(1,4)P_2], or phosphorylated to form inositol 1,3,4,5-tetrakisphosphate [I(1,3,4,5)P_4], which has been proposed to be involved in the entry of Ca^{2+} from extracellular sources [49, 52]. PKCs are ubiquitous enzymes involved in a broad spectrum of neuronal function. At rest, the PKC isozymes exist in both cytosolic and membrane-bound forms, but with partitioning predominantly in the cytosolic form. The DAG synthesized subsequent to activation of PLC-coupled receptors facilitates the translocation of cytosolic PKC to the membrane, and its activation. To date, 11 isozymes have been identified and these have been classified into three groups based on their structure and cofactor regulation [53-55]. The "classical" or "conventional" PKCs (cPKCs) consisting of four isozymes (α, two alternatively spliced variants βI and βII, and γ) are dependent on Ca^{2+} for their activity, whereas "new" PKC (nPKC) isoforms [δ, ε, η(L), θ, and μ] do not require Ca^{2+} for their activation, and two "atypical" PKC (aPKC) isoforms, ζ and λ(ι), do not respond to DAG or to phorbol esters. Such functional individuality of PKC isozymes, along with the differential tissue distribution, indicates that each isozyme exerts distinct cellular function. Although a number of targeting proteins have been described as a substrate of PKC, one of the most prominent substrates for PKC in the brain is an acidic protein, myristoylated alanine rich C kinase substrate (MARCKS), which has been implicated in cellular processes associated with neurotransmitter release and neuroplasticity [56, 57]. The degree of phosphorylation of MARCKS is thought to be used as an apparent and sensitive marker of PKC activation.

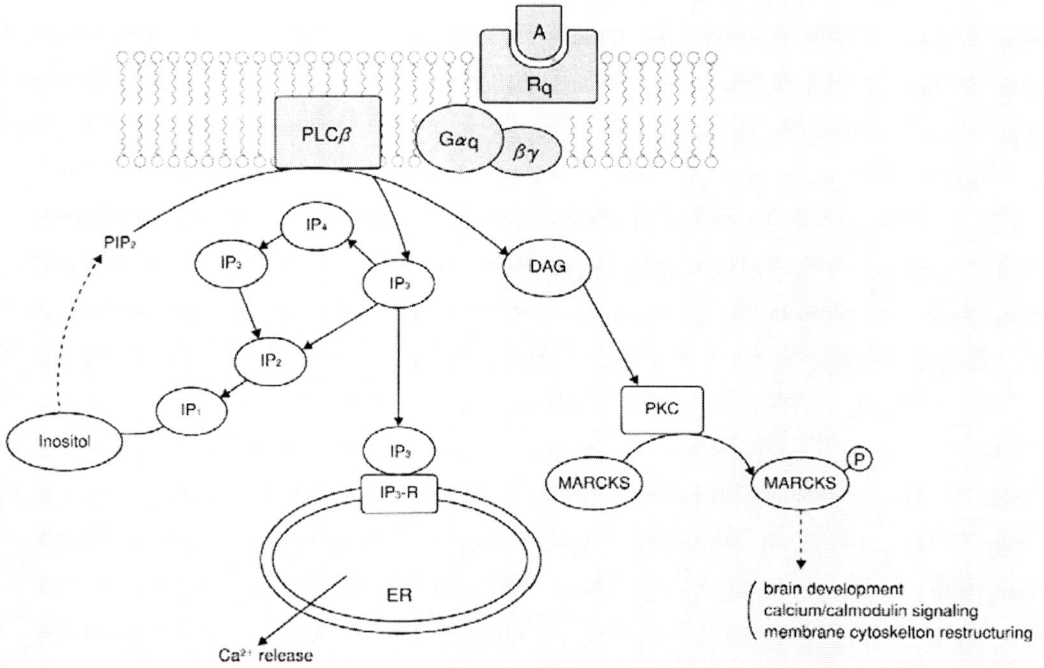

Figure 2. Schematic representation of PI signaling pathway. Occupancy of the receptor (R_q) by a specific agonist (A) activates PLC through G proteins (G_q) to hydrolyze PIP_2 to form the two major second messengers, IP_3 and DAG. IP_3 binds to IP_3 receptors to release intracellular-stored Ca^{2+} from the smooth endoplasmic reticulum (ER), whereas DAG activates PKC. IP_3 is either dephosphorylated to form inositol 1,4-bisphosphate (IP_2), inositol monophosphate (IP_1), and ultimately, free inositol, or phosphorylated to form inositol 1,3,4,5-tetrakisphosphate (IP_4), which is then dephosphorylated by sequential distinct pathway to inositol. Activated PKC is able to phosphorylate various proteins such as MARCKS, resulting in regulation of multiple cellular functions and plasticity.

G Proteins

Heterotrimeric G proteins are a ubiquitous family of proteins that serve the crucial role of transducers, amplifiers, and regulators of information across the plasma membrane, coupling receptors to above-mentioned two major intracellular signaling cascades [58, 59]. The G proteins consist of an α subunit, which binds and hydrolyzes GTP, and βγ subunits, which behave as a dimer and one functional unit in physiological milieu. The α subunits also contain the site for nicotineamide adenine nucleotide (NAD)-dependent ADP-ribosylation catalyzed by cholera or pertussis toxins. Recent cloning and sequencing of cDNAs encoding the α subunits have identified nearly 20 subtypes, and the heterogeneity of α subunits serves to divide G proteins into the major classes, i.e., G_s, G_i, G_q, and G_{12} [60]. The βγ subunits, which also have their functional roles in signal transduction [61, 62], form a tightly but noncovalently associated complex that contributes to the receptor recognition site on the G protein oligomer and facilitates the attachment of the oligomer to the inner face of the plasma membrane. When an agonist ligand binds to the G protein-coupled receptor, an activated receptor/G protein complex is formed to facilitate the GDP release from guanine nucleotide binding site on the α subunit, which is subsequently replaced with GTP. This is followed by the dissociation of G protein subunits to produce GTP-bound α subunit and βγ subunits. The GTP-bound α subunit interacts with the effector molecule such as adenylate cyclase and phospholipases and modulates their activity. As the α subunit of G protein also has intrinsic GTPase activity, GTP on the α subunit is hydrolyzed to GDP, and then, resulting GDP-bound α subunit reassociates with βγ subunits to form an inactive heterotrimer again. Thus, G protein cycles between an inactive, GDP-liganded oligomeric form ("off" position) and an active, GTP-liganded monomeric state ("on" position) (**Figure 3**).

Complexity of G Protein-coupled Signal Transduction Cascades

Although G protein-coupled signaling pathways seem to convey extracellular message to intracellular one sequentially and independently, they are interrelated with each other at multiple steps and through various mechanisms, some examples of which have been already depicted above [63-67]. Homologous regulation of the signaling efficacy subsequent to prolonged stimulation of the receptor (homologous desensitization) has also been well known [68]. In addition, these signaling cascades are connected with other multiple signaling pathways, e.g., mitogen-activated protein (MAP) kinase cascades [69] and Wnt signaling [70, 71], both of which have recently arrested much attention as novel candidate pathways involved in pathogenesis of affective disorders as well as therapeutic efficacy of some mood stabilizers. There are also a variety of accessory proteins, which play an important role for regulation of the efficacy of G protein-coupled signaling. Such molecules, i.e., β-arrestins [72], G protein-coupled receptor kinases (GRKs) [73], and regulators of G protein signaling (RGS proteins) [74], should participate in homologous and heterologous regulation of receptor-mediated intracellular signaling pathways as well as interaction with other G protein-independent intracellular signaling cascades. Thus, G protein-coupled and G protein-independent signal transduction systems construct a complex intracellular signaling network, wherein mutual interconnection at multiple molecular levels and delicate modification of the tune of the signals, via positive and negative feedback and feed-forward loops, take place, and finally resulting in maintenance of harmonious homeostasis and suitable adaptation of the cell to the external stimuli.

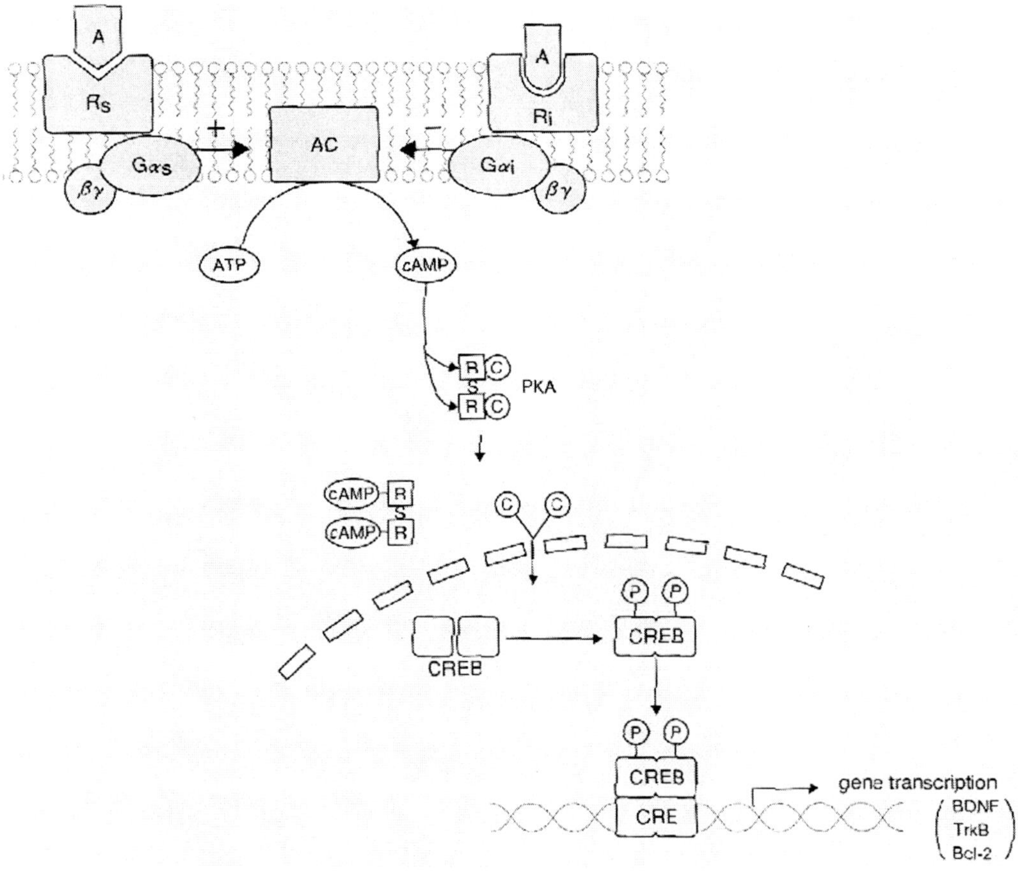

Figure 3. G protein activation/deactivation cycle. Activation of receptors (R) by an agonist (A) induces a conformational change in the receptor, allowing it to interact with the G protein, leading to the release of GDP, and the formation of a high-affinity ternary complex (A-R-G). Binding of GTP to the guanine nucleotide-binding site on the α subunit leads to a dissociation of the G protein into GTP-bound α (α_{GTP}) and βγ subunits, both of which are able to regulate the activity of various effectors such as adenylate cyclase. The continued activation of effectors by α_{GTP} is terminated by the action of a GTPase enzyme intrinsic to the α subunit, which hydrolyzes GTP on the α subunit. The GDP-bound α (α_{GDP}) reassociates with βγ subunits to form inactive heterotrimeric G protein.

Post-Receptor Components as a Molecular Target of Psychotropic Agents Prescribed for Affective Disorders

Most therapeutic psychoactive agents, at least their prototypes, have been discovered accidentally with careful clinical observations, and clarification of the modes of action of these drugs has made meaningful contributions to the understanding of the potential pathophysiology of psychiatric disorders. In the case of antidepressants, their acute effects on monoamine reuptake or monoamine oxidase, and then their subchronic effects on monoamine receptors, bore classical hypotheses on the etiology or pathophysiology of depressive illness. More recently, interest of researchers shifted downstream to intracellular signaling driven by these monoamine receptors, finally leading to regulation of gene expression, and newer theory of pathophysiology of affective disorders and molecular mechanisms of action of antidepressants and mood stabilizers lays emphasis on the importance of neurotrophic factor-mediated neurogenesis or neural plasticity in the brain [75-81]. In line with the notion supposing impairments of neuroplasticity and cellular resilience involved in affective disorders, most recent accumulating morphometric neuroimaging as well as neuropathological studies, if not all, have clearly shown the existence of gross volumetric reduction and microscopic abnormalities in neuronal and/or glial cells in some brain regions in affective disorders [78, 81].

In the pharmacological treatment for bipolar affective disorders, lithium still remains the most widely and effectively used drug with antimanic as well as prophylactic properties, though more than half a century has passed since the re-discovery of its efficacy. Although there have been numerous reports investigating its mechanisms of action from several points of view, the cellular and molecular basis for its beneficial effects have yet to be elucidated. As it is beyond the scope of this article to detail the preclinical reports on intracellular mechanisms of action of lithium, interested readers should be referred to many excellent reviews on this topic [9-19]. Some other review articles focus on searching a common mechanism or target molecule of lithium and other psychoactive drugs with mood-stabilizing properties such as valproate or carbamazepine [82-90].

Although a number of plausible molecular targets of acute lithium's effects have been identified, including inositol monophosphatase, a family of structurally related phosphomomoesterases, and the protein kinase glycogen synthase kinase-3 (GSK-3) [19], its therapeutic effects in the treatment of affective disorders are observed only after chronic administration, thereby precluding any simple mechanistic interpretations based on its acute biochemical effects. The most compelling hypothesis to explain lithium's action was formerly the inositol depletion hypothesis [10, 91], in which inhibition of inositol monophosphatase by lithium [92] was supposed to reduce the pool of free inositol, and thereby suppressing inositol-based signaling. Although this hypothesis is an attractive model for explaining the effects of lithium in some settings, it is still obscure whether therapeutic efficacy of lithium as an antimanic or prophylactic agent could be explained solely by this hypothesis. Inositol depletion by lithium appears to trigger long-term events through modulation of downstream components of intracellular signaling pathways, such as PKC. Some researchers stressed the importance of a reduction of the expression of some kinds of PKC isozymes as well as a reduction in the expression of a major PKC substrate, MARCS, which was observed after chronic treatment with lithium [82, 85]. More recently, as with the effects of long-term administration of antidepressants, regulation of gene expression and the factors involved in neurotrophic/neuroprotective process have been noticeable as plausible therapeutic targets of mood stabilizers. Activator protein 1 (AP-1) is a family of transcription factors consisting of homodimeric and heterodimeric complexes of c-Jun and c-Fos proteins, which regulates expression of many target genes for various neuropeptides, neurotrophins, receptors, transcription factors, enzymes involved in neurotransmitter synthesis and proteins binding to cytoskeletal elements [93], and it has been demonstrated that AP-1 DNA binding activity and

AP-1-dependent transcription are increased by mood stabilizers such as lithium and valproate [83-89]. Both mood stabilizers have also been reported to increase the levels of the major neuroprotective protein bcl-2 (B-cell lymphoma/leukemia-2) genes and to inhibit GSK-3β, an enzyme known to regulate the levels of phosphorylated tau and β-catenin, both of which should be related to the neuroprotective effects of mood stabilizers against diverse insults observed in some settings [88, 89].

One research group has exclusively emphasized the critical roles of G proteins implicated in pathophysiology of affective disorders [30, 33-35, 94], based on the results of a series of their own experiments following the epoch-making finding that lithium impairs receptor-coupled G protein function in vitro as well as ex vivo [95]. In general, however, the search for the mechanisms of action of mood stabilizing agents has been facilitated by a growing appreciation that, rather than any single target protein, many interacting and overlapping systems are affected, irrespective which one plays a primary role. It would be acceptable that most psychoactive drugs, in particular mood stabilizers like lithium, are unlikely to work on any particular neurotransmitter system in isolation, but rather, affect the functional balance between interacting systems at multiple levels and through complicated interacting mechanism in post-receptor signaling pathways.

Postmortem Brain Studies

Cyclic AMP Signaling

There exist several reports wherein adenylate cyclase activity has been studied in postmortem brains from patients with affective disorders. Cowburn et al. [96] demonstrated reduced basal, GTPγS-stimulated, and forskolin-stimulated adenylate cyclase activity in suicide victims, especially in those with violent suicide means or a history of depression. Similar tendency, though statistically not significant, was observed in frontal and parietal cortex obtained from depressed suicides [97]. Forskolin-stimulated cAMP formation, when expressed as a percent increase above the basal, was reduced in temporal cortex of depressed suicide victims, which might be, however, attributable to the higher basal adenylate cyclase activity in this group [98]. As for bipolar affective disorders, Young et al. [99] found elevated forskolin-stimulated adenylate cyclase activity in some cerebral cortical regions compared with matched controls. There was a significant correlation between forskolin-stimulated cAMP formation and $G_{\alpha s\text{-}L}$, which was also shown to be elevated in bipolar affective disorders. It is somewhat puzzling that increased cAMP formation in bipolar group was found solely in response to forskolin (a direct activator of adenylate cyclase), but not to GTPγS (a non-hydrolyzable GTP analogue), in spite of the elevated $G_{\alpha s\text{-}L}$. Curiously, in the subsequent report from the same laboratory group, forskolin-stimulated cAMP formation was not increased, but rather decreased, in bipolar and major depressive disorder subjects compared with controls [100].

To summarize these reports, although adenylate cyclase activity appears to be reduced in the depressed, or suicide-prone, subjects, the tone of cAMP signaling in the brain of bipolar disorder patients is still controversial. As already mentioned in the Introduction, it is clearly preferable to deal with bipolar subjects in consideration of the pathophysiological heterogeneity of affective disorders, but it is often very difficult in the case of postmortem studies. Even if substantial number of brains from bipolar affective disorder subjects can be obtained, it should be impossible to uniformize the antemortem mood state. Provided that the targeted measures are state-dependent rather than trait-dependent, the results become varied and embarrassing. In such studies, furthermore, the effects of antemortem therapeutic intervention, especially long-term treatment with psychotropic agents including lithium, antidepressants, and antipsychotics, could not be excluded. These problems are essentially unconquerable, and also apply to the all biochemical studies with postmortem brains from bipolar subjects described below.

Some isoforms of adenylate cyclase were determined by western blotting in postmortem temporal cortex from bipolar disorder subjects, depressed suicide victims, and age-matched controls [98]. Of the isoforms investigated, only adenylate cyclase type IV (Ca^{2+}/calmodulin-insensitive) [38] was lower in depressed suicides, but not in bipolar affective disorders, as compared to the controls [98]. Specific [^{3}H]cAMP binding was reported to be reduced in cytosolic fractions, but not in the membrane fractions, across all brain regions in bipolar affective disorder subjects, probably indicative of decreased number of the R subunits of PKA in bipolar patients [101]. In the subsequent study, the same laboratory investigated PKA activity both in cytosolic and membrane fractions. The basal as well as cAMP-stimulated PKA activities in bipolar subjects were augmented in cytosolic fractions in temporal cortex, with a reduced EC_{50} for cAMP [102]. On the other hand, it has been reported that both basal and cAMP-stimulated PKA activities in nuclear fraction in prefrontal cortex and hippocampus are significantly reduced in suicide victims, and specifically in those with a diagnosis of major depression [102]. In another paper, Dwivedi et al. [104] also reported that cytosolic and membranous PKA activities, either basal or when stimulated by cAMP, were significantly reduced in prefrontal cortex in suicide victims, again especially those with a history of major depression, compared with comparison subjects, and that these alterations were associated with significant decrease in the number of [^{3}H]cAMP binding sites. Using immunolabeling techniques with specific antisera against PKA RIα, RIβ, RIIα, RIIβ, and Cα subunits, Chang et al. [105] revealed significant higher levels of cytosolic Cα in temporal and frontal cortices and of cytosolic RIIβ in temporal cortex in bipolar subjects compared with the matched control brains. Although these alterations in cAMP signaling components seen in the brain of affective disorder subjects are apparently associated with each other, it has not been fully understood which common mechanisms underlie these changes or which abnormalities are the primary to induce secondary adaptive alterations in the other components.

Since CREB proteins serve as the primary substrates of PKA to play an important role in regulation of transcriptional activity of numerous genes, it is of great interest to investigate them in affective disorders. In the temporal cortex, CREB levels were decreased in the major depressive disorder subjects who had not been treated with antidepressants at the time of death, but not in antidepressant-treated major depressive disorder, bipolar disorder or schizophrenic groups, compared to the controls [106]. In the subsequent investigation, the same authors reported that CREB immunoreactivities were not different among major depressive disorder, bipolar affective disorder, and control groups, and that lower CREB levels were associated with suicides as well as treatment with anticonvulsants [100]. Recently, Dwivedi et al. [103] found significant reduction in mRNA and protein levels of CREB as well as in CRE-DNA binding activity in both prefrontal cortex and hippocampus in suicide victims. They concluded that these alterations were related to suicidal behavior, since the changes were seen irrespective of diagnosis when the suicide victims were divided into those with a diagnosis of major depression and those with a diagnosis of other psychiatric disorders.

Odagaki et al. [107] determined CREB proteins, both as a whole and as a phosphorylated form, in the prefrontal cortex from depressed suicide victims. The depressed suicide victims had increased levels of total CREB as well as phosphorylated CREB compared to the matched controls. Although the possibility that the increase in CREB was induced by long-term treatment with antidepressants [108] could not be entirely excluded, these alterations were also observed in the antidepressant drug-free subjects, indicative of pathophysiological relevance instead of the consequence of antidepressant administration. There was also a trend, though statistically not significant, for increase in PKA Cα subunits in the depressed suicide victims, and these three measures were correlated with each other. On the other hand, another research group recently reported that both total and phosphorylated CREB immunoreactive levels in postmortem orbitofrontal cortex were significantly lower in the subjects with major depressive disorder who were in remission and free from antidepressant treatment than in the control subjects [109].

Most recently, an interesting report was published wherein mRNA and protein levels of BDNF and its receptor tyrosine kinase B (trk B) were determined in postmortem brains [110]. Both in prefrontal cortex and hippocampus, mRNA levels of BDNF and trk B receptors were significantly reduced in suicide victims as compared with control subjects, and there was concurrent decrease in protein levels of BDNF and full-length, but not truncated, trk B receptors. These alterations were seen in all suicide victims irrelevant to whether they were diagnosed as major depression, as in the case of decrease of CREB mRNA and protein levels in suicide victims reported by the same authors in the preceding paper [103], suggesting close linkage among these phenomena.

PI Signaling

Immunoreactive levels of PLC-β_1 in postmortem brains of bipolar affective disorder subjects were found higher in occipital cortex, but not in frontal or temporal cortex, than those in the controls [111]. Interestingly, this increase in PLC-β_1, though statistically only marginally significant, correlated with the increase in $G_{\alpha q/11}$ (described below) in occipital cortex, indicating a certain interrelation between the two alterations. The reason of region-specific alteration only in occipital cortex remains unclear. Ca^{2+}-dependent PLC activity was not significantly different between bipolar and control subjects in any of cortical brain regions examined (frontal, temporal, and occipital) [112]. On the other hand, G protein-stimulated PLC activity, as determined by [^{3}H]PI hydrolysis induced by GTPγS, was decreased only in occipital cortex, but not in temporal or frontal cortex, in bipolar affective disorder subjects [112]. Since NaF-stimulated [^{3}H]PI hydrolysis and the increments of the activity elicited by several agonists were found similar between the bipolar subjects and the controls [112], they concluded that the PI signaling system in bipolar disorder patients might be impaired at the level of GTP-GDP exchange on G proteins, selectively in occipital cortex.

As for the depressed suicide victims, Ca^{2+}-dependent PLC-β was not different, functionally as well as quantitatively, from that of the controls in postmortem prefrontal cortex [113]. Only GTPγS-stimulated [^{3}H]PI hydrolysis was decreased in depressed suicide victims in prefrontal cortex (Broadmann's area 10), but not in area 8/9 [113]. It appears difficult to integrate these experimental results in postmortem brains from bipolar and depressed suicide subjects to specify the molecular component(s) of PI signaling in specialized brain region(s) underlying pathogenesis of affective disorders.

Although decreased brain inositol levels were reported in frontal cortex, but not in occipital cortex or cerebellum, in bipolar disorder patients and suicide victims, with inositol monophosphatase activity unaltered [114], this could not be replicated later [115]. Thus, the relevance of this finding is obscure, though some preliminary trials have been reported wherein inositol was administered as a possible antidepressive agent to affective disorder patients [116, 117]. The relationship between affective disorders and brain inositol levels may be more complex than expected from the so-called inositol depletion hypothesis as originally posited based on the effects of lithium on PI metabolism by Berridge et al. [10, 91].

As for the key enzyme of PI signaling pathway, PKC, Wang and Friedman [118] reported that PKC activity in frontal cortex of the bipolar affective disorder subjects was higher in the membrane fraction, but not in the cytosolic fraction than that of the control subjects, and that translocation of PKC from cytosolic to membrane fraction in response to a phorbol ester was potentiated in the bipolar subjects. Of PKC isozymes investigated, bipolar affective disorder subjects had increased cytosolic α isoform, decreased cytosolic ε, and elevated membrane-associated γ and ζ isoforms compared to the control subjects [118]. Membrane PKC α immunoreactive levels in prefrontal cortex were reported to be similar between depressed suicide victims and controls [113], while PKC levels determined by [^{3}H]phorbol dibutyrate binding were significantly reduced both in membrane and cytosolic fractions in prefrontal cortex from teenage suicide victims as compared to control subjects [119]. Another report failed to detect significant differences in PKC isoenzyme (α, β, γ, and ε) levels in any of the brain regions examined (prefrontal cortex, amygdala, substantia nigra, and putamen) between depressed suicide victims and controls [120].

As mentioned previously, the PKC substrate MARCKS has been postulated as one of the molecular targets of lithium [82, 85]. According to this notion, McNamara et al. [121] determined mRNA expression for MARCKS and MARCKS-related protein (MRP) by quantitative in situ hybridization in postmortem brains from suicide victims. Neither MARCKS nor MRP mRNA expression levels differed in any subregions examined in prefrontal cortex and hippocampus in suicide victims relative to normal controls. However, since these suicide victims were described as nonpsychotic, alterations in quantity and/or function of either proteins still remain to be determined in affective disorder subjects.

Another major substrate of PKC, growth-associated protein (GAP-43), is also of particular interest, because this protein plays an important role in structural and functional plasticity of mature brain. It has been reported that the levels of GAP-43 protein as well as its mRNA are significantly decreased in prefrontal cortex (Brodmann area 9), but not in frontopolar cortex (Brodmann area 10), amygdala, substantia nigra or putamen, in depressed suicide victims than those in the control subjects [120].

There has been no postmortem research report aiming at evaluating the involvement of intracellular Ca^{2+} signaling in pathophysiology of affective disorders for lack of appropriate method.

G Proteins

There have been several reports on the levels of G protein subtypes in postmortem brains determined by western blotting with specific antibodies in affective disorder subjects, as summarized in **Table 1** [99, 100, 113, 122-127]. In the earlier studies, it was emphasized that $G_{\alpha s}$ proteins were quantitatively elevated in specific brain regions in bipolar affective disorder subjects [99, 122]. However, this finding has not necessarily been replicated in subsequent studies (**Table 1**). In the same brain samples, in which bipolar disorder subjects were reported to have increased levels of $G_{\alpha s}$ proteins compared with the controls [99], Young et al. [128] determined their mRNA levels by reverse transcriptase polymerase chain reaction (RT-PCR) and could not find significant differences in $G_{\alpha s}$ mRNA levels in frontal, temporal, or occipital cortex, between both groups.

Interestingly, receptor-G protein coupling determined by agonist-induced [^{35}S]GTPγS bindings was shown to be enhanced in postmortem prefrontal cortex of bipolar affective disorder subjects [123]. This hyperactive receptor-G protein coupling in bipolar subjects was universally seen in physiologically relevant combinations, regardless of agonists used (isoproterenol, carbachol, and 5-HT) and G_{α} subtypes investigated ($G_{\alpha s}$, $G_{\alpha i}$, $G_{\alpha o}$, $G_{\alpha z}$, and $G_{\alpha q}$). These functional alterations do not derive solely from the quantitative changes of G protein α subtypes, since it was reported in the same study that only $G_{\alpha s}$ levels were elevated whereas immunoreactive levels of other G_{α} subtypes were unaltered in bipolar subjects compared to controls (**Table 1**) [123].

Gonzalez-Maeso et al. [125] investigated agonist-induced and receptor-independent stimulation of [^{35}S]GTPγS binding in frontal cortical membranes from suicide victims with affective disorders (6/28 bipolar, 22/28 major depressive or dysthymic) and matched control subjects. The results indicated that only α_{2A}-adrenoceptor-mediated stimulation of [^{35}S]GTPγS binding displayed significantly greater sensitivity to the agonist UK14304 in suicide victims than in controls, with many other signaling pathways coupled with 5-HT_{1A}, μ-opioid, $GABA_B$, and muscarinic acetylcholine receptors as well as receptor-independent G protein activation unaltered.

It appears thus plausible that at least some G proteins are changed, whether quantitatively or functionally, in postmortem brains in affective disorder subjects. However, results of postmortem brain studies reported thus far have been still inconsistent with regard to the subtypes of G proteins affected, mode of alterations, and brain regions involved, to simply support the hypothesis that specific patterns of up- and down-regulated levels and/or function of selective G protein subtypes determine mood states of affective disorders [33-35]

Table 1. Levels of G Protein Subtypes in Postmortem Studies

	$G_{\alpha s\text{-}L}$	$G_{\alpha s\text{-}S}$	$G_{\alpha i}$	$G_{\alpha o}$	$G_{\alpha q/11}$	$G_{\alpha z}$	G_{β}	References
Bipolar affective disorders								
Frontal cortex								
	⇔	↑	⇔	⇔	⇔	n.d.	⇔	Young et al. [122]
	↑	⇔	⇔	⇔	n.d.	n.d.	⇔	Young et al. [99]
	↑	↑	⇔	⇔	⇔	⇔	⇔	Friedman and Wang [123]
	n.d.	n.d.	n.d.	n.d.	⇔	n.d.	⇔	Mathews et al. [111]
Occipital cortex								
	↑	↑	n.d.	n.d.	n.d.	n.d.	n.d.	Young et al. [122]
	↑	↑	⇔	⇔	n.d.	n.d.	⇔	Young et al. [99]
	n.d.	n.d.	n.d.	n.d.	↑	n.d.	⇔	Mathews et al. [111]
	⇔	⇔	⇔	n.d.	n.d.	n.d.	n.d.	Dowlatshahi et al. [100]
Temporal cortex								
	↑	⇔	⇔	⇔	n.d.	n.d.	⇔	Young et al. [99]
	n.d.	n.d.	n.d.	n.d.	⇔	n.d.	⇔	Mathews et al. [111]
	⇔	⇔	⇔	n.d.	n.d.	n.d.	n.d.	Dowlatshahi et al. [100]
Hippocampus								
	⇔	⇔	⇔	⇔	n.d.	n.d.	⇔	Young et al. [99]
Thalamus								
	⇔	⇔	⇔	⇔	n.d.	n.d.	⇔	Young et al. [99]
Cerebellar cortex								
	⇔	⇔	n.d.	n.d.	n.d.	n.d.	n.d.	Young et al. [122]
	⇔	⇔	⇔	⇔	n.d.	n.d.	⇔	Young et al. [99]
Depressed subjects or suicide victims								
Frontal cortex								
	⇔	⇔/↑ *	⇔	n.d.	n.d.	n.d.	n.d.	Cowburn et al. [96]
	n.d.	n.d.	↑	n.d.	n.d.	n.d.	n.d.	Garcma-Sevilla et al. [124]
	⇔	⇔	⇔	⇔	n.d.	n.d.	n.d.	Gonzalez-Maeso et al. [125]
	n.d.	n.d.	n.d.	n.d.	n.d.	n.d.	⇔	Grange-Midroit et al. [126]
Occipital cortex								
	⇔	⇔	⇔	n.d.	n.d.	n.d.	n.d.	Dowlatshahi et al. [100]
Temporal cortex								
	⇔	⇔	⇔	⇔	⇔	n.d.	⇔	Ozawa et al. [127]
	⇔	⇔	⇔	n.d.	n.d.	n.d.	n.d.	Dowlatshahi et al. [100]
Parietal cortex								
	⇔	⇔	⇔	⇔	⇔	n.d.	⇔	Ozawa et al. [127]

↑ : significantly increased compared to controls; ⇔: not significantly different from controls; n.d.: not determined.

*Unaltered in total suicide cases, but significantly increased in subgroup with violent death and in subgroup with a history of depression.

Miscellaneous

Among accessory proteins involved in G protein-coupled signaling networks, immunodensity of membrane-associated GRK 2 in postmortem prefrontal cortex was elevated in drug-free depressed subjects, but not in antidepressant-treated ones [124, 126]. The densities of membrane-associated GRK 6, β-arrestin-2, and protein phosphatase 2A were not significantly altered in depressed subjects [126].

Based on the newer hypothesis that bipolar affective disorder is associated with GSK-3-mediated signaling events [70], a few studies measuring levels of this enzyme and its substrates begin to emerge. Lesort et al. [129] reported there were no significant differences between bipolar disorder subjects and controls in GSK-3β, β-catenin, and tau immunoreactive levels in postmortem prefrontal cortex. Another research group reported that GSK-3β immunoreactivity in postmortem frontal cortex was lower in schizophrenic patients, but not in affective disorder patients, than in the comparison subjects [130].

There is one report showing no alteration in the levels of Bcl-2 protein in the temporal cortex from subjects with bipolar disorder [131].

Peripheral Blood Sample Studies

Cyclic AMP Signaling

Increase in cAMP formation in leukocytes stimulated by isoproterenol, but not by prostaglandin E_1, was reported to be significantly lower in unipolar depressed patients as well as in manic patients than in normal subjects [132]. This finding was replicated by the following investigation using lymphocytes, in which concomitant decrease of β-adrenoceptor binding sites in depressed and manic patients was also reported [133]. On the other hand, another research group [134, 135] reported that decreased β-adrenoceptor-mediated cAMP production observed in lymphocytes from depressed patients was not accompanied with an alteration in β-adrenoceptor binding. It was also reported that basal, isoproterenol-stimulated, and forskolin-stimulated cAMP accumulation in lymphocytes was reduced in depressed patients, especially in depressed patients who did not respond to antidepressant treatment [136]. Prostaglandin E_1- or prostaglandin D_2-stimulated cAMP response in platelet was significantly reduced in the depressed patients compared to the control subjects [137-141]. Other investigators, however, could not find significant difference in prostaglandin E_1-stimulated [142, 143] or forskolin-stimulated [144, 145] cAMP response in platelets between depressed patients and controls. From these data, though it could be concluded that cAMP production system is desensitized in affective disorder patients, it remains still unclear whether these alterations only reflect down-regulated β-adrenoceptors and which abnormally regulated post-receptor signaling components, if any, underlie these phenomena.

Since there have been a lot of reports indicating some abnormalities in PI signaling involved in pathophysiology of affective disorders and the existence of crosstalk between the two major signaling pathways at multiple levels and in different ways has been demonstrated as mentioned previously, there arises a question how these disturbances in cAMP signaling pathway and PI cascades are associated with each other. To address this matter,

Emamghoreishi et al. [146] determined cAMP production in B lymphoblasts from bipolar I patients, who were divided into two subgroups according to basal intracellular Ca^{2+} concentration. Isoproterenol-stimulated cAMP formation in B lymphoblasts was lower in bipolar patients with high Ca^{2+} concentrations, but not in those with normal Ca^{2+} concentrations, compared to healthy subjects. The basal (and probably as a result, also NaF-stimulated) adenylate cyclase activity was higher in bipolar I patients with higher Ca^{2+} concentrations, but not in patients with normal Ca^{2+} concentrations, compared to the controls. Thus, these results seem to indicate that trait-dependent disordered processes seen in both cAMP and Ca^{2+} signaling pathways in affective disorders occur in conjunction with each other, irrespective to which abnormality is the primary one.

The inhibition of adenylate cyclase activity in platelets has been probed by stimulating α_2-adrenoceptors, which are coupled with G_i proteins to decrease cAMP formation. The α_2-adrenoceptor-mediated inhibition of adenylate cyclase activity in platelets from depressed patients was reported to be attenuated in some studies [137-139, 141, 145], but to be unaltered in others [140, 142-144, 147].

A series of studies have been reported by Perez and colleagues, wherein PKA-mediated phosphorylation cascades in platelets were assessed in affective disorder patients and controls. It was reported that cyclic AMP stimulated phosphorylation of platelet endogenous proteins with molecular weight of 22 kDa and 38 kDa, and that only the phosphorylation of 22 kDa band was significantly higher in euthymic bipolar patients than in comparison subjects [148-150]. This PKA substrate of 22 kDa was identified as Rap 1, a Ras-like protein belonging to the family of small GTP-binding proteins [149]. These alterations appear to derive from increase in Rap 1 levels per se [150], and the increase in Rap 1 levels was detected in bipolar affective disorder patients irrespective of mood states, thus indicative of trait-dependent marker [151]. With regard to PKA subunits, C subunit levels were increased in bipolar patients in depressed or manic phase, but not in those in euthymic state, whereas neither RI nor RII subunit levels were altered in bipolar patients compared to the respective control values in healthy subjects [151]. However, these results are not so easy to interpret when the data concerning the patients with unipolar depression [152] and depressed patients with psychotic features were taken into consideration [153]. **Table 2** summarizes the complex pattern of alterations in these proteins in platelets from various subtypes of affective disorder patients.

PI Signaling

In lymphoblastoid cell lines established from patients with bipolar affective disorder, the incorporation of inositol into the PI intracellular pools was decreased compared with those from control subjects, albeit the uptake of inositol and free intracellular inositol levels were similar in both groups [154]. On the other hand, Belmaker et al. [155] reported that, although inositol uptake was unaltered, inositol levels of lymphocyte-derived cell lines from bipolar patients were significantly lower than those from controls. The relevance of these findings is unclear.

Some researches focused on stimulant-induced PI hydrolysis in platelets. It has been reported that PI hydrolysis in platelets is, when stimulated by agonists for α_2-adrenoceptor [156, 157] and 5-HT_2 receptors [158], and by thrombin [157], but not by NaF [157], significantly higher in depressed (mostly unipolar) patients than in the controls. I am not aware of the same type of experiments conducted on the bipolar affective disorders.

Table 2. Levels of PKA subunits and PKA substrate in platelets

	RI	RII	C	Rap 1	References
Bipolar patients					Perez et al. [150, 151]
Euthymic	⇔	⇔	⇔	↑	
Depressed	⇔	⇔	↑	↑	
Manic	⇔	⇔	↑	↑	
Unipolar patients					Perez et al. [152]
Euthymic	⇔	⇔	⇔	⇔	
Depressed	⇔	↓	⇔	↓	
Depressed patients with psychotic features					Perez et al. [153]
Bipolar	↓	⇔	↑	⇔	
Unipolar	↓	↑	↑	⇔	

↑ : significantly increased compared to controls.

↓ : significantly decreased compared to controls

⇔: not significantly different from controls

As described previously, PIP_2 serves as a substrate for the enzyme PLC to form the two second messengers, i.e., DAG and IP_3, and then, alterations in the levels of this phospholipid in membrane fraction should affect the PI signaling pathway to an substantial extent. In 1993, Brown et al. [159] reported that platelet membrane PIP_2 was significantly higher in drug-free manic patients than in the comparison subjects. In a subsequent single case study, PIP_2 levels have been shown to fluctuate in parallel with mood states (euthymic, then manic before treatment, and again euthymic during lithium treatment), indicating that the increase in PIP_2 in mania is state-dependent [160]. Elevated levels of PIP_2 in platelet membranes were also observed in drug-free depressed bipolar patients [161]. It has been shown that lithium treatment reduces PIP_2 levels [162], and that lithium-treated euthymic bipolar patients have lower levels of PIP_2 in platelets than the controls [163, 164].

Inositol monophosphatase is an enzyme inhibited by lithium at therapeutically relevant concentrations [92], which serves an important basis of the inositol depletion hypothesis [10, 91]. Though this enzyme activity in red blood cells was indeed inhibited during treatment with lithium in bipolar patients in line with the preclinical studies, there appeared no difference in the activity between bipolar patients without lithium treatment and healthy controls [165].

It was reported that the ratio of PKC activities (membrane-bound to cytosolic) at rest in platelets was elevated in manic bipolar patients compared to that in the controls and schizophrenic patients, and that 5-HT-elicited PKC translocation through 5-HT_2 receptors [166] was also enhanced in manic bipolar patients [167]. These preliminary results were later confirmed in larger samples [168]. In this report, they showed that this finding was restrictively found in manic patients, but not in unipolar depressed patients or in schizophrenic patients. Further analysis of re-distribution of PKC activities induced by 5-HT, phorbol 12-myristate 13-acetate (PMA), and thrombin provided a possibility that PKC-mediated signaling was heightened in mania and rather impaired in unipolar depression or schizophrenia [168].

Pandey et al. [169] reported that [^{3}H]phorbol dibutyrate binding to PKC was significantly higher in cytosolic fraction, but not in membrane fraction, obtained from platelets of depressed patients compared to normal control subjects. As for the levels of PKC isozymes in platelets determined by western blotting, Soares et al. [164] demonstrated lower cytosolic PKC α in lithium-treated euthymic bipolar patients, whereas Young et al. [170] could not find any difference in PKC α levels, either membranous or cytosolic, among unmedicated bipolar patients (depressed or hypomanic/manic), lithium-treated euthymic bipolar patients, and healthy comparison subjects.

IP_3, another second messenger of PI signaling, which is generated from cleavage of PIP_2 catalyzed by activated PLC, stimulates the release of intracellular-stored calcium from the smooth endoplasmic reticulum into the cytosol. Given the pivotal roles of this ion in regulating many cellular processes, it is of particular importance to investigate possible disturbances in intracellular Ca^{2+} signaling involved in pathophysiology of affective disorders. Abnormalities of Ca^{2+} homeostasis in affective disorders have been supposed for a long time [171], and calcium concentrations in serum or cerebrospinal fluid were determined in relation to the various behavioral or emotional states of psychiatric diseases. To give an example, transient increases in serum Ca^{2+} levels were observed to precede the onset of manic or excitement episodes [172]. However, measures of Ca^{2+} levels in the extracellular fluid do not necessarily reflect the activity of the intracellular free Ca^{2+} ($[Ca^{2+}]_i$) which is maintained in the 100 nM range at rest, a concentration 10,000 times lower than serum calcium. Analysis of $[Ca^{2+}]_i$ was greatly facilitated by the advent of fluorescent intracellular calcium chelators such as Fura 2 in the early 1980s [173], and this technique was adapted by Dubovsky et al. [174] for the first time to study intracellular calcium dynamics in the platelets of patients suffering from affective disorders. Following this research, many studies on $[Ca^{2+}]_i$ at rest as well as after stimulation in peripheral blood cells of affective disorder patients have emerged to date [174-195], as summarized in **Table 3**. Although there are substantial differences in study design as to materials (platelets, lymphocytes, and neutrophils), subjects selection (bipolar, unipolar, and their mixture), their mood states at the blood sampling (euthymic, manic, depressed, and their mixture), and therapeutic history (drug-naïve, drug-free for a certain period, and under treatment with antidepressants or mood stabilizers) among these reports, most investigators revealed elevated levels of basal and/or stimulated $[Ca^{2+}]_i$ in some types of affective disorders, in particular bipolar affective disorder patients in active phase (manic or depressed). As with other biochemical markers, it remains to be clarified whether this alteration is trait-dependent or state-dependent.

Table 3. Intracellular Calcium Concentrations in Peripheral Blood Cells in Affective Disorder Patients

	Basal	Stimulant 5-HT	Stimulant Thrombin	Stimulant Others	References
Platelets					
Bipolar patients					
Euthymic					
	⇔	n.d.	⇔*1	n.d.	Duvovsky et al. [174]
	↑	n.d.	↑	n.d.	Tan et al. [175]
	⇔	n.d.	⇔	n.d.	Duvovsky et al. [176]
	↑	n.d.	n.d.	⇔*2	Berk et al. [177]
	⇔	⇔	⇔	⇔*3	Bothwell et al. [178]
	↑	⇔	n.d.	n.d.	Berk et al. [179]
	⇔	⇔	n.d.	n.d.	Okamoto et al. [180]
Depressed					
	⇔	n.d.	↑ *1	n.d.	Duvovsky et al. [174]
	↑	n.d.	↑	n.d.	Duvovsky et al. [176]
	⇔	n.d.	↑	n.d.	Kusumi et al. [181]
	↑	n.d.	n.d.	⇔*2	Berk et al. [177]
	⇔	↑	n.d.	n.d.	Kusumi et al. [182]
	↑	↑ *4	n.d.	n.d.	Berk et al. [179]
	⇔	↑	n.d.	n.d.	Kusumi et al. [183]
Manic					
	↑	n.d.	↑ *1	n.d.	Duvovsky et al. [174]
	↑	n.d.	n.d.	⇔*2	Berk et al. [177]
	↑	↑ *4	n.d.	n.d.	Berk et al. [179]
	⇔	↑	n.d.	n.d.	Okamoto et al. [180]
Manic/depressed or uninformed					
	↑	n.d.	n.d.	n.d.	Dubovsky et al. [184]
	⇔	↑	n.d.	n.d.	Yamawaki et al. [185]
	↑	↑	↑	↑ /⇔*5	Hough et al. [186]
	⇔	↑	n.d.	n.d.	Suzuki et al. [187]
Unipolar patients					
Euthymic					
	⇔	⇔	⇔	⇔*3	Bothwell et al. [178]
Depressed					
	⇔	n.d.	⇔*1	n.d.	Duvovsky et al. [174]
	⇔	n.d.	⇔	n.d.	Duvovsky et al. [184]
	⇔	n.d.	⇔	n.d.	Kusumi et al. [181]
	⇔	↑	n.d.	⇔*6	Mikuni et al. [188]
	⇔	↑ /⇔*7	n.d.	n.d.	Kusumi et al. [182]
	↑	↑	n.d.	n.d.	Konopka et al. [189]
	⇔	↑	n.d.	n.d.	Yamawaki et al. [185]
	⇔	⇔	⇔	⇔*8	Hough et al. [186]
	⇔	⇔	n.d.	n.d.	Kusumi et al. [183]
	⇔	⇔	n.d.	n.d.	Suzuki et al. [187]

Table 3. Intracellular Calcium Concentrations in Peripheral Blood Cells in Affective Disorder Patients (Continued)

	Basal	Stimulant: 5-HT	Stimulant: Thrombin	Stimulant: Others	References
Mixed					
Depressed					
	⇔	↑	⇔	n.d.	Kusumi et al. [190]
	⇔	↑	⇔	n.d.	Eckert et al. [191, 192]
Lymphocytes					
Bipolar patients					
Manic/depressed or uninformed					
	↑	n.d.	n.d.	n.d.	Dubovsky et al. [184]
	↑ /⇔*9	n.d.	n.d.	↓ /⇔*10	Emamghoreishi et al. [193]
	↑	⇔	n.d.	↑ /⇔*11	Hough et al. [194]
Unipolar patients					
Depressed					
	⇔	n.d.	n.d.	↓ *12	Emamghoreishi et al. [193]
	⇔	⇔	n.d.	⇔*13	Hough et al. [194]
Mixed					
Depressed					
	⇔	n.d.	n.d.	↓ *14	Eckert et al. [192]
Neutrophils					
Mixed					
Euthymic					
	⇔	n.d.	n.d.	↓ *15	Fvrstner et al. [194]
Manic/depressed or uninformed					
	n.d.	n.d.	n.d.	EC_{50}↑ ↓ *16	van Calker et al. [195]

↑ : significantly increased compared to controls; ↓ : significantly decreased compared to controls; □: not significantly different from controls; n.d.: not determined.

*1 Platelet-activating factor (PAF) coadministered with thrombin.
*2 Dopamine
*3 PAF
*4 ↑ as compared with euthymic bipolar group.
*5 ↑ in response to thapsigargin, but □ in response to NaF.
*6 Norepinephrine
*7 ↑ in subjects with melancholia, but □ in subjects without melancholia.
*8 NaF or thapsigargin
*9 ↑ in B lymphoblasts in bipolar I, but □ in bipolar II; ↑ in T lymphocytes in male bipolar I, but □ in female bipolar I and bipolar II.
*10 %Stimulation by phytohemagglutinin (PHA) in T lymphocytes. ↓ in bipolar I, but □ in bipolar II.
*11 ↑ in response to thapsigargin, but □ in response to concanavalin A (Con A) or NaF.
*12 %Stimulation by PHA in T lymphocytes
*13 Con A, NaF, or thapsigargin
*14 PHA
*15 Formylmethyonylleucylphenylalanin (fMLP)
*16 Increased EC_{50} for fMLP in lithium-treated group and decreased EC_{50} in medication-free group.

Prior to the advent of fluorescent calcium chelators, many investigators tried to elucidate abnormalities of intracellular calcium dynamics postulated in affective disorder patients by indirect methods. For instance, it was reported that the activity of Ca^{2+}-ATPase pump in red blood cells was increased in manic and depressed bipolar disorder patients [196, 197] as well as in lithium-treated bipolar patients [198]. The last finding [198] should, however, be attributable to lithium's effect, but not to disease process per se, because higher calmodulin-activated Ca^{2+}-ATPase activity was observed only in lithium-treated bipolar patients, but not in bipolar subjects without lithium treatment [199]. Another well-established abnormality associated with affective disorders is a state-dependent decrease in Na^{+}-K^{+}-ATPase activity, which has been reported consistently in red blood cells in depressed bipolar patients and less consistently in mania [200]. It was reported that the uptake of $^{45}Ca^{2+}$ into platelets, which was inhibited by 1 mM lithium, was not significantly different between bipolar patients (either in manic or depressed state) and healthy controls [201].

G Proteins

As in the postmortem brain studies described above, the most intriguing finding as to the alterations in G protein subtype levels associated with affective disorders is the increase in $G_{\alpha s}$ in platelets or in lymphocytes from bipolar patients (**Table 4**) [202-210]. However, accumulating results are not necessarily consistent to let us reach a conclusion on the problem of whether this phenomenon is dependent on bipolar trait or associated with manic state. Nevertheless, a series of studies from the laboratory of Avissar and colleagues have provided the data supporting the notion of state-dependent alterations of both $G_{\alpha s}$ and $G_{\alpha i}$ in mononuclear leukocytes. Thus, both protein levels were significantly increased in manic state and inversely decreased in depressed state compared with healthy controls [208], and the reductions in both protein levels were significantly correlated with the severity of depressed symptoms [210]. Furthermore, the reduced levels of $G_{\alpha s}$ and $G_{\alpha i}$ in mononuclear leukocytes in depressed patients were normalized by repeated treatments with electroconvulsive therapy, followed by clinical improvement [211].

As for mRNA expression of G protein subtypes in granulocytes, Spleiss et al. [212] demonstrated that both $G_{\alpha s}$ and $G_{\alpha i2}$ mRNA levels were significantly elevated in bipolar patients, but not in unipolar patients, compared with those in controls. Levels of $G_{\alpha q}$ mRNA in bipolar or unipolar patients were similar to those in the control subjects. Interestingly, elevated $G_{\alpha s}$ mRNA levels were seen in bipolar patients irrespective to the medication with lithium, whereas $G_{\alpha i2}$ mRNA levels were increased only in lithium-treated bipolar patients, but not in unmedicated bipolar patients, making the interpretation of these results rather complicated.

G protein functionality evaluated by agonist-induced increase in [^{3}H]Gpp(NH)p in mononuclear leukocytes was reported to be associated well with mood states. Both isoproterenol-induced and carbamylcholine-induced increases in [^{3}H]Gpp(NH)p binding capacity were significantly higher in untreated manic patients [208, 213], but not in lithium-treated euthymic patients [213], and in reverse significantly lower in depressed patients [208-210], as compared with those in healthy volunteers. There was a significant correlation between isoproterenol-stimulated [^{3}H]Gpp(NH)p binding and $G_{\alpha s}$, and also between carbamylcholine-stimulated [^{3}H]Gpp(NH)p binding and $G_{\alpha i}$, in mononuclear leukocytes from depressed patients [210], indicating that state-dependent G protein impairment occurs in affective disorder patients quantitatively as well as functionally in parallel. These results, along with the preclinical findings about the effects of lithium [95], carbamazepine [214], electroconvulsive therapy [214], and antidepressants [30] on agonist-induced G protein activation, led them to the attractive hypothesis that manic states are associated with hyperfunctional β-adrenoceptor/G_s (derived from elevated amount of $G_{\alpha s}$) plus hyperfunctional muscarinic acetylcholine receptor/G_i (derived from elevated amount of $G_{\alpha i}$) and vice versa as to depressed states [33-35].

Table 4. Levels of G Protein Subtypes in Peripheral Blood Cells in Affective Disorder Patients

	$G_{\alpha s\text{-}L}$	$G_{\alpha s\text{-}S}$	$G_{\alpha i}$	$G_{\alpha q/11}$	$G_{\alpha z}$	G_β	References
Platelets							
Bipolar patients							
Manic/euthymic/depressed*1							
	↑	↑	⇔*2	⇔	⇔	n.d.	Mitchell et al. [202]
Unipolar patients							
Depressed							
	n.d.	n.d.	↑ *2	↑	n.d.	↑	Karege et al. [203]
	⇔	⇔	↑ ↓ *3	⇔	n.d.	⇔	Garcma-Sevilla et al. [204]
Lymphocytes							
Bipolar patients							
Euthymic							
	n.d.	↓ /⇔*4	n.d.	n.d.	n.d.	n.d.	Karege et al. [205]
	⇔*5	⇔*5	n.d.	n.d.	n.d.	n.d.	Alda et al. [206]
Depressed							
	n.d.	↑	↑ *2	n.d.	n.d.	n.d.	Young et al. [207]
	n.d.	↓	↓ *2	n.d.	n.d.	⇔	Avissar et al. [208]
Manic							
	n.d.	↑	↑ *2	n.d.	n.d.	⇔	Avissar et al. [208]
Manic/euthymic/depressed*1							
	⇔	⇔	⇔*2	⇔	⇔	n.d.	Mitchell et al. [202]
Unipolar patients							
Depressed							
	n.d.	⇔	⇔*2	n.d.	n.d.	n.d.	Young et al. [207]
Mixed							
Depressed							
	n.d.	↓	n.d.	n.d.	n.d.	n.d.	Avissar et al. [209]
	n.d.	↓	↓ *2	n.d.	n.d.	⇔	Avissar et al. [210]

↑ : significantly increased compared to controls; ↓ : significantly decreased compared to controls; □: not significantly different from controls; n.d.: not determined.

*1 Euthymic in most cases.

*2 $G_{\alpha i1/2}$

*3 ↑ in $G_{\alpha i1/2}$, but ↓ in $G_{\alpha i3}$.

*4 ↓ in lithium-treated patients, but □ in haloperidol-treated patients.

*5 In lymphoblasts from euthymic bipolar patients with an excellent response to lithium prophylaxis.

Parallel alterations between quantitative and functional measures for G protein subtypes were not always found in affective disorders. As mentioned above (**Table 4**), Karege et al. [203] reported elevated immunoreactive levels of $G_{\alpha i2}$ in the platelets from drug-free major depressed patients. Using the same platelet membranes, however, epinephrine-stimulated [^{35}S]GTPγS binding (α_{2A}-adrenoceptor/G_{i2} coupling) was shown to be decreased in the depressed patient group, indicative of a dissociation of the two measures.

The author utilized agonist-induced increase in high-affinity GTPase activity to assess functional receptor/G protein coupling in platelet membranes. Neither epinephrine-stimulated high-affinity GTPase activity (α_{2A}-adrenoceptor/G_{i2} coupling) nor thrombin-stimulated high-affinity GTPase activity [thrombin receptor/(G_{i2} + G_q) coupling] was altered in affective disorder patients (mostly unipolar patients in depressed phase) compared with healthy controls [215].

Concluding Remarks and Future Perspective

As partly mentioned previously, there are many unavoidable limitations in the clinical studies utilizing postmortem human brains and peripheral tissue as research materials. In postmortem studies, it is often very difficult to gather enough number of subjects with homogeneous clinical features with reference to lifelong psychiatric diagnosis, mood states just before the death, cause of death, premortal somatic conditions and therapeutic intervention, history of antemortem treatment with psychotropic drugs, postmortem storage conditions before autopsy, and so on. In the studies with peripheral tissue, there is an essential problem of whether detected abnormalities in peripheral tissue represent the primary pathogenetically relevant alterations in the central nervous systems or not. It is well known that mood states influence hormonal homeostasis including hypothalamo-pituitary-adrenal axis, immune systems, daily activity, appetite, sleep, and circadian rhythm and so on, all of which are potentially alter in turn the intracellular signaling pathways in circulating blood cells.

Despite these limitations, lots of postmortem studies and peripheral tissue studies have, as overviewed above, provided convincing evidence of signal transduction abnormalities associated with affective disorders, in particular bipolar affective disorders. Among them, hyperactive PI signaling pathway resulting in PKC hyperactivity and elevated intracellular Ca^{2+} homeostasis observed in bipolar affective disorder, particularly in manic state, seems the most reliable finding. The cAMP-mediated signaling is also implicated in pathophysiology of affective disorders. Given the complexity of intracellular communication network and well-harmonized tuning of cascading signals, multiple alterations observed in affective disorder patients may be the results of interplay between diverse interrelated signaling components.

Biological psychiatric research always followed the development of novel techniques and knowledge in basic neurobiology, and usually preclinical investigations preceded adapting the techniques to clinical settings. Considering recent trends in preclinical studies as to the mechanisms of action of antidepressants and mood stabilizers, gene expression related to neurogenesis and neuroprotective factors would be the center of interest in the future clinical studies. Direct evidence supporting the hypothesis in which impairment of structural neuroplasticity and cellular resilience is associated with pathogenesis of affective disorders has been still scarce thus far.

Although molecular genetic studies have produced numerous interesting findings, they have not yet succeeded to identify specific genes that are so far responsible for the vulnerability to bipolar disorders. On the other hand, recent development in molecular biological techniques has made it possible to screen large number of genes for differential regulation of factors that may be relevant to the underlying disease process or vulnerability [216, 217] as well as treatment with psychotropic drugs such as lithium [218] and antidepressant [219].

Further research efforts aiming at elucidating molecular abnormalities in affective disorders, step by step at multiple levels downward in intracellular signaling cascades, leading finally to targeted gene expressions in the nucleus, will reach the pivotal findings relevant to the pathogenesis of these illnesses. In combination with genetic and molecular biological studies, such work will provide newer understanding of pathophysiology of affective disorders as well as clue to development of novel therapeutic agents for these diseases.

ACKNOWLEDGEMENTS

The author is supported by grant (No.13671030) from the Ministry of Education, Culture, Sports, Science and Technology of Japan.

REFERENCES

[1] Akiskal HS. The prevalent clinical spectrum of bipolar disorders: beyond DSM-IV. *J Clin Pcyshopharmacol.* 1996;16(suppl 1):4S-14S.

[2] Perugi G, Akiskal HS, Micheli C, Musetti L, Paiano A, Quilici C, Rossi L, Cassano GB. Clinical subtypes of bipolar mixed stated: validating a broader European definition in 143 cases. *J Affect Disord.* 1997;43:169-180.

[3] Perugi G, Akiskal HS, Lattanzi L, Cecconi D, Mastrocinque C, Patronelli A, Vignoli S, Bemi E. The high prevalence of "soft" bipolar (II) features in atypical depression. *Compr Psychiatry.* 1998;39:63-71.

[4] Bunney WE Jr, Davis JM. Norepinephrine in depressive reactions. *Arch Gen Psychiatry.* 1965;13:483-494.

[5] Schildkraut JJ. The catecholamine hypothesis of affective disorders: a review of supporting evidence. *Am J Psychiatry.* 1965;122:509-522.

[6] Sulser F. Functional aspects of the norepinephrine receptor coupled adenylate cyclase system in the limbic forebrain and its modification by drugs which precipitate or alleviate depression: molecular approaches to an understanding of affective disorders. *Pharmakopsychiat.* 1978;11:43-52.

[7] Coppen A, Wood K. 5-Hydroxytryptamine in the pathogenesis of affective disorders. *Adv Biochem Psychopharmacol.* 1982;34:249-258.

[8] Charney D. Monoamine dysfunction and the pathophysiology and treatment of depression. *J Clin Psychiatry.* 1998;59(suppl 14):11-14.

[9] Baraban JM, Worley PF, Snyder SH. Second messenger systems and psychoactive drug action: focus on the phosphoinositide system and lithium. *Am J Psychiatry.* 1989;146:1251-1260.

[10] Berridge MJ, Downes CP, Hanley MR. Neural and developmental action of lithium: a unifying hypothesis. *Cell*. 1989;59:411-419.
[11] Mxrk A, Geisler A, Hollund P. Effects of lithium on second messenger systems in the brain. *Pharmacol Toxicol*. 1992;71(suppl 1):4-17.
[12] Manji HK, Potter WZ, Lenox RH. Signal transduction pathways. Molecular targets for lithium's actions. *Arch Gen Psychiatry*. 1995;52:531-543.
[13] Lenox RH, McNamara RK, Papke RL, Manji HK. Neurobiology of lithium: an update. *J Clin Psychiatry*. 1998;59(suppl 6):37-47.
[14] Odagaki Y, Nishi N, Koyama T. Postreceptor signal-transduction systems as potential targets of lithium. In: Ozawa H, Saito T, Takahata N, eds. *Signal Transduction in Affective Disorders*. Tokyo: Springer-Verlag; 1998;97-119.
[15] Chen G, Masana MI, Manji HK. Lithium regulates PKC-mediated intracellular cross-talk and gene expression in the CNS *in vivo*. *Bipol Disord*. 2000;2:217-236.
[16] Jope RS. Anti-bipolar therapy: mechanism of action of lithium. *Mol Psychiatry*. 1999;4:117-128.
[17] Lenox RH, Hahn C-G. Overview of the mechanism of action of lithium in the brain: fifty-year update. *J Clin Psychiatry*. 2000;61(suppl 9):5-15.
[18] Manji HK, Moore GJ, Chen G. Lithium up-regulates the cytoprotective protein Bcl-2 in the CNS in vivo: a role for neurotrophic and neuroprotective effects in manic depressive illness. *J Clin Psychiatry*. 2000;61(suppl 9):82-96.
[19] Phiel CJ, Klein PS. Molecular targets of lithium action. *Ann Rev Pharmacol Toxicol*. 2001;41:789-813.
[20] Li PP, Andreopoulos S, Warsh JJ. Signal transduction abnormalities in bipolar affective disorders. In: Reith MEA, ed. *Cerebral Signal Transduction: From First to Fourth Messengers*. Totowa: Humana Press Inc; 2000;283-309.
[21] Manji HK, Chen G. Post-receptor signaling pathways in the pathophysiology and treatment of mood disorders. *Curr Psychiatry Rep*. 2000;2:479-489.
[22] Manji HK, Lenox RH. Signalling: cellular insights into the pathophysiology of bipolar disorder. *Biol Psychiatry*. 2000;48:518-530.
[23] Manji HK, Lenox RH. The nature of bipolar disorder. *J Clin Psychiatry*. 2000;61(suppl 13):42-57.
[24] Bezchlibnyk Y, Young LT. The neurobiology of bipolar disorder: focus on signal transduction pathways and the regulation of gene expression. *Can J Psychiatry*. 2002;47:135-148.
[25] Gould T, Manji HK. Signaling networks in the pathophysiology and treatment of mood disorders. *J Psychosom Res*. 2002;53:687-697.
[26] Perez J, Tardito D, Mori S, Racagni G, Smeraldi E, Zanardi R. Abnormalities of cAMP signaling in affective disorders: implications for pathophysiology and treatment. *Bipolar Disord*. 2000;2:27-36.
[27] Stewart RJ, Chen B, Dowlatshahi D, MacQueen GM, Young LT. Abnormalities in the cAMP signaling pathway in *post-mortem* brain tissue from the Stanley Neuropathology Consortium. *Brain Res Bull*. 2001;55:625-629.
[28] Pacheco MA, Jope RS. Phosphoinositide signaling in human brain. *Prog Neurobiol*. 1996;50:255-273.
[29] Soares JC, Mallinger AG. Intracellular phosphatidylinositol pathway abnormalities in bipolar disorder patients. *Psychopharmacol Bull*. 1997;33:685-691.

[30] Avissar S, Schreiber G. The involvement of guanine nucleotide binding proteins in the pathogenesis and treatment of affective disorders. *Biol Psychiatry*. 1992;31:435-459.

[31] Manji HK. G proteins: implications for psychiatry. *Am J Psychiatry*. 1992;149:746-760.

[32] Manji HK, Chen G, Shimon H, Hsiao JK, Potter WZ, Belmaker RH. Guanine nucleotide-binding proteins in bipolar affective disorder. *Arch Gen Psychiatry*. 1995;52:135-144.

[33] Avissar S, Schreiber G. Toward molecular diagnostics of mood disorders in psychiatry. *Trends Mol Med*. 2002;8:294-300.

[34] Schreiber G, Avissar S. Application of G-proteins in the molecular diagnosis of psychiatric disorders. *Expert Rev Mol Diagn*. 2003;3:89-100.

[35] Schreiber G, Avissar S. G proteins as a biochemical tool for diagnosis and monitoring treatments of mental disorders. *Isr Med Assoc J*. 2000;2:86-91.

[36] Daniel P, Walker WH, Habener JF. Cyclic AMP signaling and gene regulation. *Annu Rev Nutr*. 1998;18:353-383.

[37] Beavo JA. Cyclic nucleotide phosphodiesterases: functional implications of multiple isoforms. *Physiol Rev*. 1995;75:725-748.

[38] Taussig R, Gilman AG. Mammalian membrane-bound adenylyl cyclases. *J Biol Chem*. 1995;270:1-4.

[39] Premont RT, Matsuoka I, Mattei M-G, Pouille Y, Defer N, Hanoune J. Identification and characterization of a widely expressed form of adenylyl cyclase. *J Biol Chem*. 1996;271:13900-13907.

[40] Scott JD. Cyclic nucleotide-dependent protein kinases. *Pharmacol Ther*. 1991;50:123-145.

[41] Spaulding SW. The way in which hormones change cyclic adenosine 3',5'-monophosphate-dependent protein kinase subunits, and how such changes affect cell behavior. *Endocr Rev*. 1993;14:632-650.

[42] Herdegen T, Leah JD. Inducible and constitutive transcription factors in the mammalian nervous system: control of gene expression by Jun, Fos and Krox, and CREB/ATF proteins. *Brain Res Rev*. 1998;28:370-490.

[43] Shaywitz AJ, Greenberg ME. CREB: a stimulus-induced transcription factor activated by a diverse array of extracellular signals. *Annu Rev Biochem*. 1999;68:821-861.

[44] Catt KJ, Balla T. Phosphoinositide metabolism and hormone action. *Annu Rev Med*. 1989;40:487-509.

[45] Chuang D-M. Neurotransmitter receptors and phosphoinositide turnover. *Annu Rev Pharmacol Toxicol*. 1989;29:71-110.

[46] Fain JN. Regulation of phosphoinositide-specific phospholipase C. *Biochim Biophys Acta*. 1990;1053:81-88.

[47] Rana RS, Hokin LE. Role of phosphoinositides in transmembrane signaling. *Physiol Rev*. 1990;70:115-164.

[48] Cockcroft S, Thomas GMH. Inositol-lipid-specific phospholipase C isoenzymes and their differential regulation by receptors. *Biochem J*. 1992;288:1-14.

[49] Fisher SK, Heacock AM, Agranoff BW. Inositol lipids and signal transduction in the nervous system: an update. *J Neurochem*. 1992;58:18-38.

[50] Exton JH. Phosphoinositide phospholipases and G proteins in hormone action. *Annu Rev Physiol*. 1994;56:349-369.

[51] Supattapone S, Danoff SK, Theibert A, Joseph SK, Steiner J, Snyder SH. Cyclic AMP-dependent phosphorylation of a brain inositol trisphosphate receptor decreases its release of calcium. *Proc Natl Acad Sci USA*. 1988;85:8747-8750.

[52] Berridge MJ, Irvine RF. Inositol phosphates and cell signalling. *Nature*. 1989;341:197-205.

[53] Nishizuka Y. Intracellular signaling by hydrolysis of phospholipids and activation of protein kinase C. *Science*. 1992;258:607-614.

[54] Tanaka C, Nishizuka Y. The protein kinase C family for neuronal signaling. *Annu Rev Neurosci*. 1994;17:551-567.

[55] Nishizuka Y. Protein kinase C and lipid signaling for sustained cellular response. *FASEB J*. 1995;9:484-496.

[56] Aderem A. The MARCKS brothers: a family of protein kinase C substrates. *Cell*. 1992;71:713-716.

[57] Blackshear PJ. The MARCKS family of cellular protein kinase C substrates. *J Biol Chem*. 1993;268:1501-1504.

[58] Gilman AG. G proteins: transducers of receptor-generated signals. *Ann Rev Biochem*. 1987;56:615-649.

[59] Gudermann T, Schvneberg T, Schultz G. Functional and structural complexity of signal transduction via G-protein-coupled receptors. *Annu Rev Neurosci*. 1997;20:399-427.

[60] Simon MI, Strathmann MP, Gautam N. Diversity of G proteins in signal transduction. *Science*. 1991;252:802-808.

[61] Birnbaumer L. Receptor-to-effector signaling through G proteins: roles for βγ dimmers as well as α subunits. *Cell*. 1992;71:1069-1072.

[62] Clapham DE, Neer EJ. New roles for G-protein βγ-dimers in transmembrane signalling. *Nature*. 1993;365:403-406.

[63] Hill SJ, Kendall DA. Cross-talk between different receptor-effector systems in the mammalian CNS. *Cell Signal*. 1989;1:135-141.

[64] Houslay MD. 'Crosstalk': a pivotal role for protein kinase C in modulating relationships between signal transduction pathways. *Eur J Biochem*. 1991;195:9-27.

[65] Bygrave FL, Roberts HR. Regulation of cellular calcium through signaling cross-talk involves an intricate interplay between the actions of receptors, G-proteins, and second messengers. *FASEB J*. 1995;9:1297-1303.

[66] Fisher SK. Homologous and heterologous regulation of receptor-stimulated phosphoinositide hydrolysis. *Eur J Pharmacol*. 1995;288:231-250.

[67] Selbie LA, Hill SJ. G protein-coupled-receptor cross-talk: the fine-tuning of multiple receptor-signalling pathways. *Trends Pharmacol Sci*. 1998;19:87-93.

[68] Sibley DR, Lefkowitz RJ. B-Adrenergic receptor-coupled adenylate cyclase. Biochemical mechanisms of regulation. *Mol Neurobiol*. 1987;1:121-154.

[69] Stork PJS, Schimitt JM. Crosstalk between cAMP and MAP kinase signaling in the regulation of cell proliferation. *Trends Cell Biol*. 2002;12:258-266.

[70] Grimes CA, Jope RS. The multifaceted roles of glycogen synthase kinase 3β in cellular signaling. *Prog Neurobiol*. 2001;65:391-426.

[71] Gould TD, Manji HK. The Wnt signaling pathway in bipolar disorder. *Neuroscientist*. 2002;8:497-511.

[72] Luttrell LM, Lefkowitz RJ. The role of β-arrestins in the termination and transduction of G-protein-coupled receptor signals. *J Cell Sci.* 2002;115:455-465.
[73] B|nemann M, Hosey MM. G-protein coupled receptor kinases as modulators of G-protein signalling. *J Physiol.* 1999;517:5-23.
[74] Hollinger S, Hepler JR. Cellular regulation of RGS proteins: modulators and integrators of G protein signaling. *Pharmacol Rev.* 2002;54:527-559.
[75] Duman RS, Heninger GR, Nestler EJ. A molecular and cellular theory of depression. *Arch Gen Psychiatry.* 1997;54:597-606.
[76] Duman RS, Malberg J, Thome J. Neural plasticity to stress and antidepressant treatment. *Biol Psychiatry.* 1999;46:1181-1191.
[77] Duman RS, Malberg J, Nakagawa S, D'Sa C. Neuronal plasticity and survival in mood disorders. *Biol Psychiatry.* 2000;48:732-739.
[78] Manji HK, Duman RS. Impairment of neuroplasticity and cellular resilience in severe mood disorders: implications for the development of novel therapeutics. *Psychopharmacol Bull.* 2001;35:5-49.
[79] Vaidya VA, Duman RS. Depression – emerging insights from neurobiology. *Brit Med Bull.* 2001;57:61-79.
[80] Nestler EJ, Barrot M, DiLeone RJ, Eisch AJ, Gold SJ, Monteggia LM. Neurobiology of depression. *Neuron.* 2002;34:13-25.
[81] Manji HK, Quiroz JA, Sporn J, Payne JL, Denicoff K, Gray NA, Zarate CA Jr, Charney DS. Enhancing neuronal plasticity and cellular resilience to develop novel, improved therapeutics for difficult-to-treat depression. *Biol Psychiatry.* 2003;53:707-742.
[82] Lenox RH, McNamara RK, Watterson JM, Watson DG. Myristoylated alanine-rich C kinase substrate (MARCKS): a molecular target for the therapeutic action of mood stabilizers in the brain? *J Clin Psychiatry.* 1996;57(suppl 13):23-31.
[83] Manji HK, Chen G, Hsiao JK, Risby ED, Masana MI, Potter WZ. Regulation of signal transduction pathways by mood-stabilizing agents: implications for the delayed onset of therapeutic efficacy. *J Clin Psychiatry.* 1996;57(suppl 13):34-46.
[84] Chen G, Hasanat KA, Bebchuk JM, Moore GJ, Glitz D, Manji HK. Regulation of signal transduction pathways and gene expression by mood stabilizers and antidepressants. *Psychosom Med.* 1999;61:599-617.
[85] Manji HK, Lenox RH. Protein kinase C signaling in the brain: molecular transduction of mood stabilization in the treatment of manic-depressive illness. *Biol Psychiatry.* 1999;46:1328-1351.
[86] Manji HK, Bebchuk JM, Moore GJ, Glitz D, Hasanat KA, Chen G. Modulation of CNS signal transduction pathways and gene expression by mood-stabilizing agents: therapeutic implications. *J Clin Psychiatry.* 1999;60(suppl 2):27-39.
[87] Manji HK, McNamara R, Chen G, Lenox RH. Signalling pathways in the brain: cellular transduction of mood stabilisation in the treatment of manic-depressive illness. *Aust NZ J Psychiatry.* 1999;33:S65-S83.
[88] Manji HK, Moore GJ, Chen G. Bipolar disorder: leads from the molecular and cellular mechanisms of action of mood stabilisers. *Brit J Psychiatry.* 2001;178(suppl 41):S107-S119.
[89] Gurvich N, Klein PS. Lithium and valproic acid: parallels and contrasts in diverse signaling contexts. *Pharmacol Ther.* 2002;96:45-66.

[90] Harwood AJ, Agam G. Search for a common mechanism of mood stabilizers. *Biochem Pharmacol.* 2003;66:179-189.

[91] Berridge MJ, Downes CP, Hanley MR. Lithium amplifies agonist-dependent phosphatidylinositol responses in brain and salivary glands. *Biochem J.* 1982;206:587-595.

[92] Hallcher LM, Sherman WR. The effects of lithium ion and other agents on the activity of *myo*-inositol-1-phosphatase from bovine brain. *J Biol Chem.* 1980;255:10896-10901.

[93] Hughes P, Dragunow M. Induction of immediate-early genes and the control of neurotransmitter-regulated gene expression within the nervous system. *Pharmacol Rev.* 1995;47:133-178.

[94] Schreiber G, Avissar S. Lithium sensitive G protein hyperfunction: a dynamic model for the pathogenesis of bipolar affective disorder. *Med Hypoth.* 1991;35:237-243.

[95] Avissar S, Schreiber G, Danon A, Belmaker RH. Lithium inhibits adrenergic and cholinergic increases in GTP binding in rat cortex. *Nature.* 1988;331:440-442.

[96] Cowburn RF, Marcusson JO, Eriksson A, Wiehager B, O'Neill C. Adenylyl cyclase activity and G-protein subunit levels in postmortem frontal cortex of suicide victims. *Brain Res.* 1994;633:297-304.

[97] Lowther S, Crompton MR, Katona CLE, Horton RW. GTPγS and forskolin-stimulated adenylyl cyclase activity in post-mortem brain from depressed suicides and controls. *Mol Psychiatry.* 1996;1:470-477.

[98] Reiach JS, Li PP, Warsh JJ, Kish SJ, Young LT. Reduced adenylyl cyclase immunolabeling and activity in postmortem temporal cortex of depressed suicide victims. *J Affect Disord.* 1999;56:141-151.

[99] Young LT, Li PP, Kish SJ, Siu KP, Kamble A, Hornykiewicz O, Warsh JJ. Cerebral cortex $G_s\alpha$ protein levels and forskolin-stimulated cyclic AMP formation are increased in bipolar affective disorder. *J Neurochem.* 1993;61:890-898.

[100] Dowlatshahi D, MacQueen GM, Wang J-F, Reiach JS, Young LT. G protein-coupled cyclic AMP signaling in postmortem brain of subjects with mood disorders: effects of diagnosis, suicide, and treatment at the time of death. *J Neurochem.* 1999;73:1121-1126.

[101] Rahman S, Li PP, Young LT, Kofman O, Kish SJ, Warsh JJ. Reduced [^{3}H]cyclic AMP binding in postmortem brain from subjects with bipolar affective disorder. *J Neurochem.* 1997;68:297-304.

[102] Fields A, Li PP, Kish SJ, Warsh JJ. Increased cyclic AMP-dependent protein kinase activity in postmortem brain from patients with bipolar affective disorder. *J Neurochem.* 1999;73:1704-1710.

[103] Dwivedi Y, Rao JS, Rizavi HS, Kotowski J, Conley RR, Roberts RC, Tamminga CA, Pandey GN. Abnormal expression and functional characteristics of cyclic adenosine monophosphate response element binding protein in postmortem brain of suicide subjects. *Arch Gen Psychiatry.* 2003;60:273-282.

[104] Dwivedi Y, Conley RR, Roberts RC, Tamminga CA, Pandey GN. [^{3}H]cAMP binding sites and protein kinase A activity in the prefrontal cortex of suicide victims. *Am J Psychiatry.* 2002;159:66-73.

[105] Chang A, Li PP, Warsh JJ. Altered cAMP-dependent protein kinase subunit immunolabeling in post-mortem brain from patients with bipolar affective disorder. *J Neurochem.* 2003;84:781-791.
[106] Dowlatshahi D, MacQueen GM, Wang JF, Young LT. Increased temporal cortex CREB concentrations and antidepressant treatment in major depression. *Lancet.* 1998;352:1754-1755.
[107] Odagaki Y, Garcma-Sevilla JA, Huguelet P, La Harpe R, Koyama T, Guimsn J. Cyclic AMP-mediated signaling components are upregulated in the prefrontal cortex of depressed suicide victims. *Brain Res.* 2001;898:224-231.
[108] Nibuya M, Nestler EJ, Duman RS. Chronic antidepressant administration increases the expression of cAMP response element binding protein (CREB) in rat hippocampus. *J Neurosci.* 1996;16:2365-2372.
[109] Yamada S, Yamamoto M, Ozawa H, Riederer P, Saito T. Reduced phosphorylation of cyclic AMP-responsive element binding protein in the postmortem orbitofrontal cortex of patients with major depressive disorder. *J Neural Transm.* 2003;110:671-680.
[110] Dwivedi Y, Rizavi HS, Conley RR, Roberts RC, Tamminga CA, Pandey GN. Altered gene expression of brain-derived neurotrophic factor and receptor tyrosine kinase B in postmortem brain of suicide subjects. *Arch Gen Psychiatry.* 2003;60:804-815.
[111] Mathews R, Li PP, Young LT, Kish SJ, Warsh JJ. Increased $G\alpha_{q/11}$ immunoreactivity in postmortem occipital cortex from patients with bipolar affective disorder. *Biol Psychiatry.* 1997;41:649-656.
[112] Jope RS, Song L, Li PP, Young LT, Kish SJ, Pacheco MA, Warsh JJ. The phosphoinositide signal transduction system is impaired in bipolar affective disorder brain. *J Neurochem.* 1996;66:2402-2409.
[113] Pacheco MA, Stockmeier C, Meltzer HY, Overholser JC, Dilley GE, Jope RS. Alterations in phosphoinositide signaling and G-protein levels in depressed suicide brain. *Brain Res.* 1996;723:37-45.
[114] Shimon H, Agam G, Belmaker RH, Hyde TM, Keinman JE. Reduced frontal cortex inositol levels in postmortem brain of suicide victims and patients with bipolar disorder. *Am J Psychiatry.* 1997;154:1148-1150.
[115] Shapiro J, Belmaker RH, Biegon A, Seker A, Agam G. Scyllo-inositol in post-mortem brain of bipolar, unipolar and schizophrenia patients. *J Neural Transm.* 2000;107:603-607.
[116] Levine J, Barak Y, Gonzalves M, Szor H, Elizur A, Kofman O, Belmaker RH. Double-blind, controlled trial of inositol treatment of depression. *Am J Psychiatry.* 1995;152:792-794.
[117] Chengappa KNR, Levine J, Gershon S, Mallinger AG, Hardan A, Vagnucci A, Pollock B, Luther J, Buttenfield J, Verfaille S, Kupfer DJ. Inositol as an add-on treatment for bipolar depression. *Bipolar Disord.* 2000;2:47-55.
[118] Wang H-Y, Friedman E. Enhanced protein kinase C activity and translocation in bipolar affective disorder brains. *Biol Psychiatry.* 1996;40:568-575.
[119] Pandey GN, Dwivedi Y, Pandey SC, Conley RR, Roberts RC, Tamminga CA. Protein kinase C in the postmortem brain of teenage suicide victims. *Neurosci Lett.* 1997;228:111-114.

[120] Hrdina P, Faludi G, Li Q, Bendotti C, Tekes K, Sotonyi P, Palkovits M. Growth-associated protein (GAP-43), its mRNA, and protein kinase C (PKC) isoenzymes in brain regions of depressed suicides. *Mol Psychiatry*. 1998;3:411-418.

[121] McNamara RK, Hyde TM, Kleinman JE, Lenox RH. Expression of the myristoylated alanine-rich C kinase substrate (MARCKS) and MARCKS-related protein (MRP) in the prefrontal cortex and hippocampus of suicide victims. *J Clin Psychiatry*. 1999;60(suppl 2):21-26.

[122] Young LT, Li PP, Kish SJ, Siu KP, Warsh JJ. Postmortem cerebral cortex G_s α-subunit levels are elevated in bipolar affective disorder. *Brain Res*. 1991;553:323-326.

[123] Friedman E, Wang H-Y. Receptor-mediated activation of G proteins is increased in postmortem brains of bipolar affective disorder subjects. *J Neurochem*. 1996;67:1145-1152.

[124] Garcma-Sevilla JA, Escriba PV, Ozaita A, La Harpe R, Walzer C, Eytan A, Guimsn J. Up-regulation of immunolabeled α_{2A}-adrenoceptors, G_i coupling proteins, and regulatory receptor kinases in the prefrontal cortex of depressed suicides. *J Neurochem*. 1999;72:282-291.

[125] Gonzalez-Maeso J, Rodrmguez-Puertas R, Meana JJ, Garcma-Sevilla JA, Guimsn J. Neurotransmitter receptor-mediated activation of G-proteins in brains of suicide victims with mood disorders: selective supersensitivity of α_{2A}-adrenoceptors. *Mol Psychiatry*. 2002;7:755-767.

[126] Grange-Midroit M, Garcma-Sevilla JA, Ferre-Alcsn M, La Harpe R, Huguelet P, Guimsn J. Regulation of GRK 2 and 6, β-arrestin-2 and associated proteins in the prefrontal cortex of drug-free and antidepressant drug-treated subjects with major depression. *Mol Brain Res*. 2003;111:31-41.

[127] Ozawa H, Gsell W, Frvlich L, Zvchling R, Pantucek F, Beckmann H, Riederer P. Imbalance of the G_s and $G_{i/o}$ function in post-mortem human brain of depressed patients. *J Neural Transm*. 1993;94:63-69.

[128] Young LT, Asghari V, Li PP, Kish SJ, Fahnestock M, Warsh JJ. Stimulatory G-protein α-subunit mRNA levels are not increased in autopsied cerebral cortex from patients with bipolar disorder. *Mol Brain Res*. 1996;42:45-50.

[129] Lesort M, Greendorfer A, Stockmeier C, Johnson GVW, Jope RS. Glycogen systhase kinase-3β, β-catenin, and tau in postmortem bipolar brain. *J Neural Transm*. 1999;106:1217-1222.

[130] Kozlovsky N, Belmaker RH, Agam G. Low GSK-3β immunoreactivity in postmortem frontal cortex of schizophrenic patients. *Am J Psychiatry*. 2000;157:831-833.

[131] Jarskog LF, Gilmore JH, Selinger ES, Lieberman JA. Cortical Bcl-2 protein expression and apoptotic regulation in schizophrenia. *Biol Psychiatry*. 2000;48:641-650.

[132] Pandey GN, Dysken MW, Garver DL, Davis JM. Beta-adrenergic receptor function in affective illness. *Am J Psychiatry*. 1979;136:675-678.

[133] Extein I, Tallman J, Smith CC, Goodwin FK. Changes in lymphocyte beta-adrenergic receptors in depression and mania. *Psychiatry Res*. 1979;1:191-197.

[134] Mann JJ, Brown RP, Halper JP, Sweeney JA, Kocsis JH, Stokes PE, Bilezikian JP. Reduced sensitivity of lymphocyte beta-adrenergic receptors in patients with endogenous depression and psychomotor agitation. *New Eng J Med*. 1985;313:715-720.

[135] Halper JP, Brown RP, Sweeney JA, Kocsis JH, Peters A, Mann JJ. Blunted β-adrenergic responsivity of peripheral blood mononuclear cells in endogenous depression. *Arch Gen Psychiatry*. 1988;45:241-244.

[136] Ebstein RP, Lerer B, Shapira B, Shemesh Z, Moscovich DG, Kindler S. Cyclic AMP second-messenger signal amplification in depression. *Brit J Psychiatry*. 1988;152:665-669.

[137] Siever LJ, Kafka MS, Targum S, Lake R. Platelet al.pha-adrenergic binding and biochemical responsiveness in depressed patients and controls. *Psychiatry Res*. 1984;11:287-302.

[138] Kafka MS, Siever LJ, Nurnberger JI, Uhde TW, Targum S, Cooper DMJ, van Kammen DP, Tokola NS. Platelet al.pha-adrenergic receptor function in affective disorders and schizophrenia. *Psychopharmacol bull*. 1985;21:599-602.

[139] Kafka MS, Nurnberger JI, Siever L, Targum S, Uhde TW, Gershon ES. Alpha$_2$-adrenergic receptor function in patients with unipolar and bipolar affective disorders. *J Affect Disord*. 1986;10:163-169.

[140] Kanof PD, Johns CA, Davidson M, Siever LJ, Coccaro EF, Davis KL. Platelet al.pha$_2$-adrenergic receptor function in psychiatric disorders. *Psychiatry Res*. 1988;23:11-22.

[141] Mooney JJ, Schatzberg AF, Cole JO, Kizuka PP, Salomon M, Lerbinger J, Pappalardo KM, Gerson B, Schildkraut JJ. Rapid antidepressant response to alprazolam in depressed patients with high catecholamine output and heterologous desensitization of platelet adenylate cyclase. *Biol Psychiatry*. 1988;23:543-559.

[142] Murphy DL, Donnelly C, Moskowitz J. Catecholamine receptor function in depressed patients. *Am J Psychiatry*. 1974;131:1389-1391.

[143] Wang Y-C, Pandey GN, Mendels J, Frazer A. Platelet adenylate cyclase response in depression: implications for a receptor defect. *Psychopharmacologia*. 1974;36:291-300.

[144] Garcma-Sevilla JA, Padrs D, Giralt T, Guimsn J, Areso P. α_2-Adrenoceptor-mediated inhibition of platelet adenylate cyclase and induction of aggregation in major depression. *Arch Gen Psychiatry*. 1990;47:125-132.

[145] Karege F, Bovier P, Widmer J, Gaillard J-M, Tissot R. Decrease in epinephrine-induced attenuation of platelet adenylate cyclase activity in depressed patients: relation with plasma electrolytes. *Neuropsychobiology*. 1992;26:129-135.

[146] Emamghoreishi M, Li PP, Schlichter L, Parikh SV, Cooke R, Warsh JJ. Associated disturbances in calcium homeostasis and G protein-mediated cAMP signaling in bipolar I disorder. *Biol Psychiatry*. 2000;48:665-673.

[147] Lenox RH, Ellis JE, van Riper DA, Ehrlich YH, Peyser JM, Shipley JE, Weaver LA. Platelet α_2-adrenergic receptor activity in clinical studies of depression. In: Usdin E, Goldstein M, Friedhoff AJ, Georgotas A, eds. *Frontiers in Neuropsychiatric Research*. London: MacMillan Press; 1983;331-356.

[148] Perez J, Zanardi R, Mori S, Gasperini M, Smeraldi E, Racagni G. Abnormalities of cAMP-dependent endogenous phosphorylation in platelets from patients with bipolar disorder. *Am J Psychiatry*. 1995;152:1204-1206.

[149] Zanardi R, Racagni G, Smeraldi E, Perez J. Differential effects of lithium on platelet protein phosphorylation in bipolar patients and healthy subjects. *Psychopharmacology*. 1997;129:44-47.

[150] Perez J, Tardito D, Mori S, Racagni G, Smeraldi E, Zanardi R. Altered Rap1 endogenous phosphorylation and levels in platelets from patients with bipolar disorder. *J Psychiat Res*. 2000;34:99-104.
[151] Perez J, Tardito D, Mori S, Racagni G, Smeraldi E, Zanardi R. Abnormalities of cyclic adenosine monophosphate signaling in platelets from untreated patients with bipolar disorder. *Arch Gen Psychiatry*. 1999;56:248-253.
[152] Perez J, Tardito D, Racagni G, Smeraldi E, Zanardi R. Protein kinase A and Rap1 levels in platelets of untreated patients with major depression. *Mol Psychiatry*. 2001;6:44-49.
[153] Perez J, Tardito D, Racagni G, Smeraldi E, Zanardi R. cAMP signaling pathway in depressed patients with psychotic features. *Mol Psychiatry*. 2002;7:208-212.
[154] Banks RE, Aiton JF, Cramb G, Naylor GJ. Incorporation of inositol into the phosphoinositides of lymphoblastoid cell lines established from bipolar manic-depressive patients. *J Affect Disord*. 1990;19:1-8.
[155] Belmaker RH, Shapiro J, Vainer E, Nemanov L, Ebstein RP, Agam G. Reduced inositol content in lymphocyte-derived cell lines from bipolar patients. *Bipolar Disord*. 2002;4:67-69.
[156] Mori H, Koyama T, Yamashita I. Platelet al.pha-2 adrenergic receptor-mediated phosphoinositide responses in endogenous depression. *Life Sci*. 1991;48:741-748.
[157] Karege F, Bovier P, Rudolph W, Gaillard J-M. Platelet phosphoinositide signaling system: an overstimulated pathway in depression. *Biol Psychiatry*. 1996;39:697-702.
[158] Mikuni M, Kusumi I, Kagaya A, Kuroda Y, Mori H, Takahashi K. Increased 5-HT-2 receptor function as measured by serotonin-stimulated phosphoinositide hydrolysis in platelets of depressed patients. *Prog Neuro-Psychopharmacol Biol Psychiatry*. 1991;15:49-61.
[159] Brown AS, Mallinger AG, Renbaum LC. Elevated platelet membrane phosphatidylinositol-4,5-bisphosphate in bipolar mania. *Am J Psychiatry*. 1993;150:1252-1254.
[160] Soares JC, Dippold CS, Mallinger AG. Platelet membrane phosphatidylinositol-4,5-bisphosphate alterations in bipolar disorder – evidence from a single case study. *Psychiatry Res*. 1997;69:197-202.
[161] Soares JC, Dippold CS, Wells KF, Frank E, Kupfer DJ, Mallinger AG. Increased platelet membrane phosphatidylinositol-4,5-bisphosphate in drug-free depressed bipolar patients. *Neurosci Lett*. 2001;299:150-152.
[162] Soares JC, Mallinger AG, Dippold CS, Wells KF, Frank E, Kupfer DJ. Effects of lithium on platelet membrane phosphoinositides in bipolar disorder patients: a pilot study. *Psychopharmacology*. 2000;149:12-16.
[163] Soares JC, Mallinger AG, Dippold CS, Frank E, Kupfer DJ. Platelet membrane phospholipids in euthymic bipolar disorder patients: are they affected by lithium treatment? *Biol Psychiatry*. 1999;45:453-457.
[164] Soares JC, Chen G, Dippold CS, Wells KF, Frank E, Kupfer DJ, Manji HK, Mallinger AG. Concurrent measures of protein kinase *C* and phosphoinositides in lithium-treated bipolar patients and healthy individuals: a preliminary study. *Psychiatry Res*. 2000;95:109-118.

[165] Moscovich DG, Belmaker RH, Agam G, Livne A. Inositol-1-phosphatase in red blood cells of manic-depressive patients before and during treatment with lithium. *Biol Psychiatry*. 1990;27:552-555.

[166] Wang H-Y, Friedman E. Protein kinase C translocation in human blood platelets. *Life Sci*. 1990;47:1419-1425.

[167] Friedman E, Wang H-Y-W, Levinson D, Connell TA, Singh H. Altered platelet protein kinase C activity in bipolar affective disorder, manic episode. *Biol Psychiatry*. 1993;33:520-525.

[168] Wang H-Y, Markowitz P, Levinson D, Undie AS, Friedman E. Increased membrane-associated protein kinase C activity and translocation in blood platelets from bipolar affective disorder patients. *J Psychiat Res*. 1999;33:171-179.

[169] Pandey GN, Dwivedi Y, Kumari R, Janicak PG. Protein kinase C in platelets of depressed patients. *Biol Psychiatry*. 1998;44:909-911.

[170] Young LT, Wang J-F, Woods CM, Robb JC. Platelet protein kinase C alpha levels in drug-free and lithium-treated subjects with bipolar disorder. *Neuropsychobiology*. 1999;40:63-66.

[171] Carman JS, Wyatt RJ. Calcium: bivalent cation in the bivalent psychoses. *Biol Psychiatry*. 1979;14:295-336.

[172] Carman JS, Post RM, Runkle DC, Bunney WE Jr, Wyatt RJ. Increased serum calcium and phosphorus with the 'Switch' into manic or excited psychotic states. *Brit J Psychiatry*. 1979;135:55-61.

[173] Grynkiewics G, Poenie M, Tsien RY. A new generation of Ca^{2+} indicators with greatly improved fluorescence properties. *J Biol Chem*. 1985;260:3440-3450.

[174] Dubovsky SL, Christiano J, Daniell LC, Franks RD, Murphy J, Adler L, Baker N, Harris RA. Increased platelet intracellular calcium concentration in patients with bipolar affective disorders. *Arch Gen Psychiatry*. 1989;46:632-638.

[175] Tan CH, Javors MA, Seleshi E, Lowrimore PA, Bowden CL. Effects of lithium on platelet ionic intracellular calcium concentration in patients with bipolar (manic-depressive) disorder and healthy controls. *Life Sci*. 1990;46:1175-1180.

[176] Dubovsky SL, Lee C, Christiano J, Murphy J. Elevated platelet intracellular calcium concentration in bipolar depression. *Biol Psychiatry*. 1991;29:441-450.

[177] Berk M, Bodemer W, van Oudenhove T, Butkow N. Dopamine increases platelet intracellular calcium in bipolar affective disorder and controls. *Int Clin Psychopharmacol*. 1994;9:291-293.

[178] Bothwell RA, Eccleston D, Marshall E. Platelet intracellular calcium in patients with recurrent affective disorders. *Psychopharmacology*. 1994;114:375-381.

[179] Berk M, Bodemer W, van Oudenhove T, Butkow N. The platelet intracellular calcium response to serotonin is augmented in bipolar manic and depressed patients. *Human Psychopharmacol*. 1995;10:189-193.

[180] Okamoto Y, Kagaya A, Shinno H, Motohashi N, Yamawaki S. Serotonin-induced platelet calcium mobilization is enhanced in mania. *Life Sci*. 1995;56:327-332.

[181] Kusumi I, Koyama T, Yamashita I. Thrombin-induced platelet calcium mobilization is enhanced in bipolar disorders. *Biol Psychiatry*. 1992;32:731-734.

[182] Kusumi I, Koyama T, Yamashita I. Serotonin-induced platelet intracellular calcium mobilization in depressed patients. *Psychopharmacology*. 1994;113:322-327.

[183] Kusumi I, Suzuki K, Sasaki Y, Kameda K, Koyama T. Treatment response in depressed patients with enhanced Ca mobilization stimulated by serotonin. *Neuropsychopharmacology*. 2000;23:690-696.

[184] Dubovsky SL, Murphy J, Thomas M, Rademacher J. Abnormal intracellular calcium ion concentration in platelets and lymphocytes of bipolar patients. *Am J Psychiatry*. 1992;149:118-120.

[185] Yamawaki S, Kagaya A, Okamoto Y, Shimizu M, Nishida A, Uchitomi Y. Enhanced calcium response to serotonin in platelets from patients with affective disorders. *J Psychiatry Neurosci*. 1996;21:321-324.

[186] Hough C, Lu S-J, Davis CL, Chuang D-M, Post RM. Elevated basal and thapsigargin-stimulated intracellular calcium of platelets and lymphocytes from bipolar affective disorder patients measured by a fluorometric microassay. *Biol Psychiatry*. 1999;46:247-255.

[187] Suzuki K, Kusumi I, Sasaki Y, Koyama T. Serotonin-induced platelet intracellular calcium mobilization in various psychiatric disorders: is it specific to bipolar disorder? *J Affect Disord*. 2001;64:291-296.

[188] Mikuni M, Kagaya A, Takahashi K, Meltzer HY. Serotonin but not norepinephrine-induced calcium mobilization of platelets is enhanced in affective disorders. *Psychopharmacology*. 1992;106:311-314.

[189] Konopka LM, Cooper R, Crayton JW. Serotonin-induced increases in platelet cytosolic calcium concentration in depressed, schizophrenic, and substance abuse patients. *Biol Psychiatry*. 1996;39:708-713.

[190] Kusumi I, Koyama T, Yamashita I. Serotonin-stimulated Ca^{2+} response is increased in the blood platelets of depressed patients. *Biol Psychiatry*. 1991;30:310-312.

[191] Eckert A, Gann H, Riemann D, Aldenhoff J, M|ller WE. Elevated intracellular calcium levels after 5-HT_2 receptor stimulation in platelets of depressed patients. *Biol Psychiatry*. 1993;34:565-568.

[192] Eckert A, Gann H, Riemann D, Aldenhoff J, M|ller WE. Platelet and lymphocytes free intracellular calcium in affective disorders. *Eur Arch Psychiatry Clin Neurosci*. 1994;243:235-239.

[193] Emamghoreishi M, Schlichter L, Li PP, Parikh S, Sen J, Kamble A, Warsh JJ. High intracellular calcium concentrations in transformed lymphoblasts from subjects with bipolar I disorder. *Am J Psychiatry*. 1997;154:976-982.

[194] Fvrstner U, Bohus M, Gebicke-Hdrter PJ, Baumer B, Berger M, van Calker D. Decreased agonist-stimulated Ca^{2+} response in neutrophils from patients under chronic lithium therapy. *Eur Arch Psychiatry Clin Neurosci*. 1994;243:240-243.

[195] van Calker D, Fvrstner U, Bohus M, Gebicke-Hdrter, Hecht H, Wark H-J, Berger M. Increased sensitivity to agonist stimulation of the Ca^{2+} response in neutrophils of manic-depressive patients: effect of lithium therapy. *Neuropsychobiology*. 1993;27:180-183.

[196] Linnoila M, MacDonald E, Reinila M, Leroy A, Rubinow DR, Goodwin FK. RBC membrane adenosine triphosphatase activities in patients with major affective disorders. *Arch Gen Psychiatry*. 1983;40:1021-1026.

[197] Bowden CL, Huang LG, Javors MA, Johnson JM, Seleshi E, McIntyre K, Contreras S, Maas JW. Calcium function in affective disorders and healthy controls. *Biol Psychiatry*. 1988;23:367-376.

[198] Meltzer HL, Kassir S, Goodnick PJ, Fieve RR, Chrisomalis L, Feliciano M, Szypula D. Calmodulin-activated calcium ATPase in bipolar illness. *Neuropsychobiology*. 1988;20:169-173.

[199] Meltzer HL, Kassir S. Abnormal calmodulin-activated CaATPase in manic-depressive subjects. *J Psychiat Res*. 1982;17:29-35.

[200] Dubovsky S, Murphy J, Christiano J, Lee C. The calcium second messenger system in bipolar disorders: data supporting new research directions. *J Neuropsychiatry Clin Neurosci*. 1992;4:3-14.

[201] Berk M, Kirchmann NH, Butkow N. Lithium blocks $^{45}Ca^{2+}$ uptake into platelets in bipolar affective disorder and controls. *Clin Neuropharmacol*. 1996;19:48-51.

[202] Mitchell PB, Manji HK, Chen G, Jolkovsky L, Smith-Jackson E, Denicoff K, Schmidt M, Potter WZ. High levels of $G_s\alpha$ in platelets of euthymic patients with bipolar affective disorder. *Am J Psychiatry*. 1997;154:218-223.

[203] Karege F, Bovier P, Stepanian R, Gaillard J-M. Change in platelet GTP-binding protein in drug-free depressed patients. *Human Psychopharmacol*. 1996;11:115-121.

[204] Garcma-Sevilla JA, Walzer C, Busquets X, Escriba PV, Balant L, Guimsn J. Density of guanine nucleotide-binding proteins in platelets of patients with major depression: increased abundance of the $G\alpha_{i2}$ subunit and down-regulation by antidepressant drug treatment. *Biol Psychiatry*. 1997;42:704-712.

[205] Karege F, Golaz J, Schwald M, Malafosse A. Lithium and haloperidol treatments differently affect the mononuclear leukocyte $G\alpha s$ protein levels in bipolar affective disorder. *Neuropsychobiology*. 1999;39:181-186.

[206] Alda M, Keller D, Grof E, Turecki G, Cavazzoni P, Duffy A, Rouleau GA, Grof P, Young LT. Is lithium response related to $G_s\alpha$ levels in transformed lymphoblasts from subjects with bipolar disorder? *J Affect Disord*. 2001;65:117-122.

[207] Young LT, Li PP, Kamble A, Siu KP, Warsh JJ. Mononuclear leukocyte levels of G proteins in depressed patients with bipolar disorder or major depressive disorder. *Am J Psychiatry*. 1994;151:594-596.

[208] Avissar S, Nechamkin Y, Barki-Harrington L, Roitman G, Schreiber G. Differential G protein measures in mononuclear leukocytes of patients with bipolar mood disorder are state dependent. *J Affect Disord*. 1997;43:85-93.

[209] Avissar S, Barki-Harrington L, Nechamkin Y, Roitman G, Schreiber G. Reduced β-adrenergic receptor-coupled Gs protein function and $Gs\alpha$ immunoreactivity in mononuclear leukocytes of patients with depression. *Biol Psychiatry*. 1996;39:755-760.

[210] Avissar S, Nechamkin Y, Roitman G, Schreiber G. Reduced G protein functions and immunoreactive levels in mononuclear leukocytes of patients with depression. *Am J Psychiatry*. 1997;154:211-217.

[211] Avissar S, Nechamkin Y, Roitman G, Schreiber G. Dynamics of ECT normalization of low G protein function and immunoreactivity in mononuclear leukocytes of patients with major depression. *Am J Psychiatry*. 1998;155:666-671.

[212] Spleiss O, van Calker D, Schdrter L, Adamovic K, Berger M, Gebicke-Haerter PJ. Abnormal G protein α_s- and α_{i2}-subunit mRNA expression in bipolar affective disorder. *Mol Psychiatry*. 1998;3:512-520.

[213] Schreiber G, Avissar S, Danon A, Belmaker RH. Hyperfunctional G protein mononuclear leukocytes of patients with mania. *Biol Psychiatry*. 1991;29:273-280.

[214] Avissar S, Schreiber G, Aulakh CS, Wozniak KM, Murphy DL. Carbamazepine and electroconvulsive shock attenuate β-adrenoceptor and muscarinic cholinoceptor coupling to G proteins in rat cortex. *Eur J Pharmacol.* 1990;189:99-103.

[215] Odagaki Y, Koyama. Epinephrine- and thrombin-stimulated high-affinity GTPase activity in platelet membranes from patients with psychiatric disorders. *Psychiatry Res.* 2002;112:111-119.

[216] Kakiuchi C, Iwamoto K, Ishiwata M, Bundo M, Kasahara T, Kusumi I, Tsujita T, Okazaki Y, Nanko S, Kunugi H, Sasaki T, Kato T. Impaired feedback regulation of XBP1 as a genetic risk factor for bipolar disorder. *Nature Gen.* 2003;35:171-175.

[217] Tkachev D, Mimmack ML, Ryan MM, Wayland M, Freeman T, Jones PB, Starkey M, Webster MJ, Yolken RH, Bahn S. Oligodendrocyte dysfunction in schizophrenia and bipolar disorder. *Lancet.* 2003;362:798-805.

[218] Detera-Wadleigh SD. Lithium-related genetics of bipolar disorder. *Ann Med.* 2001;33:272-285.

[219] Yamada M, Higuchi T. Functional genomics and depression research. Beyond monoamine hypothesis. *Eur Neuropsychopharmacol.* 2002;12:235-244.

In: Focus on Bipolar Disorder Research
Editor: Malcomb R. Brown, pp. 113-129
ISBN 1-59454-059-4

Chapter 6

ANTIEPILEPTIC DRUGS IN THE MANAGEMENT OF NEUROPSYCHIATRIC DISORDERS

Edward Kim

University of Medicine and Dentistry of New Jersey,
Robert Wood Johnson Medical School, Medical Director, Adult Services, University Behavioral HealthCare

Mona Bijlani

University of Medicine and Dentistry of New Jersey,
Robert Wood Johnson Medical School

ABSTRACT

Numerous neurological conditions may be complicated by behavioral symptoms such as aggression, mania and psychosis. Antiepileptic drugs (AEDs) are emerging as safe and effective agents in the management of these complex disorders. The purported mechanism for such therapeutic effects is attributed to mood stabilizing properties of these medications. The authors will describe the results of a retrospective chart review and a prospective clinical trial of two different AEDs, sodium divalproex and oxcarbazepine, and discuss the pathophysiology of these syndromes and the role of AEDs in effective treatment. Both studies support the use of AEDs in the management of a range of neuropsychiatric complications of acquired brain injuries.

INTRODUCTION

Our increasing understanding of the complex relationship between brain function and behavior has promoted the use of multiple psychotropic medications for behavioral complications of neurological disorders. These uses often extend beyond those approved by the Food and Drug Administration (FDA). Neurological conditions such as dementia, traumatic brain injury (TBI), developmental disorders, and stroke may be associated with an increased incidence of bipolar symptoms [1, 2], aggression [3], and psychosis [4, 5]. Often there are considerable phenomenological similarities between these syndromes, making accurate and consistent diagnosis challenging [6]. This in turn makes generalizations about treatment efficacy ambiguous. The continuing development of newer anticonvulsants has led to increased interest in the psychotropic properties of this entire class of medications and their respective roles in the management of psychiatric and neuropsychiatric syndromes [7, 8]. Lithium is a salt with an unclear mechanism of action that has been reported to reduce aggressive behaviors in brain-injured patients [9]. Despite its lengthy history as the prototypical mood stabilizer, lithium treatment may be limited by tremor, nausea, and cognitive impairment. Brain-injured patients appear to be more vulnerable to the neurotoxic effects of lithium even at therapeutic serum levels [10]. As a result, the role of anticonvulsant medications in neuropsychiatric syndromes may present a useful alternative to lithium. This chapter will discuss the benefits and limitations of anti-epileptic drugs (AEDs) in managing psychiatric complications of neurological syndromes.

Neural Substrates of Behavioral Syndromes

Animal and human data suggest that aggression and other neurobehavioral disturbances are mediated through complex interconnections between cortical and subcortical structures that comprise the limbic system, including the orbitofrontal cortex, hippocampus, parahippocampal gyrus, insula, temporal pole, olfactory cortex, cingulate cortex, amygdala, septal nuclei, hypothalamus, and select thalamic nuclei [11]. The prefrontal cortex is involved in executive cognitive processes such as planning, initiative, evaluation, and regulation of impulses [12, 13]. Decreased metabolism in the orbitofrontal cortex has been associated with aggression in subjects with personality disorders [14] and has been transiently induced in healthy subjects while they imagine aggressive behavior [15]. Damage to the prefrontal cortex, particularly the in orbitofrontal and ventromedial regions, has been associated with increased hostility, impulsivity, and aggression [2, 3, 16]. In functional neuroimaging studies of TBI survivors, agitation is associated with hypoperfusion in the orbitofrontal and basotemporal regions [17, 18]. Functional neuroimaging studies in elderly demented patients have noted an association between hypoperfusion in the dorsolateral frontal cortex and anterior cingulate gyrus and the emergence of psychotic and aggressive symptoms [4, 19, 20].

These findings suggest that deactivation of key prefrontal cortical structures and their associated limbic connections may lead to a failure of impulse control and affect regulation. This deactivation may be mediated by a number of mechanisms from acquired brain injury to self-induced imagined aggressive states. The precise mechanism by which such deactivation mediates aggression in neuropsychiatric conditions is unclear. One hypothesis implicates the loss of tonic balance between inhibitory pathways in the orbitofrontal cortex and limbic structures that mediate impulse and drive expression [2]. Alternatively, orbitofrontal damage may disrupt efferent projections to limbic structures, leading to denervation hypersensitivity and limbic kindling. The resulting hyperactivity or kindling of these structures may lead to an increase in aggression [21].

Chronic neurochemical changes may contribute to behavioral syndromes, though the nature and role of these changes are less well-understood. Cholinergic dysfunction is related to behavioral disturbances in Alzheimer's disease [22]. The role of serotonin in aggression is well-documented in non-brain-injured patients. Impaired serotonergic functioning is a common marker in individuals with impulsive aggression. Aggression and impulsivity are associated with decreased levels of the serotonin metabolite 5-hydroxyindoleacetic acid (5-HIAA) in the cerebrospinal fluid (CSF) as well as blunted neuroendocrine response to serotonin agonists [23]. Increases in dopamine and norepinephrine may be associated with increased aggression in animal models [24]. Stanislav [25] compared aggressive brain-injured patients with non-aggressive brain-injured controls. There were no significant differences between the two groups in CSF levels of 5-HIAA or the dopamine metabolite homovanillic acid (HVA). There was a trend toward significantly higher levels of the norepinephrine metabolite 3-methoxy-4-hydroxymethylphenylglycol (MHPG) within the aggressive group. The use of valproic acid (VPA) in the management of schizophrenia spectrum disorders has led to the hypothesis of a sub-type of VPA-responsive schizophrenia characterized by irritability, hyperresponsiveness to external stimuli, and agitation [26]. Given the heterogeneous nature of schizophrenia, one wonders if responsiveness to VPA signifies a neuropsychiatric etiology of psychotic symptoms. Mental health providers do not traditionally screen for neuropsychiatric factors such as head trauma or other sources of congenital or acquired brain dysfunction [27].

These findings underscore the complex, multifactorial interactions between environment, neurochemistry, and neuroanatomy that result in neurobehavioral disorders. Moreover, syndromal classification is quite challenging due to the overlap of symptom presentation across multiple neuropsychiatric syndromes that involve behavioral dyscontrol, psychotic symptomatology, and affective instability [6]. The role of anticonvulsants in managing these complex and heterogeneous symptoms derives from phenomenological similarities to idiopathic psychiatric disorders.

Spectrum of Neuropsychiatric Disorders

The symptomatic presentation in neuropsychiatric disorders is complex and made further problematic by the lack of a consistent and reliable nosology for symptom definition. These syndromes are at times indistinguishable from their idiopathic counterparts. Moreover, as stated previously, they may also be difficult to differentiate from one another, making clinical assessment and management challenging.

Aggression

Aggression in neuropsychiatric disorders is one of the most powerful predictors of institutionalization and social dysfunction. The nosology of aggression and "agitation" is problematic, with a general lack of rigorous definition in the literature. The DSM-IV classification system provides the diagnosis of Personality Change Secondary to a General Medical Condition, with several subtypes to clarify the type of behavior changes manifested. The Aggressive type is characterized by predominantly aggressive behavior, which may be directed toward self, others, or inanimate objects. The Disinhibited type is characterized primarily by disinhibition and sexual indiscretions, but patients may become aggressive when redirected or frustrated. Patients with the Labile type primarily demonstrate affective lability, which may include verbal outbursts with minimal provocation, but without substantial threatening or violent behaviors. To further complicate the diagnostic challenge, impulsive aggression may also occur in the context of a mixed bipolar syndrome.

Pre-morbid risk factors for aggression following TBI include a history of arrest [28] and substance abuse [29, 30]. A prior history of impulsive aggression is also correlated with post-TBI aggression [30, 31]. Another risk factor for post-TBI aggression appears to be prior episodes of head injuries. Patients sustaining multiple head injuries over time appear to develop increased irritability with each subsequent injury, particularly when injuries are associated with loss of consciousness [32]. There is some evidence that more severe injuries increase the likelihood of post-traumatic aggression [33].

Mania

Mania in neuropsychiatric conditions tends to be associated with more irritability and aggression [6, 34]. Some studies of TBI have found an increased association between aggression and injury severity as well as seizures [34]. In patients with focal vascular lesions, mania is associated with right orbitofrontal, basotemporal, caudate, and thalamic injuries [35]. In patients with head trauma, mania has been reported in 9.1% of patients, and associated with multifocal and basotemporal lesions [36]. Post-TBI mania was not associated with brain injury severity, physical or cognitive impairment, social functioning, or previous family or personal history of psychiatric disorder. Mania is a relatively infrequent complication of Alzheimer's disease, occurring in approximately 2.2% of cases [37].

Psychosis

Psychosis is a relatively infrequent but potentially serious and debilitating consequence of TBI. In some cases, the constellation of symptoms may produce a clinical syndrome that is virtually indistinguishable from schizophrenia [38]. The incidence of psychosis among individuals who have suffered traumatic brain injury has ranged from 0.7% to 26.5%, depending on the diagnostic criteria used [39-42]. There is often a considerable delay between TBI and the onset of psychotic symptoms, with mean latencies of 4-5 years and a range of 2 weeks to 19 years [38, 40, 43, 44]. The onset of psychotic illness in patients with TBI is later than the onset of schizophrenia in the general population [44], which may be helpful in differentiating injury-related psychoses from idiopathic disorders.

Paranoia and delusions are common symptoms in post-TBI psychosis [45], with a relative absence of formal thought disorder and affect blunting. Delusions appear to be more common than hallucinations, with the most common delusions being persecutory, and the most common hallucinations auditory [38, 46, 47]. Injuries to the left hemisphere and temporal lobes are associated with post-TBI psychosis [38, 41]. Severity of TBI has been linked to the development of psychotic symptoms in some studies [38, 41]. However, other studies have reported no relationship between injury severity and onset of psychosis [41, 44].

Mechanisms of Anticonvulsant Psychotropic Efficacy

Animal models indicate that many of the anticonvulsants with psychotropic efficacy are also potent inhibitors of amygdala-kindled seizures. Kindling is a model of epileptogenesis, in which repeated sub-convulsive electrical stimuli leads to the development of spontaneous seizures. Kindling, particularly within limbic structures, has been hypothesized to play a role in the development of idiopathic psychiatric disorders [48]. Anticonvulsant medications that inhibit amygdala-kindled seizures include carbamazepine and valproic acid [49], topiramate [50], lamotrigine [51], and vigabatrin [52]. An additional mechanism by which anticonvulsants may exert beneficial psychotropic effects is through modulation of central serotonergic functioning. Carbamazepine is an inhibitor of serotonin reuptake at higher dosages [53], and valproic acid has been reported to increase brain serotonin levels [54]. Lamotrigine has been reported to inhibit serotonin reuptake [55]. Gabapentin increases CSF levels of 5-HIAA in healthy human subjects [56]. Finally, GABA, the principle inhibitory neurotransmitter in the brain, appears to play a role in the modulation of aggression in animal models [57]. In the limbic system GABA has a stimulatory effect on norepinephrine transmission [58], and directly increases brain serotonin levels [59].

Topiramate

Topiramate is a sulfamate-substituted monosaccharide antiepileptic that is approved for monotherapy and adjunctive treatment of partial complex seizures. It has several mechanisms of action, including blockade of voltage-dependent sodium channels, antagonism of non-N-methyl-D-Aspartate (NMDA) glutamate receptors, increasing GABA-a receptor activity, and inhibition of carbonic anhydrase [60]. Topiramate has demonstrated antimanic efficacy in monotherapy and as an adjunctive treatment for partial response [61-63]. Its tendency to induce weight loss through dulling of the appetite may be a beneficial side effect in patients prone to gain weight on other anticonvulsants such as valproic acid [64]. However, topiramate treatment has been associated with the emergence of psychotic symptoms [65] and, more commonly, cognitive impairment [66]. The latter reaction is particularly problematic in the context of neuropsychiatric conditions such as dementia, TBI, and mental retardation, where cognitive deficits are already present. The author has noted substantial cognitive improvements following discontinuation of topiramate therapy in TBI patients, consistent with similar reports in epileptic patients. However, if cognitive side effects do not emerge, topiramate may be a useful medication for affective and behavioral dysregulation, particularly in patients who have experienced treatment-emergent weight gain.

Carbamazepine

Carbamazepine is a tricyclic compound with a variety of mechanisms of action, including stabilization of voltage-dependent sodium channels. It has been used to reduce agitation and aggression in TBI patients, both in the acute rehabilitative and post-acute setting [67, 68]. In demented patients, carbamazepine has demonstrated efficacy in randomized controlled trials for the treatment of agitation at doses of 300-400mg/d [69, 70]. In these studies, the drug was well-tolerated with no functional or cognitive decline noted. Chronic administration of carbamazepine leads to increased clearance of hepatically metabolized medications. Additional side effects include nausea, rash, and rare hepatotoxicity and agranulocytosis. Additionally, carbamazepine has been reported to cause cognitive impairment in some brain-injured patients [71]. The etiology of carbamazepine-induced side effects has been hypothesized to be due to the formation of an epoxide intermediate breakdown product [72]. At stable doses, carbamazepine may be well-tolerated, but requires routine monitoring of drug levels, hepatic and hematological parameters. However, in patients who have become accustomed to this regimen there may be little motivation to change medications. Substituting another anticonvulsant for carbamazepine is particularly complicated when patients are taking multiple hepatically metabolized medications whose clearance will be altered as the hepatic enzymes return to their baseline activity.

Gabapentin

Gabapentin is a novel anticonvulsant structurally related to GABA. Gabapentin is minimally processed in the liver and excreted in urine, making it particularly suitable for patients with liver disease due to alcohol abuse or hepatitis. The role of gabapentin in management of neuropsychiatric disorders is somewhat less clear, though its favorable metabolic pathway and side effect profile make it quite attractive to many clinicians. In bipolar disorders, gabapentin has been reported to reduce manic symptoms in several open label studies [73, 74]. However, anti-manic efficacy was not established in one double-blind study [75]. This alone does not disqualify gabapentin as a potential anti-aggressive medication. In agitation associated with dementia, several case series have suggested that gabapentin may be at least partially efficacious at doses ranging from 200-2400mg/d [76-78]. In one report, less than half of patients were determined to have at least minimal improvement, and there was a high prevalence of ataxia and sedation [78]. The literature on gabapentin's use for agitation in patients with mental retardation is also mixed; one report of an adult patient receiving 800mg bid noted a significant reduction in agitation and aggression [79]. However, a case series of 12 children with developmental disorders who were treated with gabapentin for seizures, noted an increase in tantrums, hyperactivity, and aggression [80]. The author has observed substantial reductions in agitation and affective lability in TBI patients treated with gabapentin 900-3600mg/d in both acute and post-acute settings. Based on these findings, gabapentin may represent a useful adjunctive medication for the management of neuropsychiatric aggression and agitation, particularly in patients with compromised hepatic functioning. Its efficacy has yet to be determined in randomized controlled trials.

Lamotrigine

Lamotrigine has demonstrated efficacy in treated both mania and bipolar depression in randomized controlled trials [81-83]. Moreover, in brain injured patients, the use of lamotrigine for seizure control was associated with more rapid rehabilitative progress, suggesting some treatment-associated cognitive enhancement [84]. Lamotrigine does not cause significant weight gain, in contrast to valproic acid, and may cause fewer cognitive side effects than carbamazepine [85]. The most notable adverse reaction to this drug is a skin rash that may evolve into the more serious Stevens - Johnson syndrome. However, the occurrence of this serious condition appears to be less than 0.3% of cases and may be even less common if the medication is titrated slowly in increments of no more than 25mg/d every 2 weeks [86]. This, however, may lead to unacceptably slow rates of titration for acute agitation, necessitating adjunctive medication during dose adjustment. Lamotrigine has been associated with treatment-emergent aggression in mentally retarded epileptic patients [87], though in another case series with a similar patient population, four of the patients experienced behavioral improvement while three developed exacerbations in pre-existing aggression and affective lability [81]. A placebo-controlled study of lamotrigine in non-epileptic autistic patients demonstrated no difference between lamotrigine and placebo in autistic behaviors such as stereotypies, hyperactivity, and irritability [89]. Lamotrigine may also be useful in reducing aggression in dementia, though there is limited data [90]. Thus, while there is substantial support for the use of lamotrigine in idiopathic bipolar disorders, treatment data in neuropsychiatric conditions is limited and demonstrates mixed results.

Vigabatrin

Vigabatrin is a structural analogue of gamma amino butyric acid (GABA), which binds irreversibly to GABA-transaminase causing increased brain levels of GABA [91]. It is currently available in Canada. While there is no available data regarding its use for idiopathic psychiatric disorders, vigabatrin has been reported to be associated with an increased incidence of depression and psychosis in patients treated for epilepsy [92]. Nevertheless, vigabatrin treatment of epilepsy in mentally retarded patients with psychotic symptoms has been reported to reduce aggression, affective lability, and stereotypical behaviors [93]. Another report noted improvements in behavioral and cognitive functioning in children with tuberous sclerosis, seizures, and cognitive impairment [94]. While vigabatrin has not demonstrated efficacy in reducing target behaviors, in randomized controlled studies, naturalistic data suggests that its potential warrants further exploration.

Tiagabine and Levetiracetam

Tiagabine is an inhibitor of GABA reuptake in the synaptic cleft that demonstrations antikindling efficacy [95]. Nevertheless, it has not demonstrated antimanic efficacy [96], nor is there any available treatment data regarding antiaggressive efficacy in neuropsychiatric conditions. Levetiracetam inhibits kindling but has no known interaction with GABA or excitatory amino acids [97]. A single case report suggests that it may have some antimanic efficacy, with a favorable side effect profile [98].

Valproic Acid

Valproic acid (VPA) is a short-chain carboxylic acid that inhibits degradation of GABA and facilitates post-synaptic GABA transmission. It has been extensively used for a variety of psychiatric symptoms, including bipolar disorder, borderline personality disorder, and alcohol withdrawal [99]. Valproic acid has been used effectively to reduce agitation and aggression in both acute and post-acute TBI patients [100, 101], as well as a variety of other neuropsychiatric syndromes, including dementia and mental retardation [102].

Aggression in dementia has been reported to respond to VPA treatment in open-label [103, 104] and randomized, controlled trials [105]. Alone or in combination with neuroleptic medication, VPA appears to be efficacious and well-tolerated [106]. Typical treating doses range from 750 to 2500 mg/d, [106, 107]. While VPA is more costly per unit dose than lithium carbonate, a VA study of skilled nursing facility patients found that the reduced treatment-associated morbidity and monitoring costs led to substantial savings in the VPA-treated group. [108]. One case series reported the successful use of intravenous valproic acid to treat three geriatric inpatients: two acutely manic patients who refused oral medication and one dementia patient with agitation and dysphagia receiving end-of-life care for Alzheimer's disease.

Valproic acid also effectively reduced aggression and self-injurious behavior in adult patients with severe mental retardation [109]. Valproic acid appears to be well-tolerated with respect to cognitive functioning [110], but may cause weight gain, thrombocytopenia, alopecia, and, more rarely, pancreatitis and hepatotoxicity. The author has noted valproic acid to be generally well-tolerated in TBI, dementia, and developmental disorders complicated by aggression and agitation at serum levels of 80-100 mcg/l. Lower serum levels appear to be somewhat less efficacious, though with fewer side effects, particularly in elderly patients. Treatment may be initiated at 20mg/kg or slightly less, which typically results in serum levels at or near the optimal therapeutic range. The relatively short half-life of the drug enables rapid achievement of steady-state kinetics, usually within 2 days. Treatment-emergent weight gain and alopecia are the typical reasons that patients request a change in their medication regimen. In summary, valproic acid is clearly the most rigorously studied anticonvulsant in both bipolar and neuropsychiatric disorders, and has demonstrated substantial efficacy and a fairly benign side effect profile.

Valproic Acid in Neuropsychiatric Syndromes Following Acquired Brain Injury (ABI)

A retrospective chart review was conducted on 11 patients referred to an acute psychiatric inpatient/partial hospital program or neuropsychiatry clinic with a history of ABI. The history of ABI was known at the time of referral in only 3 cases; in the other 8, ABI was discovered at the time of initial evaluation. All selected patients were treated with divalproex sodium alone or in combination with other psychotropic medications.

Results

The sample consisted of 7 males and 4 females with a mean age of 40.7 years (SD=7.8). The mean age of onset of psychiatric disturbance was 30.9 years (SD=10). All patients were neurologically intact and living in the community. Psychiatric diagnoses included Bipolar Disorder (n=3), Psychotic Disorder Not Otherwise Specified (n=2), Personality Change Due to Acquired Brain Injury (n=2), Adjustment Disorder (n=2), Schizoaffective Disorder (n=1), and Impulse Control Disorder Not Otherwise Specified (n=1). Four (36.4%) patients had concomitant substance abuse disorders. Symptoms upon initial evaluation included physical and verbal aggression (N=7), psychosis (N=6), impulsivity (N=5), elevated mood (N=4), and depression (N=1). The age at time of injury ranged from 4 to 43. Concomitant psychoactive medications included: antipsychotics (n=5), antidepressants (n=4), sedative-hypnotics (n=2), mood stabilizers (n=2), and buspirone (n=1).

The mean daily dose of divalproex was 1818 mg/d (SD=791), with a mean serum valproic acid level of 85.6 μg/ml (SD=29.6). Mean CGI improvement score was 1.9 (SD=0.5). Two patients were rated as extremely improved, eight patients were much improved, and one patient was minimally improved. There was a weak negative correlation between serum valproate level and CGI improvement score suggesting a possible association between higher serum levels and better response, but the sample size did not permit statistical inference.

Comment

This study is limited by its uncontrolled retrospective design, small sample size and patient heterogeneity. Injury mechanisms ranged from repetitive physical abuse to spontaneous subarachnoid hemorrhage. The presenting psychiatric symptoms varied considerably, and patients were receiving a wide range of concomitant psychoactive medications. ABI frequently causes changes in personality, emotion, and impulse control that may cause significant family distress and poor longitudinal outcomes [7]. Despite the diagnostic heterogeneity of our sample, aggression, psychosis, and impulsivity, either alone or in combination, were observed in all patients.

Valproic acid inhibits limbic kindling in animal models [111]. Single and multiple case series cite its effectiveness in reducing agitation, aggression, and affective lability in patients with organic brain disorders [112-115]. Total daily dosages of 750-1500mg with serum levels of 50-110 μg/ml were described in these reports. Valproic acid is well tolerated with respect to cognitive functioning in patients with TBI [116]. None of the patients experienced adverse side effects or significant drug-drug interactions. The mean dosages of divalproex and serum levels in this sample were substantially higher than those described in previous reports.

Oxcarbazepine

Oxcarbazepine is a 10-keto-analog of carbamazepine with similar anticonvulsant and antimanic efficacy [117]. Although hepatically metabolized, oxcarbazepine causes much less autoinduction of cytochrome enzymes and therefore does not substantially influence the metabolism of other hepatically-excreted medications. Agranulocytosis has not been reported, though there is a slightly increased incidence of hyponatremia that is usually not clinically significant [118]. The side effect profile is similar to that of carbamazepine, though in the author's experience, these symptoms are much milder. The metabolism of oxcarbazepine does not produce the 10, 11-epoxide that has been implicated in the etiology of many of the untoward side effects of carbamazepine. The efficacy of oxcarbazepine in the treatment of acute mania has been found to be comparable to that of lithium, haloperidol, and valproic acid in randomized controlled trials [117, 119]. The author has noted considerable efficacy of oxcarbazepine for agitation and aggression in patients with TBI, anoxic brain injury, and stroke at doses of 900-2400 mg/d. In several patients with psychotic symptoms and atypical mixed bipolar syndromes, monotherapy with oxcarbazepine was effective in reducing affective and psychotic symptoms. Titration typically starts at 150-300mg bid and is increased by 300-600mg/d every 3-5 days until symptom relief or side effects emerge. Because there are no clinically relevant serum levels and hyponatremia is uncommon and rarely significant clinically, treatment with oxcarbazepine typically does not require blood tests.

Oxcarbazepine in Aggression and Irritability Following Closed Head Injury

Five subjects were enrolled in a flexible dose, open-label clinical trial. Oxcarbazepine was started at 150mg bid and titrated over 5 weeks, followed by a 3-week maintenance phase. Primary outcome measures were the Overt Aggression Scale – Modified (OAS-M) and Clinical Global Impression Severity of Illness Scale (CGI). Secondary outcome measures included the Montgomery-Asberg Depression Rating Scale (MADRS) and the Repeatable Battery for the Assessment of Neuropsychological Status (RBANS).

Results

The mean OAS score decreased from 67.4 (SD = 55.23) to 4.00 (SD = 3.61) ($t=2.51$, $p=.066$), with 4 subjects' scores decreasing by 50% or more at 2 weeks, and one subject's score diminishing by 50% or more at 4 weeks. The mean MADRS score decreased from 22.88 (SD = 17.62) to 7.60 (SD = 8.20) ($t=2.49$, $p=0.067$), with 4 subjects' scores decreasing by 50% or more at 2 weeks. The mean dosage at week two was 1020 mg/day. The mean CGI severity score improved from 4.20 (SD = 0.45) to 2.5 (SD = 0.58) ($t=3.66$, $p=0.035$). The mean total score on the RBANS increased from 70.4 ± 18.7 to 79.0 ± 19.6 ($p=0.081$), primarily due to improvements in immediate memory performance.

Comment

This study provides preliminary evidence that oxcarbazepine is a well-tolerated and effective agent for treating aggression resulting from TBI. All of the study participants showed clinically significant improvement in aggression, and depression, the majority of them after two weeks of treatment. None of the subjects experienced any cognitive deterioration during treatment with oxcarbazepine. On the contrary, there was a trend towards improvement in the patients' neuropsychological status that was primarily due to improvements in immediate memory. It is possible that these cognitive improvements were due to subjects' improved mood state, since depression may lead to impaired attention and immediate recall. There were no adverse events reported by the study participants, suggesting that oxcarbazepine is well-tolerated in this patient population.

Conclusion

The psychotropic efficacy of anticonvulsant medications appears to be mediated by mechanisms similar to that of their anticonvulsant effects. As a result, mood stabilizing properties may often be translated into anti-aggressive effects in patients with neuropsychiatrically-mediated syndromes. However, there are notable exceptions to this rule, which makes generalization of clinical knowledge derived from the use of AEDs in the treatment of idiopathic psychiatric disorders challenging and at times inconsistent. Additionally, the kindling hypothesis of psychiatric illness appears to be just one aspect of the psychotropic benefits of anticonvulsant agents. Antikindling efficacy does not suffice to ensure antimanic efficacy. Moreover, a lack of antimanic efficacy does not predict failure of an anticonvulsant in reducing behavioral complications of neurological illness.

Psychiatric complications of neurological disorders frequently involve changes in personality, impulse control, and affective regulation. The wide range of variability in presentations requires the thoughtful integration of a fairly limited body of rigorous trial data. The current state of the art is rich in retrospective and non-controlled studies, with few well-designed trials. An agenda for future research would require the development and validation of a consistent nosology to address various types of neuropsychiatric syndromes. This nosology would be vital in designing studies to clarify the efficacy of various medications for target symptoms. In addition, adequately powered randomized controlled trials to assess the efficacy and tolerability of AEDs would help clarify first line, adjunctive, and non-supported medications in patients who are highly vulnerable to medication side effects. The evidence base for rational prescribing of AEDs for neurobehavioral disorders will likely occur outside of the parameters of FDA approval. Nevertheless, rigorous and well-designed studies are necessary to clarify their important role in the armamentarium of neurobehavioral specialists.

References

[1] Vanstraelen M, Tyrer SP: Rapid cycling bipolar affective disorder in people with intellectual disability: a systematic review. *J Intellect Disabil Res* 1999, 43:349-59.

[2] Starkstein SE, Mayberg HS, Berthier ML, et al.: Secondary mania: neuroradiological and metabolic findings. *Ann Neurol* 1990, 27:652-659.

[3] Starkstein SE, Robinson RG: Mechanism of disinhibition after brain lesions. *J Nerv Ment Dis 1997*, 185:108-114.

[4] Mega MS, Lee L, Dinov ID, et al.: Cerebral correlates of psychotic symptoms in Alzheimer's disease. *J Neurol Neurosurg Psychiatry* 2000, 69:167-171.

[5] McAllister TW: Traumatic brain injury and psychosis: what is the connection? *Semin Clin Neuropsychiatry* 1998, 3:211-223.

[6] Zwil AS, McAllister TW, Raimo E: The expression of bipolar affective disorders in brain-injured patients. *Int J Psychiatry Med* 1992, 22:377-395.

[7] Yatham LN, Kusumakar V, Calabrese JR: Third generation anticonvulsants in bipolar disorder: A review of efficacy and summary of clinical recommendations. *J Clin Psychiatry* 2002, 63:275-283.

[8] DiMartino A, Tuchman RF: Antiepileptic drugs: affective use in autism spectrum disorders. *Pediatr Neurol* 2001, 25:199-207.

[9] Glenn MB, Wroblewski B, Parziale J, et al.: Lithium carbonate for aggressive behavior or affective instability in ten brain-injured patients. *Am J Phys Med Rehabil* 1989, 68:221-226.

[10] Moskowitz AS, Altshuler L: Increased sensitivity to lithium-induced neurotoxicity after stroke. *J Clin Psychopharmacol* 1991, 11:272-273.

[11] Mesulam MM: *Principles of Behavioral and Cognitive Neurology*, 2nd Edition. New York: Oxford University Press, 2000.

[12] Hawkins KA, Trobst KK: Frontal lobe dysfunction and aggression: conceptual issues and research findings. *Aggression and Violent Behavior* 2000; 5:147-157.

[13] Hornstein A, Seliger G: Cognitive side effects of lithium in closed head injury (letter). *J Neuropsychiatry Clin Neurosci* 1989; 1:446-447.

[14] Goyer PF, Andreason PJ, Semple WE, et al.: Positron-emission tomography and personality disorders. *Neuropsychopharmacol* 1994, 10:21-28.

[15] Pietrini P, Guazzelli M, Basso G, et al.: Neural correlates of imaginal aggressive behavior assessed by positron emission tomography in healthy subjects. *Am J Psychiatry* 2000;157:1772-1781.

[16] Grafman J, Schwab K, Warden D, et al.: Frontal lobe injuries, violence, and aggression: a report of the Vietnam Head Injury Study. *Neurology* 1996;46:1231-1238.

[17] Oder W, Goldenberg G, Spatt J, et al.: Behavioural and psychosocial sequelae of severe closed head injury and regional cerebral blood flow: a SPECT study. *J Neurol Neurosurg Psychiatry* 1992, 55:475-480.

[18] Van der Naalt J, Van Zomeren AH, Sluiter WJ, Minderhoud JM: Acute behavioural disturbances related to imaging studies and outcome in mild-to-moderate head injury. *Brain Inj* 1999, 14:781-788.

[19] Lopez OL, Zivkovic S, Smith G, et al.: Psychiatric symptoms associated with cortical-subcortical dysfunction in Alzheimer's disease. *J Neuropsychiatry Clin Neurosci 2001*, 13:56-60.

[20] Hirono N, Mega MS, Dinov ID, et al.: Left frontotemporal hypoperfusion is associated with aggression in patients with dementia. *Arch Neurol* 2000, 57:861-866.

[21] Jorge RE, Robinson RG, Starkstein SE, et al.: Secondary mania following traumatic brain injury. *Am J Psychiatry* 1993, 150:916-921.

[22] Minger SL, Esiri MM, McDonald B, et al.: Cholinergic deficits contribute to behavioral disturbance in patients with dementia. *Neurology* 2000, 55:1460-1467.

[23] Coccaro EF, Kavoussi RJ, Berman ME, Hauger RL: Relationship of prolactin response to d-fenfluramine to behavioral and questionnaire assessments of aggression in personality disordered males. *Biol Psychiatry* 1996, 40:157-164.

[24] Eichelman B: *Neurochemical and psychopharmacological aspects of aggressive behavior. Psychopharmacology: The Third Generation of Progress*. Edited by Meltzer HY. New York: Raven Press; 1987:697-704.

[25] Stanislav SW, Crismon ML, Childs NL: Cerebrospinal fluid monoamine metabolites and glucose metabolism in posttraumatic aggression. *Biol Psychiatry* 1998; 43: 619-621.

[26] Winterer G, Hermann WM: Valproate and the symptomatic treatment of schizophrenia spectrum patients. *Pharmacopsychiatry* 2000, 33:182-188.

[27] McAllister TW: Evaluation of brain injury related behavioral disturbances in community mental health centers. *Comm Ment Health J* 1997, 33:341-364.

[28] Kreutzer JS, Marwitz JH, Witol AD: Interrelationship between crime, substance abuse, and aggressive behaviours among persons with traumatic brain injury. *Brain Inj* 1995; 9:757-768.
[29] Dunlop TW, Udvarhelyi GB, Stedem AFA, O'Connor JMC, Isaacs ML, Puig JG, Mather JH: Comparison of patients with and without emotional/behavioral deterioration during the first year after traumatic brain injury. *J Neuropsychiatry Clin Neurosci* 1991; 3:150-156.
[30] Tateno A, Jorge RE, Robinson RG: Clinical correlates of aggressive behavior after traumatic brain injury. *J Neuropsychiatry Clin Neurosci.* 2003;15:155-160.
[31] Greve KW, Sherwin E, Stanford MW, Mathias C, Love J, Ramzinski P: Personality and neurocognitive correlates of impulsive aggression in long-term survivors of severe traumatic brain injury. *Brain Inj* 2001; 15:255-262.
[32] Carlsson GS, Svardsudd K, Welin L: Long-term effects of head injuries sustained during life in three male populations. *J Neurosurg* 1987; 67:197-205.
[33] Max JE, Koele SL, Smith WL Jr, Sato Y, Lindgren SD, Robin DA, Arndt S. Psychiatric disorders in children and adolescents after severe traumatic brain injury: a controlled study. *J Am Acad Child Adolesc Psychiatry.* 1998;37:832-840.
[34] Shukla S, Cook BL, Mukherjee S, Godwin C, Miller MG. Mania following head trauma. *Am J Psychiatry* 1987;144:93-96.
[35] Starkstein SE, Boston JD, Robinson RG: Mechanisms of mania after brain injury. 12 case reports and review of the literature. *J Nerv Ment Dis.* 1988;176:87-100.
[36] Jorge RE, Robinson RG, Starkstein SE, et al.: Secondary mania following traumatic brain injury. *Am J Psychiatry* 1993, 150:916-921.
[37] Lyketsos CG, Corazzini K, Steele C: Mania in Alzheimer 's disease. *J Neuropsychiatry Clin Neurosci.* 1995;7:350-352.
[38] Sachdev P, Smith JS, Cathcart S: Schizophrenia-like psychosis following traumatic brain injury: a chart-based descriptive and case-control study. *Psychol Med.* 2001;31:231-239.
[39] Thomsen IV: Late outcome of very severe blunt head trauma: a 10-15 year second follow-up. *J Neurol Neurosurg Psychiatry.* 1984;47:260-268.
[40] Violon A: Post-traumatic psychoses. *Acta Neurochir Suppl* (Wien). 1988;44:67-69.
[41] Davison K: Schizophrenia-like psychoses associated with organic cerebral disorders: a review. *Psychiatr Dev.* 1983;1:1-33.
[42] Achte KA, Hillbom E, Aalberg V: Psychoses following war brain injuries. *Acta Psychiatr Scand.* 1969;45:1-18.
[43] Ahmed I, Fujii D: Posttraumatic psychosis. *Semin Clin Neuropsychiatry.* 1998;3:23-33.
[44] Fujii DE, Ahmed I. J Risk factors in psychosis secondary to traumatic brain injury. *Neuropsychiatry Clin Neurosci.* 2001;13:61-69.
[45] Cutting J: The phenomenology of acute organic psychosis. Comparison with acute schizophrenia. *Br J Psychiatry.* 1987;151:324-332.
[46] Cummings JL: Organic delusions: phenomenology, anatomical correlations, and review. *Br J Psychiatry.* 1985;146:184-197.
[47] Fujii D, Ahmed I: Characteristics of psychotic disorder due to traumatic brain injury: an analysis of case studies in the literature. *J Neuropsychiatry Clin Neurosci.* 2002;14:130-140.

[48] Post RM, Weiss SR: Sensitization and kindling phenomena in mood, anxiety, and obsessive-compulsive disorders: The role of serotonergic mechanisms in illness progression. *Biol Psychiatry* 1998, 44:167-180.

[49] Post RM: Introduction: Emerging perspectives on valproate in affective disorders. *J Clin Psychopharmacol* 1989, 50(Suppl):3-9.

[50] Wauquier A, Zhou S: Topiramate: A potent anticonvulsant in the amygdala-kindled rat. *Epilepsy Res* 1996, 24:73-77.

[51] Otsuki K, Morimoto K, Sato K, et al.: Effects of lamotrigine and conventional antiepileptic drugs on amygdala- and hipoccampal-kindled seizures in rats. *Epilepsy Res* 1998, 31:101-112.

[52] Adamec RE: Evidence that long-lasting potentiation of amygdale efferents in the right hemisphere underlies pharmacological stressor (FG-7142) induced lasting increases in anxiety-like behaviour: role of GABA tone in initiation of brain and behavioural changes. *J Psychopharmacol* 2000, 14:323-339.

[53] Okada M, Hirano T, Mizuno K, et al.: Effects of carbamazepine on hippocampal serotonergic system. *Epilepsy Res* 1998, 31:187-198.

[54] Baf MH, Subhash MN, Lakshmana KM, et al.: Sodium valproate induced alterations in monoamine levels in different regions of the rat brain. *Neurochem Int* 1994, 24:67-72.

[55] Southam E, Kirkby D, Higgins GA: Lamotrigine inhibits monoamine uptake in vitro and modulates 5-hydroxytryptamine uptake in rats. *Eur J Pharmacol* 1998, 358:19-24.

[56] Ben-Menachem E, Persson LI, Hedner T: Selected CSF biochemistry and gabapentin concentrations in the CSF and plasma in patients with partial seizures after a single dose of gabapentin. *Epilepsy Res* 1992, 11:45-49.

[57] Miczek KA, DeBold JF, van Erp AM, et al.: Alcohol, GABA A-benzodiazepine receptor complex, and aggression. *Recent Dev Alcohol* 1997, 13:139-171.

[58] Perez MF, Nasif FJ, Marchesini GR, et al.: Hippocampus and locus coeruleus activity on rats chronically treated with diazepam. *Pharmacol Biochem Behav* 2001, 69:431-438.

[59] Varga V, Sik A, Freund TF, et al.: GABA(B) receptors in the median raphe nucleus: distribution and role in the serotonergic control of hippocampal activity. *Neuroscience* 2002, 109:119-132.

[60] Meldrum BS: Update on the mechanism of action of antiepileptic drugs. *Epilepsia* 1996, 37 (suppl):4-11.

[61] Calabrese JR, Keck PE Jr, McElroy SL, Shelton MD: A pilot study of topiramate as monotherapy in the treatment of acute mania. *J Clin Psychopharmacol* 2001, 21:340-342.

[62] Grunze HC, Normann C, Langosch J, Schaefer M, Amann B, Sterr A, Schloesser S, Kleindienst N, Walden J: Antimanic efficacy of topiramate in 11 patients in an open trial with an on-off-on design. *J Clin Psychiatry*. 2001, 62:464-468.

[63] Marcotte D: Use of topiramate, a new anti-epileptic as a mood stabilizer. *J Affect Disord* 1998, 50:245-251.

[64] Glauser TA: Topiramate. *Epilepsia* 1999, 40(Suppl 5):S71-80.

[65] Khan A, Faught E, Gilliam F, Kuzniecky R: Acute psychotic symptoms induced by topiramate. *Seizure* 1999, 8:235-237.

[66] Tatum WO 4th, French JA, Faught E, et al.: Postmarketing experience with topiramate and cognition. *Epilepsia* 2001, 42:1134-1140.

[67] Azouvi P, Jokic C, Attal N, et al.: Carbamazepine in agitation and aggressive behaviour following severe closed-head injury: results of an open trial. *Brain Inj* 1999, 13:797-804.

[68] Chatham-Showalter PE: Carbamazepine for combativeness in acute traumatic brain injury. *J Neuropsychiatry Clin Neurosci* 1996, 8:96-99.

[69] Olin JT, Fox LS, Pawluczyk S, et al.: A pilot randomized trial of carbamazepine for behavioral symptoms in treatment-resistant outpatients with Alzheimer disease. *Am J Geriatr Psychiatry* 2001, 9:400-405.

[70] Tariot PN, Erb R, Podgorski CA, et al.: Efficacy and tolerability of carbamazepine for agitation and aggression in dementia. *Am J Psychiatry* 1998, 155:54-61.

[71] Smith KR Jr, Goulding PM, Wilderman D, et al.: Neurobehavioral effects of phenytoin and carbamazepine in patients recovering from brain trauma: a comparative study. *Arch Neurol* 1994, 51:635-660.

[72] Eadie MH, Tyrer JH: *Carbamazepine. Anticonvulsant Therapy – Pharmacological Basis and Practice*, 3rd Ed. Oxford: Churchill Livingston; 1989:142-143.

[73] Sokolski KN, Green C, Maris DE, DeMet EM: Gabapentin as an adjunct to standard mood stabilizers in outpatients with mixed bipolar symptomatology. *Ann Clin Psychiatry* 1999, 11:217-222.

[74] Carta MG, Hardoy MC, Dessi I, Hardoy MJ, Carpiniello B: Adjunctive gabapentin in patients with intellectual disability and bipolar spectrum disorders. *J Intellect Disabil Res* 2001, 45:139-145.

[75] Pande AC, Crockatt JG, Janney CA, et al.: Gabapentin in bipolar disorder: a placebo-controlled trial of adjunctive therapy. Gabapentin Bipolar Disorder Study Group. *Bipolar Disord* 2000, 2:249-255.

[76] Roane DM, Feinberg TE, Meckler L, et al.: Treatment of dementia-associated agitation with gabapentin. *J Neuropsychiatry Clin Neurosci* 2000, 12:40-43.

[77] Dallocchio C, Buffa C, Mazzarello P: Combination of donepezil and gabapentin for behavioral disorders in Alzheimer's disease. *J Clin Psychiatry* 2000, 61:64 .

[78] Hermann N, Lanctot K, Myszak M: Effectiveness of gabapentin for the treatment of behavioral disorders in dementia. *J Clin Psychopharmacol* 2000, 20:90-93.

[79] Bozikas V, Bascialla F, Yulis P, et al.: Gabapentin for behavioral dyscontrol with mental retardation. *Am J Psychiatry* 2001, 158:965-966.

[80] Lee DO, Steingard RJ, Cesna M, et al.: Behavioral side effects of gabapentin in children. *Epilepsia* 1996, 37:87-90.

[81] Bowden CL, Calabrese JR, McElroy SL, et al.: The efficacy of lamotrigine in rapid cycling and non-rapid cycling patients with bipolar disorder. *Biol Psychiatry* 1999, 45:953-958.

[82] Calabrese JR, Bowden CL, Sachs GS, et al.: A double-blind placebo-controlled study of lamotrigine monotherapy in outpatients with bipolar I depression. Lamictal 602 Study Group. *J Clin Psychiatry* 1999, 60:79-88.

[83] Calabrese JR, Suppes T, Bowden CL, et al.: A double-blind, placebo-controlled, prophylaxis study of lamotrigine in rapid-cycling bipolar disorder. *J Clin Psychiatry* 2000, 61:841-850.

[84] Showalter PE, Kimmel DN: Stimulating consciousness and cognition following severe brain injury: a new potential clinical use for lamotrigine. *Brain Inj* 2000, 14:997-1001.

[85] Meador KJ, Loring DW, Ray PG, et al.: Differential cognitive and behavioral effects of carbamazepine and lamotrigine. *Neurology* 2001, 56:1177-1182.

[86] Messenheimer JA: Rash in adult and pediatric patients treated with lamotrigine. *Can J Neurol Sci* 1998, 25:S14-18.

[87] Beran RG, Gibson RJ: Aggressive behaviour in intellectually challenged patients with epilepsy treated with lamotrigine. *Epilepsia* 1998, 39:280-282.

[88] Ettinger AB, Weisbrot DM, Saracco J, et al.: Positive and negative psychotropic effects of lamotrigine in patients with epilepsy and mental retardation. *Epilepsia* 1998, 39:874-877.

[89] Belsito KM, Law PA, Kirk KS, et al.: Lamotrigine therapy for autistic disorder: A randomized, double-blind, placebo-controlled trial. *J Autism Dev Disord* 2001, 31:175-181.

[90] Devarajan S, Dusrun S: Aggression in dementia with lamotrigine treatment (letter). *Am J Psychiatry* 2000, 157:1178.

[91] Shields WD, Sankar R: Vigabatrin. *Semin Pediatr Neurol* 1997, 4:43-50.

[92] Levinson DF, Devinsky O: Psychiatric adverse events during vigabatrin therapy. *Neurology* 1999, 53:1503-1511.

[93] Veggiotti P, De Agostini G, Muzio C, et al.: Vigabatrin use in psychotic epileptic patients: report of a prospective pilot study. *Acta Neurol Scand* 1999, 99:142-146.

[94] Jambaque I, Chiron C, Dumas C, et al.: Mental and behavioural outcome of infantile epilepsy treated by vigabatrin in tuberous sclerosis patients. *Epilepsy Res* 2000, 38:151-160.

[95] Dalby NO, Nielsen EB: Tiagabine exerts an anti-epileptogenic effect in amygdala kindling epileptogenesis in the rat. *Neurosci Lett* 1997, 229:135-137.

[96] Grunze H, Erfurth A, Marcuse A, et al.: Tiagabine appears not to be efficacious in the treatment of acute mania. *J Clin Psychiatry* 1999, 60:759-762.

[97] Loscher W, Honack D, Rundfeldt C: Antiepileptogenic effects of the novel anticonvulsant levetiracetam (UCB L059) in the kindling model of temporal lobe epilepsy. *J Pharmacol Exp Ther* 1998, 284:474-479.

[98] Goldberg JF, Burdick KE: Levetiracetam for acute mania (letter). *Am J Psychiatry* 2002, 159:148.

[99] Davis LL, Ryan W, Adinoff B, et al.: Comprehensive review of the psychiatric uses of valproate. *J Clin Psychopharmacol* 2000, 20(Suppl 1):1S-17S.

[100] Chatham-Showalter PE, Netsky-Kimmel D: Agitated symptom response to divalproex following acute brain injury. *J Neuropsychiatry Clin Neurosci* 2000; 12:395-397.

[101] Wroblewski BA, Joseph AB, Kupfer J, Kalliel K: Effectiveness of valproic acid on destructive and aggressive behaviours in patients with acquired brain injury. *Brain Inj* 1997, 11:37-47.

[102] Lindenmayer JP, Kotsaftis A: Use of sodium valproate in violent and aggressive behaviors: a critical review. *J Clin Psychiatry* 2000, 61:123-128.

[103] Kunik ME, Puryear L, Orengo CA, et al.: The efficacy and tolerability of divalproex sodium in elderly demented patients with behavioral disturbances. *Int J Geriatr Psychiatry* 1998, 13:29-34.

[104] Porsteinsson AP, Tariot PN, Erb R, et al.: An open trial of valproate for agitation in geriatric neuropsychiatric disorders. *Am J Geriatr Psychiatry* 1997, 5:344-351.

[105] Porsteinsson AP, Tariot PN, Erb R, et al.: Placebo-controlled study of divalproex sodium for agitation in dementia. *Am J Geriatr Psychiatry*. 2001, 9:58-66.

[106] Narayan M, Nelson JC: Treatment of dementia with behavioral disturbance using divalproex or a combination of divalproex and a neuroleptic. *J Clin Psychiatry* 1997, 58:351-354.

[107] Herrmann N: Valproic acid treatment of agitation in dementia. *Can J Psychiatry* 1998, 43:69-72.

[108] Conney J, Kaston B: Pharmacoeconomic and health outcome comparison of lithium and divalproex in a VA geriatric nursing home population: influence of drug-related morbidity on total cost of treatment. *Am J Manag Care* 1999, 5:197-204.

[109] Ruedrich S, Swales TP, Fossaceca C, et al.: Effect of divalproex sodium on aggression and self-injurious behaviour in adults with intellectual disability: a retrospective review. *J Intellect Disabil Res* 1999, 43:105-111.

[110] Dikmen SS, Machamer JE, Winn HR, et al.: Neuropsychological effects of valproate in traumatic brain injury: a randomized trial. *Neurology* 2000;54:895-902.

[111] Post RM, Weiss SR: A speculative model of affective illness cyclicity based on patterns of drug tolerance observed in amygdala-kindled seizures. *Mol Neurobiol* 1996; 13:33-60.

[112] Geracioti TD: Valproic acid treatment of episodic explosiveness related to brain injury. *J Clin Psychiatry* 1994;55:9:416-417.

[113] Monji A, Yoshida I, Koga H, Tashiro K, Tashiro N: Brain injury induced rapid-cycling affective disorder successfully treated with valproate. *Psychosomatics* 1999;40:5:448-449.

[114] Geracioti TD: Valproic acid treatment of episodic explosiveness related to brain injury. *J Clin Psychiatry* 1994;55:9:416-417.

[115] Chatham-Showalter PE, Netsky-Kimmel D: Agitated symptom response to divalproex following acute brain injury. *J Neuropsychiatry Clin Neurosci* 2000; 12:395-397.

[116] Dikmen SS, Machamer JE, Winn HR, Anderson GD, Temkin NR: Neuropsychological effects of valproate in traumatic brain injury: a randomized trial. *Neurology* 2000; 54:895-902.

[117] Emrich HM, Dose M, von Zerssen D: The use of sodium valproate, carbamazepine, and oxcarbazepine in patients with affective disorders. *J Affect Disord* 1985, 8:243-250.

[118] Grant SM, Faulds D: Oxcarbazepine. A review of its pharmacology and therapeutic potential in epilepsy, trigeminal neuralgia and affective disorders. *Drugs* 1992, 43:873-888.

[119] Emrich HM: Studies with oxcarbazepine (Trileptal) in acute mania. *Intern Clin Psychopharmacol* 1990, 5:83-88.

In: Focus on Bipolar Disorder Research
Editor: Malcomb R. Brown, pp. 131-151
ISBN 1-59454-059-4

Chapter 7

THE BECH-RAFAELSEN MANIA AND MELANCHOLIA SCALES IN CLINICAL TRIALS: A 25-YEAR REVIEW OF THEIR USE AS OUTCOME MEASURE IN BIPOLAR AND UNIPOLAR PATIENTS

Per Bech
Frederiksborg General Hospital

ABSTRACT

Background

The Bech-Rafaelsen Mania and Melancholia Scales are the psychometrically most validated rating scales for mood disorders as they have been accepted for dimensionality (total score being a sufficient outcome statistic) by item response models.

Objective

Clinical trials in which the two scales have been used as outcomes have been reviewed to evaluate the efficacy of the various treatments.

Results

In the acute therapy of mania, antipsychotics are superior to lithium in severe mania. However, in mild to moderate mania lithium is as effective as antipsychotics or anticonvulsants.

In the acute therapy of unipolar depression tricyclics (TCAs) are superior to serotonin selective reuptake inhibitors (SSRIs) in severe depression. However, in mild to moderate depression SSRIs are equal to TCAs.

In the acute therapy of mixed depressive-manic states ECT (electroconvulsive therapy) is the most effective as ECT, in contrast to pharmacological treatment, is effective in both manic and depressive states. However, the atypical antipsychotics (e.g. risperidone) may also be effective in depressive states. The atypical antidepressant trimipramine seems also to have an antipsychotic effect, which may be important in mixed states.
In the medium-term continuation therapy lithium is superior to anticonvulsants in bipolar depression in combination with SSRIs. In the continuation therapy of mania, lithium is equal to anticonvulsants such as carbamazepine.
In the continuation therapy of unipolar depression, SSRIs are superior to TCAs. In the long-term prophylactic therapy of bipolar patients, lithium is superior to anticonvulsants, also at suicide risk. In unipolar patients the SSRIs are the most effective.

Conclusion

This non-industry-based review of pharmacological outcomes in bipolar and unipolar mood disorders with reference to psychometric one-dimensional rating scales has supported the effect of lithium in moderate mania, in bipolar depression in combination with SSRIs, and in medium-term and especially in long-term treatment of bipolar disorders. The review has also supported the medium-term and long-term effects of SSRIs in unipolar, recurrent depression.

INTRODUCTION

The interest in developing clinician-related rating scales for measuring manic states has been much lower than the interest for scales measuring states of melancholia. Thus, Hamilton never developed a rating scale for mania although he successfully developed both a depression [1] and an anxiety [2] scale nearly five decades ago. These scales, the Hamilton Depression Rating Scale (HAM-D) and the Hamilton Anxiety Rating Scale (HAM-A) are still the most frequently used scales in clinical trials with antidepressants [3]. Hamilton was, however, involved in the development of the Bech-Rafaelsen Mania Scale (MAS) [4] twenty-five years ago, and he accepted the version of the Bech-Rafaelsen Melancholia Scale [5] which was combined with his own HAM-D. Hamilton's argument for not developing a mania scale himself was that he found manic states occurring too rarely and he, therefore, found such a scale of less interest.

However, during the last decades, a need for psychometrically valid scales for manic states has been growing because bipolar disorder is of a much more progressive nature than recurrent depressive disorder (unipolar disorder). Thus, a recent follow-up analysis of the causes of mood disorders has shown that while around 40% of the bipolar patients are hospitalised more than ten times, only 10% of the unipolar patients (including patients with more than four depressive episodes) are hospitalised more than ten times [6].

On this background it was found important to make a review of those controlled clinical trials in which the MAS or the MES have been used. The review of the MAS included both short-term and long-term trials in bipolar disorder in which lithium has been most penetratingly evaluated. The review of the MES included also short-term as well as long-term trials, with special focus on the selective serotonin reuptake inhibitors (SSRIs), predominantly evaluated in patients with recurrent depressive episodes or in unipolar patients.

The selection of trials in bipolar and unipolar patients was solely based on the inclusion of the MAS or MES. In the present review, the results of these studies have been integrated. This has been possible because the anti-manic outcome on the MAS and the anti-depressive outcome on the MES are directly comparable as these scales have the same number of items, have both been shown to be unidimensional (indicating that their total score is a sufficient and adequate statistic), consequently have the same theoretical score range, and have the same cut-off scores for response, remission or relapse, and recurrence.

From the separate reviews with MAS [4] and MES [5] an integrated overview of these results is outlined. However, new data have been included to give an updated version covering a time frame of 25 years.

Psychometric Background for the MAS and MES

The rating scales developed for depression and mania have traditionally been psychometrically validated by use of factor analysis. Thus, the HAM-D was validated by factor analysis by Hamilton and others (for a review see ([7]). Mania scales such as the Beigel Scale [8] and the Young Mania Rating Scale [9] have also been validated by factor analysis [10]. These analyses identified more than one factor in both scales, indicating that the total scores of the scales are not sufficient statistics as in this case the individual factor scores or factor profiles should be considered.

There have, however, been very few attempts to compare the various mania scales. Recently, an attempt has been made [11] to include the MAS and the Young Mania Rating Scale in a mania rating guide (MRG). A pilot study on manic inpatients with the MRG has shown a Cronbach coefficient alpha of only 0.66 for the Young Mania Scale, but an adequate coefficient of 0.79 for the MAS [13].

For the validation of the Turkish version of the Young Mania Rating Scale the MAS was used as the index of validity [13]. The results showed an interscale correlation coefficient of 0.72, implying that the two scales only partially overlap.

Both the MAS and the MES have been developed on the basis of existing scales. Thus, the MAS was developed from the Beigel Mania Scale to constitute a dimension of manic states, and the MES was developed from the HAM-D on the basis of the six-item melancholia factor to constitute a dimension of depressive states [5]. These six items are included in both the HAM-D_6, in the MES (Table 1), and in the Montgomery-Åsberg Depression Scale ($MADRS_6$), as discussed elsewhere [14]. Attempts to establish other subscales from the Hamilton Depression Scale in order to capture the core symptoms of depressive states [15] are not transferable to the $MADRS_6$ or MES or are not adequately psychometrically tested.

The psychometric analysis used to test for dimensionality of both the MAS and the MES included the Rasch item analysis, which is the simplest version of the item response theory [16]. The Rasch analysis assumes a linear structure of patient disability and item difficulty (the prevalence of items). When developing a rating scale in accordance with the Rasch item response theory, the developer should have shown that it is possible to conceptualise a dimension, a simple unidimensional construct represented by a line. In our first studies we used experienced clinicians to measure on a line from 0 (no mania or no depression) to 10 (the most extreme states of mania or of depression). The items of the MAS and MES were developed by analysing the association between the Beigel Mania Scale and the Hamilton

Depression Scale. The Rasch analysis was then performed to validate whether the prevalence of items showed a range from very frequent (i.e. measuring the very mild mania or depression) to less frequent (i.e. measuring moderate mania and depression) and very rare (i.e. measuring the severe degree of mania or depression). The results showed that both the MAS [4, 17] and the MES [5] fulfilled the Rasch item response criteria.

Table 1.

MAS	Score	MES	Score
Elevated mood	0-4	*Lowered mood	0-4
Increased verbal activity	0-4	Decreased verbal activity	0-4
Increased social contact	0-4	Decreased social contact	0-4
Increased motor activity	0-4	*Decreased motor activity	0-4
Sleep disturbances	0-4	Sleep disturbances	0-4
Social activities (distractibility)	0-4	*Decreased social activities	0-4
Hostility, irritable mood	0-4	*Guilt feelings	0-4
Increased sexual activity	0-4	*Tiredness	0-4
Increased self-esteem	0-4	Suicidal thoughts	0-4
Flight of thoughts	0-4	Poor concentration	0-4
Noise level	0-4	*Anxiety	0-4
Total theoretical score range	0-44	Total theoretical score range	0-44

*The six items of the melancholia subscale (MES-S)

Mania	**MAS total score**	**Depression**	**HAM-D_{17}**	**MES**	**Melancholia subscale: MES-S**
Mild	15-20	Mild	18-24	15-20	9-11
Moderate	21-28	Moderate	25-28	21-28	12-14
Severe	29-44	Severe	29-52	29-44	15-22

It is as a consequence of these findings that factor analysis has to identify the structure manifested by the MAS and MES when applied to patients with bipolar disorders. Recently, Rossi et al. [18] have used factor analysis in bipolar patients with the MAS and MES supporting their unidimensional structures. A comparison of the MAS and the Young Mania Rating Scale has also indicated a superiority of explained variance by factor analysis of MAS [12].

Table 1 shows the items included in the MAS and the MES. For the MES, the six items identified to fulfil the Rasch response criteria within the Hamilton Depression Scale have been indicated as the melancholia subscale. These items constitute the HAM-D_6 which now seems to have outperformed the HAM-D and which is measuring pure antidepressant effect [19]. Table 1 also shows the standardization in terms of cut-off scores for mild, moderate and severe states for the MES and the MAS. Also the 17-item-Hamilton Depression Scale's (HAM-D_{17}) corresponding cut-off scores are shown.

Sensitivity to change or response to treatment is part of the psychometric validity in trials of antimanic or antidepressive treatment. Kendell [20] has referred to the trial by Johnstone et al. [21] to demonstrate the use of response to treatment as an argument for the dimensional approach to mood disorders. By using the MAS in a consecutive study of hospitalised patients, Johnstone et al. [21] showed that lithium was significantly superior to placebo in patients with a MAS score of 15 or more (mean score 20), i.e. mild to moderate mania [4], independently of having the diagnosis of mania or schizoaffective disorder. Likewise, it has been shown that MES or the melancholic subscale of HAM-D (MES-S) measures depressive states across diagnoses such as poststroke depression [22] or chronic obstructive pulmonary disease [23].

Sensitivity to change in its narrow sense has been used to describe the ability of a scale to discriminate between active therapy and placebo treatment (e.g. the Johnstone et al. study on lithium versus placebo in mildly to moderately manic patients). However, in its broader sense, sensitivity is used to describe the ability of a scale to discriminate between two active treatments. In the following, it is the broader sense of sensitivity to change that has been used because it is unethical to include placebo in trials with moderate to severe mood disorders. In the continuation therapy or in long-term therapy, however, placebo is important for the evaluation of mood stabilisers.

MOOD STABILISERS USING SHORT-TERM TRIALS IN MANIC PATIENTS AS EVIDENCE OF EFFICACY

Originally, the intention with the MAS and MES was to combine them when evaluating the efficacy of mood stabilisers [24]. It was argued that rating scales may monopolise results because a scale specifically designed to measure depressive states at the same time can spuriously indicate that no manic symptoms have been present. This problem of monopolising by choice of a rating scale is therefore one of their limitations, especially in populations of bipolar patients. Kraepelin [25] described mixed affective states, of which agitated depression was found most common (the mixture of depressed mood, depressive thoughts, and increased motor activity). Currently available research evidence as discussed by Maj [26] suggests that the switching between depressive and manic symptoms during the same affective episode may have prognostic implications in bipolar disorder, as it is associated with poor long-term outcome of pharmacological treatment, including lithium.

Table 2 shows the MAS trials with lithium in the short-term therapy of manic patients. Only the Johnstone et al. [21] study is a placebo-controlled study which, as already mentioned, showed that lithium was statistically superior to placebo in patients with mild to moderate mania according to the baseline MAS scores. In the other controlled clinical trial of four weeks duration, in which lithium was compared to the typical antipsychotic zuclopenthixol [27], no difference in response was seen between the two treatments. In patients with moderate to sever mania, lithium was found as effective as oxcarbazepine (an anticonvulsant) and superior to verapamil (a calcium blocker) [28, 29]. In other trials, the effect of calcium blockers has supported the findings by Walton et al. [29] that this class of pharmacological treatments has no antimanic effect [30]. On the other hand, in other trials oxcarbazepine has been found to have an antimanic effect [31].

Table 2. The Effect of Lithium in Short-term Trials in Manic States

Mania	Authors	MAS total score: mean		Outcome
		Baseline	Endpoint	
Mild to moderate	Johnstone et al. [21]: versus Placebo	20.9	5.2	Lithium > Placebo
	Gouliaev et al. [27]: versus Zuclopenthixol	19.8	7.0	Lithium = Zuclopenthixol

Mania	Authors	MAS total score: mean		Outcome
		Baseline	Endpoint	
Moderate to severe	Emrich [28]: versus Oxcarbazepine	26.0	10.0	Lithium = Oxcarbazepine
	Walton et al. [29]: versus Verapamil	30.0	17.5	Lithium > Verapamil

Endpoint: four weeks.

Table 3 shows the effect of ECT, both in manic and in depressive patients. In mild to moderate mania, ECT was found significantly superior to lithium after eight weeks of treatment, but the endpoint score of MAS in the lithium-treated patients was within the limits of full remission [32].

Table 3. The Effect of ECT in Short-term Trials in Mania and Depression.

Mania	Authors: Small et al. [32]	MAS total score: mean	
		Baseline	Endpoint
Mild to moderate	Electroconvulsive therapy (ECT)	20	2*
	Lithium	20	4

Depression	Authors: Lauritzen et al. [33]	MES total score: mean	
		Baseline	Endpoint
Moderate to severe	ECT plus Imipramine	28	8*
	ECT plus Paroxetine	29	11

*$P \leq 0.05$.

The mania trial had an endpoint of 8 weeks while the depression trial had an endpoint of 4 weeks.

In moderate to severe depression, ECT was found very effective as early as after four weeks of treatment [33]. However, in combination with imipramine the effect after four weeks was statistically superior to a combination with paroxetine (Table 3). Of these patients, approximately 30% were bipolar.

As discussed elsewhere [4], chlorpromazine was originally introduced in psychopharmacology fifty years ago due to an "antimanic" effect in psychotic patients by reducing such symptoms as irritability, hostility, psychomotor hyperactivity, flight of ideas and expansiveness. Typical antipsychotics such as haloperidol or chlorpromazine are the most effective in manic states. In our first study 25 years ago with the MAS in manic patients a fixed dose of 10 mg haloperidol daily over a treatment period of one week was able to reduce a mean baseline score of 28 to an endpoint score of 15 [34], which is in agreement with the MAS criteria for evaluating antimanic compounds [35].

Table 4 shows the effect of anticonvulsants in moderate to severe mania in short-term trials over four weeks of therapy. For carbamazepine [36] and oxcarbazepine [28], the trials are controlled using chlorpromazine or haloperidol as active comparators. The anticonvulsants were as efficacious as the typical antipsychotics in patients with baseline MAS scores between 22 and 25 (Table 4). The first open-labelled trials with gabapentin [37] or topiramate [38] are included in Table 4. Over the four week period of therapy, patients with rather high baseline MAS scores showed an antimanic effect. However, in both trials the use of antipsychotics was allowed when needed. This is in agreement with the acute antimanic effect as measured by MAS, of lithium or valproic acid when combined with antipsychotics when needed, as shown by Fagiolini et al. [39].

Table 4. The Effect of Anticonvulsants in Moderate to Severe Mania in Short-term Trials

Controlled clinical trials		MAS total score		
Authors	**Anticonvulsant**	**Baseline**	**Endpoint**	**Outcome**
Sethi and Timari [36]	Carbamazepine	25.2	2.6	Carbamazepine = Chlorpromazine
Emrich [28]	Oxcarbazepine	22.0	10.0	Oxcarbazapine = Haloperidol

Open-labelled clinical trials		MAS total score	
Author	**Anticonvulsant**	**Baseline**	**Endpoint**
Erfurt et al. [37]	Gabapentin	37.8	7.8
Bozikars et al. [38]	Topiramate	26.2	11.6

Endpoint: four weeks.

Table 5 shows the effect of risperidone (an atypical antipsychotic) both in manic and depressive patients, analogously to the ECT results in Table 3. The effect in patients with mild to moderate mania was comparable with that of lithium or ECT [40]. Thus, after 4 weeks of therapy, the patients had a 75% reduction on the MAS, which is at the same response level as that found with lithium and in accordance with the MAS criteria for antimanic response over four weeks [35]. However, the effect in depressed patients with MES baseline scores rather similar to those treated with ECT indicated that risperidone is significantly inferior to a combination of haloperidol and amitriptyline [41]. It has previously been found that in patients with severe depression perphenazine combined with amitriptyline is more effective than amitriptyline alone [42]. From retrospective studies it appears that olanzapine has an effect similar to that of risperidone, i.e. a mild antidepressant effect which should be considered as an adjunctive to antidepressants in severe depression [43].

The term 'antidepressant' was introduced in the 1950's, based on evidence that imipramine reduced symptoms of moderate to severe depression but, unlike chlorpromazine, had no effect on the positive symptoms of schizophrenia as measured by the Brief Psychiatric Rating Scale [4]. It is of interest that trimipramine has been marketed as a tricyclic antidepressant like imipramine, but recent studies have shown that trimipramine has no serotonin or noradrenaline reuptake inhibitions such as imipramine [44]. Rather, trimipramine has antidopaminergic properties such as those of chlorpromazine or related typical antipsychotics [44]. The results are shown in Table 6 in which it can be seen that no major difference in antipsychotic or antidepressive effect was obtained. However, the depressive state in the schizophrenic patients at baseline was only of mild degree – and compared to patients with mild primary depression (Table 7) the antidepressive effect of trimipramine was only modest. Conversely, the effect is rather similar to that obtained with the atypical antipsychotics risperidone or amisulpride in schizophrenia patients with baseline MES scores of around 15 [45]. The results in Table 6 imply, however, that the use of trimipramine in mixed states of mania and depression should be evaluated. In this context it should be emphasized that in patients with major depression, trimipramine is equal to imipramine as to antidepressive effect [46].

Table 5. The Effect of Risperidone in Short-term Trials in Manic and Melancholic States

		MAS total score: mean	
Mania	Authors: Licht et al. [40]	Baseline	Endpoint
Mild to moderate	Risperidone	20.0	2.0

		MES total score: mean	
Depression	Authors: Müller-Siecheneder et al. [41]	Baseline	Endpoint
Moderate to	Risperidone	26.0	13.0
severe	Amitriptyline in combination with Haloperidol	26.0	9.0*

*$P \leq 0.05$.
Endpoint: four weeks.

Table 6. The Effect of the Atypical Antidepressant Trimipramine and the Antipsychotic Perazine in Schizophrenic Patients

	BPRS total score: mean		MES total score: mean	
	Baseline	Endpoint	Baseline	Endpoint
Trimipramine	57	44	16	10
Perazine	57	38	15	8

Endpoint four weeks. Modified after Bender et al. [44]. BPRS = Brief Psychiatric Rating Scale.

SHORT-TERM TRIALS IN UNIPOLAR DEPRESSION

The short-term trials to demonstrate the antidepressive effects of selective serotonin reuptake inhibitors (SSRIs) have been performed in patients with unipolar depression or rather by excluding patients with bipolar depression [3] Concerning the trials in which the MES has been used as outcome measure the SSRI compound paroxetine has been the most investigated within the depressive dimension from inpatients with major depression, outpatients with moderate major depression and to outpatients with mild major depression. Table 7 shows the results. The Danish University Antidepressant Group (DUAG) compared paroxetine with the tricyclic compound clomipramine and could demonstrate that paroxetine was significantly inferior to clomipramine [47]. In another DUAG study this was also shown for the SSRI compound citalopram when compared with clomipramine in hospitalised patients with major depression [48]. In outpatients with moderate major depression, paroxetine was found equal to imipramine [49] (Table 7), and this was also confirmed for citalopram when compared with imipramine in outpatients with mild major depression [50].

In outpatients with mild major depression, paroxetine was found equal to the cyclic compound maprotiline [51]. The superiority of tricyclic antidepressants (TCAs) over paroxetine in hospitalised patients with a moderate to severe degree of depression was already illustrated (Table 3) when ECT was combined either with imipramine or paroxetine. It is also in concord with a meta-analysis in which SSRIs and TCAs were compared in hospitalised patients with major depression [52].

Table 7. The Effect of Paroxetine in Short-term Trials in Unipolar Depression

		MES total score: mean	
Inpatients with major depression	Authors: DUAG [47]	Baseline	Endpoint
	Paroxetine	22	13
	Clomipramine	23	9*
		MES total score: mean	
Outpatients with moderate major depression	Authors: Øhrberg et al. [49]	Baseline	Endpoint
	Paroxetine	20	10
	Imipramine	21	11
		MES total score: mean	
Outpatients with mild major depression	Authors: Szegedi et al. [51]	Baseline	Endpoint
	Paroxetine	14	5
	Maprotiline	15	5

* $P \leq 0.05$.
Endpoint: four weeks.

Among the SSRIs, however, fluvoxamine has been shown to be as effective as clomipramine in severely depressed patients [53, 54]. In a meta-analysis of the placebo-controlled trials with fluvoxamine, the melancholia subscale of the HAM-D was used in patients with unipolar major depression [55]. The results showed (Table 8) that at endpoint (after four weeks of therapy) the difference between fluvoxamine and placebo increased with increasing baseline depression scores. Thus, with a baseline melancholia subscore of 12 to 13, indicating moderate major depression, the difference between fluvoxamine and placebo at endpoint was 4.2, while it was only 1.3 in the study with a baseline score of around 9, indicating mild major depression. In other words, the placebo effect decreases with higher baseline depression scores.

Medium-Term Trials

Figure 1 shows the terminology of clinical trials when classified into short-term, medium-term, and long-term treatment. The trials with MAS and MES within short-term treatment have typically been of four week duration. This is still the most common duration of antimanic trials, while a duration of around 6 to 8 weeks has been more common in recent years in trials with antidepressants. For both MAS and MES the response after four weeks has been scores below 10 in trials with a baseline score of 20. A response is often defined as a 50% reduction of baseline scores at endpoint (Figure 1).

Table 8. The Effect of Fluvoxamine Compared to *Placebo* in Short-term Trials in *Unipolar* Depression

Authors	Treatment	Melancholic *subscale* HAM-D_6: mean		
		Baseline	Endpoint	Difference at endpoint Fluvoxamine Placebo
Norton et al. [89]	Placebo	9.7	6.8	1.3
	Fluvoxamine	9.5	5.5*	
Dominguez et al. [90]	Placebo	11.1	7.0	1.7
	Fluvoxamine	10.5	5.3*	
Amin et al. [91]	Placebo	11.4	7.9	2.0
	Fluvoxamine	11.2	5.9*	
Lapierre et al. [92]	Placebo	12.2	8.9	4.2
	Fluvoxamine	13.0	4.7*	

*$P \leq 0.05$.
modified after Bech [55]. Endpoint: four weeks.

In both mania and depression, continuation therapy is indicated for a period of at least 6 months, or 26 weeks, as shown in Figure 1. If a patient after a response to therapy leading to remission of symptoms (which is defined as a score on MAS or MES of below 5) develops a symptomatology of 15 or more, this is considered a relapse.

The percentage of relapse in depression up to 6 months after ECT in patients with a full remission after ECT has been used to evaluate the relapse-preventive effect of antidepressants because the antidepressive effect of ECT alone has a duration of only 3 months [56].

Table 9 shows the results of such an ECT study in which patients have been followed over 6 months in a controlled, double-blind study comparing imipramine with placebo [33]. Paroxetine was found to be significantly superior to imipramine ($p \leq 0.05$) in preventing relapse. However, as shown in Table 3, imipramine was found to be superior to paroxetine in the short-term treatment phase of this study [33], as before receiving ECT the patients were severely depressed with a mean MES score of 26. It was argued [33] that patients with severe depression have an impairment involving more than one neurotransmitter than serotonin. However, when the patients have remitted at the end of the short-term treatment phase, it is then sufficient to control for impairment of the serotonin transmitter in order to prevent relapse. Both antidepressants and lithium have an effect on serotonin receptors in patients with unipolar and bipolar mood disorders [57, 58].

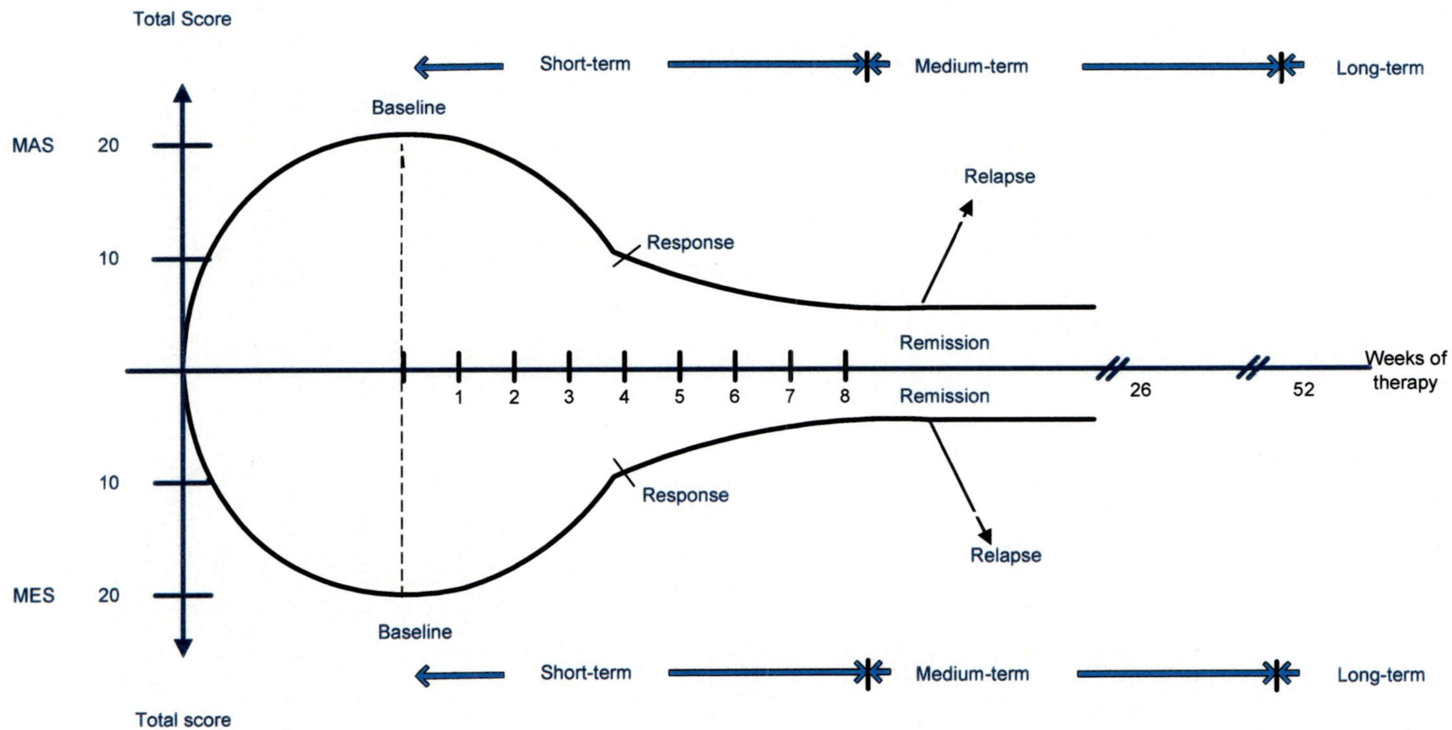

Figure 1. The model for MAS and MES in the treatment of manic and depressive episodes. Baseline scores indicate major (moderate) manic or depressive states with MAS/MES mean total scores of 20. Response after 4 weeks of therapy is a 50% reduction of baseline score (mean 10). Medium-term therapy or continuation therapy up to 52 weeks. Beyond this period of therapy is long-term or maintenance treatment.

Table 9. Prevention of Depressive Relapse (MES≥15) in the Medium-term Phase of Therapy (6 Months after ECT) in Patients who have Remitted in the Short-term Phase of Therapy [33]

Post-ECT follow-up of 6 months	Percentage of relapse
Imipramine	36.4%
Paroxetine	9.5%*

*P ≤ 0.05.

It is of great interest that lithium treatment for relapse prevention in medium-term trials after ECT in patients with major depression has been successful despite a severe co-morbid renal disease [59]. Another model in evaluating the prevention of depression in medium-term treatment trials has been post-stroke depression. In the study by Rasmussen et al. [22], patients with acute stroke were evaluated for risk of developing post-stroke depression over a period of 12 months. At baseline the patients had no signs of depression and were randomised to sertraline (an SSRI) or placebo. The results showed that the risk of developing depression was significantly greater (30% versus 10%) in the placebo group compared to the sertraline group of patients [22].This difference between sertraline and placebo in stroke patients was seen after 8 to 10 weeks when using the MES as criterion of depression (a score of 15 or more).

In unipolar depressed patients fluoxetine and sertraline have been found to be equal in the relapse prevention in a medium-term trial [60].

Long-Term or Prophylactic Trials

Figure 1 shows the treatment perspective of an affective episode. Both for mania and depression an episode typically lasts from 6 months to 12 months, and for elderly patients from 12 months to 24 months. The short-term and medium-term trials, consequently, have this time perspective. Long-term trials should, therefore, last two years or more.

Long-Term Trials in Bipolar Patients

When summarizing the major double-blind trials comparing lithium with placebo in long-term treatment, Goodwin and Jamison [61] found a recurrence rate of new episodes of 34% on lithium and 81% on placebo.

The mood-stabilising effect of lithium in long-term trials in bipolar patients has been compared to the effect of various anticonvulsants; however, trials of 24 months or more still need to be performed. The anticonvulsant most extensively studied in this respect is carbamazepine. The first study comparing lithium with carbamazepine lasted only 12 months [62]. When using the MAS to measure manic recurrence and the HAM-D for depression occurrence, the results showed no significant difference between the two treatments. However, the blood lithium concentrations indicated that with a level of 0.6 mmol/L of lithium, the recurrence percentage was only 10%.

Recently, Hartong et al. [63] have released the publication of their long-term trials of 24 months in which the prophylactic effect of lithium compared with carbamazepine was evaluated in bipolar patients, using both the MAS and the MES. The results showed that around 40% of the patients experienced recurrence of affective episodes on carbamazepine and 20% on lithium if only those patients who were prophylactically randomised were taken into consideration [63]. This result can be compared to the study by Jensen et al. [64], who evaluated the recurrence prevention of lithium in bipolar patients who had already been responding to lithium therapy but over two years were randomised to continue taking lithium tablets either once daily or every second day [64]. A cut-off score of 10 was used to measure recurrence on the MAS or MES scales. The results showed that only 10% of the patients had a recurrence when administrating lithium daily while 50% had a recurrence when administrating lithium only every second day [64].

In the long-term study over 24 months by Greil [65], lithium was found to be superior to carbamazepine when measuring inter-episodic well-being and prevention of suicides and suicide attempts. As discussed by Müller-Oerlinghausen [66], lithium appears to have an antisuicidal effect in long-term treatment. Baldessarini et al. [67] have updated the evidence for a specific, antisuicidal effect of lithium in controlled trials or follow-up studies in bipolar patients. Recently, Goodwin et al. [68] have shown that the risk of suicide attempts or death is lower in bipolar patients treated with lithium than when treated with valproic acid (divalproex).

There have been limitations to translating the results from controlled efficacy trials to effectiveness in the clinical practice in bipolar patients compared to unipolar patients. In our first investigation of the effectiveness of lithium in the daily routine [69], we showed that lithium was administered as monotherapy in only in 30-40%. The patients included had received lithium for at least two years (the patient with the longest treatment period had received lithium for 15 years). The use of combination therapy with lithium in both acute mania and in the continuation therapy has now been investigated, with lithium combined with an anticonvulsant or an atypical antipsychotic [70]. The results seem promising. However, we need long-term trials in this field.

Although oxcarbazepine does have a clear antimanic effect comparable to lithium [28] (Table 2), no long-term trials to evaluate the mood stabilising effect of oxcarbazepine have been published [31]. As concerns the other anticonvulsants, long-term trials of 24 months or longer are still missing.

Long-Term Trials in Unipolar Patients

Among the tricyclic antidepressants imipramine has been the most studied in long-term trials [71, 72, 73]. The results showed that the dose that had proven effective in short-term treatment should also be used in long-term, prophylactic treatment. Placebo-controlled trials with fluvoxamine [74] or citalopram [75] have shown that these serotonin specific reuptake inhibitors are significantly superior to placebo in preventing new episodes of depression.

When re-analysing a placebo-controlled citalopram study in elderly (unipolar) depressed patients [76], it was found (using a score on MES of 15 or more as criterion for recurrence of depression) that 12% had recurrence on citalopram and 35% on placebo. This difference was statistically significant. This study also showed that if the Montgomery-Åsberg Depression

Scale (MADRS) was used [77] to define recurrence (a score on MADRS of 22 or more) 32% had recurrence on citalopram and 67% on placebo [76]. In both the medium-term relapse prevention study with paroxetine, and in the trials with fluvoxamine [55] or sertraline [22], relapse rates of between 10% and 15% have been observed. When comparing such relapse or recurrence rates it is important to indicate the operational definition by use of unidimensional rating scales such as the MAS or MES.

Discussion

In the various guidelines for the treatment of bipolar and unipolar mood disorders the Bech-Rafaelsen Mania and Melancholia scales have been included [78, 79].

As selection criterion for inclusion of the clinical trials to be analysed, this review has used outcome measure in accordance with the Bech-Rafaelsen Mania or Melancholia Scales. However, when needed, the Bech melancholia subscale of the Hamilton Depression Scale (HAM-D_6) has also been used for inclusion as this was the instrument from which the Bech-Rafaelsen Melancholia Scale was developed, in contrast to the Young Mania Rating Scale or the HAM-D. These scales are unidimensional scales, implying that the total score is an appropriate and sufficient statistic when defining response, relapse, remission or recurrence of major affective episodes. When evaluating outcome of pharmacological treatment for bipolar disorder [80] or unipolar disorder [81, 82], these scales have been preferred to other rating scales.

The included trials have been used to cover outcomes within the three phases in the treatment of bipolar and unipolar depression: (a) the acute therapy of major affective disorder (i.e. short-term trials of mania and depression); (b) the continuation therapy (i.e. medium-term trials); and (c) the prophylactic therapy (i.e. long-term trials). In the following these issues will be discussed.

Short-Term Trials of Major Affective Episodes

In the acute therapy of mania as well as of depression, placebo is quite active in the milder affective states. However, in moderate to severe states of mania and depression, the effect of placebo decreases [83]. Severity of symptoms also seems to discriminate between the various active treatments. Thus, within mania the antipsychotics seem more effective than lithium in severe mania (MAS scores around 28). Within depression TCAs are superior to SSRIs in severe depression (hospitalised patients). However, in the most severely depressed patients, ECT or a combination of TCA and an antipsychotic are the most efficacious treatment measures (MES scores around 28).

The risk of inducing mania in bipolar depression has not been evaluated under strictly controlled conditions. However, in a consecutive study using MAS to evaluate antidepressant-induced mania in bipolar patients in the acute therapy of depression, it was found that SSRIs induced hypomanic to manic symptoms in 27% of the patients [84]. The MAS scores in these patients ranged from 10 to 30 with a mean score of around 18.

In both mania and depression the problem of placebo plays a great role when evaluating response to treatment over the acute four weeks of therapy. As the placebo effect decreases with an increase of the pre-treatment rating score, it is important to exclude mild degrees of mania or depression.

Fifty years have now passed since the first placebo-controlled study with lithium in hospitalised, severe manic patients was performed [83], showing a significant superiority of lithium. A placebo-controlled study with lithium using the MAS as outcome measure in hospitalised patients with moderate mania confirmed the superiority of lithium over placebo [21]. As discussed elsewhere [4], trials with a mixed sample of outpatients and inpatients with mild depression or mania have indicated a rather high placebo response.

In depression, the placebo response in mild to moderate depression is also rather high, implying that the advantage of antidepressants over placebo for both TCAs and SSRIs expressed in response rate is only around 15-20% [4].

The MES trial with the atypical antidepressant trimipramine (Table 6) seems to indicate that this antidepressant might be considered in bipolar disorder.

It is of great interest that the response criteria of antimanic compounds in accordance with MAS as suggested by Frank et al. [35] in the short-term treatment of bipolar patients over a period of four weeks have been supported by this review. Thus, MAS scores at endpoint between 8 and 13 are considered a partial response while endpoint MAS scores of 7 or less are considered a full response or a remission [35]. In this review the comparison of the various antidepressant compounds has also been made for a treatment period of four weeks. However, it is generally accepted that for the evaluation of full response or remission, a treatment period of six weeks is more adequate than four weeks, but the MES criteria for partial response and full response are analogue to the MAS criteria. In this context it should be emphasized that the extension of the duration of the antidepressant treatment to longer periods of the short-term treatment such as eight weeks or more is questionable [85].

Medium-Term Trials of Major Affective Episodes

The model for medium-term evaluation of antidepressants has been the ECT model, i.e. a post-ECT follow-up of 6 months in severely depressed patients who have responded to the acute ECT treatment. Using this model it was shown that paroxetine was superior to imipramine in the prevention of relapse as defined as a score of 15 or more on MES [33].

In patients with unipolar winter depression (seasonal affective disorder) light therapy has been used analogue to the ECT-model for relapse prevention in the continuation treatment. Thus, Martiny et al. [86] have shown that citalopram was superior to placebo in the prevention of relapse after response to light therapy in patients with seasonal affective disorder. The MES was found to be more sensitive than HAM-D_{17} in discriminating between citalopram and placebo over the four months' continuation phase [86].

Henry et al. [84] showed in their study that lithium was significantly superior to anticonvulsants such as carbamazepine and valproic acid in preventing hypomania or mania in patients with bipolar depression treated with SSRIs in the medium-term phase.

In the medium-term phase of mania the typical antipsychotics may induce depression and the atypical antipsychotics may have a rather high relapse rate of hypomania [87], possibly as a consequence of their antidepressive effect [41].

On this background lithium would seem to be indicated in bipolar patients in the medium-term phase in the prevention of both manic and depressive relapse.

Long-Term Trials of Major Affective Episodes

Prien et al. [88] have argued that long-term prophylactic trials of major affective episodes should have a duration of at least 24 months. In their trial [88] they showed that in bipolar disorder the recurrence of new episodes was 36% in lithium-treated patients, 80% in imipramine-treated, and 90% in placebo-treated patients. However, in unipolar disorder the recurrence of new depressive episodes was 42% in imipramine-treated patients, 57% in lithium-treated, and 90% in placebo-treated patients [88]. These results indicate the very low placebo effect in the prophylactic treatment of major affective episodes and that lithium is significantly superior to imipramine in bipolar patients while imipramine is significantly superior to lithium in unipolar patients. Very few trials comparing anticonvulsants with lithium in the long-term treatment of bipolar patients have been published. When compared to carbamazepine in a trial using both MAS and MES, lithium was found to be significantly superior when patients randomized to prophylactic treatment were considered [63]. When comparing daily to every second day administration of lithium in bipolar patients, the recurrence of new episodes was seen in only 10% in the daily administered while it was 50% in the every second day administration of lithium [64].

In unipolar depression the recurrence of new depressive episodes was seen in only around 10% of the citalopram-treated versus 36% in the placebo-treated patients when using the MES criterion of 15 or more for depression recurrence [76]. Taking the results from the ECT study [33] in which paroxetine and imipramine were compared for relapse prevention, the results favour paroxetine over imipramine (around 10% versus around 30% relapse rate).

In conclusion, lithium still seems to be the most efficacious drug in the prophylactic therapy of bipolar patients and SSSRI's to be the most efficacious class of drugs in the prophylactic therapy of unipolar depression. In mixed states of mania and depression the atypical antipsychotics and atypical antidepressants should be considered.

References

[1] Hamilton M. Development of a rating sale for primary depressive illness. *Br J Soc Clin Psychol*. 1967; 6: 278-296.

[2] Hamilton M. Diagnosis and rating of anxiety. *Br J Psychiatry*.1969 (special publ): 76-79.

[3] Bech P. Pharmacological treatment of depressive disorders: a review. In: Maj, M. & Sartorius N, eds.: *Depressive disorders. WPA Series Evidence and Experience in Psychiatry*. Chichester: John Wiley & Sons 2002, second edition; pp 89-127.

[4] Bech P. The Bech-Rafaelsen Mania Scale in Clinical Trials of Therapies for Bipolar Disorder: 20-Year Review of its Use as an Outcome Measure. *CNS Drugs*. 2002; 16: 47-63.

[5] Bech P. The Bech-Rafaelsen Melancholia Scale (MES) in clinical trials of therapies in depressive disorders: a 20-year review of its use as outcome measure. *Acta Psychiatr Scand.* 2002; 106: 252-264.

[6] Bech P, Bille J, Sondergaard S et al. *Health of the Nation Outcome Scales (HoNOS). Status report 2003* [Danish]. Psychiatric Research Unit. Frederiksborg General Hospital, Hillerød, Denmark 2003.

[7] Berrios GE, Bulbena-Villarasa A. The Hamilton Depression Scale and the numerical description of symptoms of depression. In Bech P, Coppen A, eds. *The Hamilton Scales.* Berlin: Springer;1990: 80-92.

[8] Beigel A Murphy DL Bunney WE. The manic-state rating scale. *Arch Gen Psychiat.*1971; 25: 256-262.

[9] Young RC, Biggs, JT, Ziegler VE, Meyer DA. A Rating scale for mania: Reliability, validity and sensitivity. *Br J Psychiat.* 1978; 133: 429-435.

[10] Double DB. The factor structure of manic rating scales. *J Affect Dis.* 1990; 18: 113-119.

[11] Shansis F, Grevet E, Mattevi B et al. Development and application of the mania rating guide (MRG). *Rev Bras Psiquiatr* 2003; 25: 91-95.

[12] Shansis F, Fleck M, Izquierdo I et al. Which is the best mania rating scale? *Biol Dis* 2003; 5(suppl 1): 85-86.

[13] Karadaq F, Oral T, Yalcin FA et al. Reliability and validity of Turkish translation of the Young Mania Rating Scale. *Turk Psikiatri Derg* 2002;13:107-114.

[14] Bech P, Tanghøj P, Andersen HF el al. Citalopram dose-response revisited using an alternative psychometric approach to evaluate clinical effects of four fixed citalopram doses compared to placebo in patients with major depression. *Psychopharmacol* 2002; 163: 20-25.

[15] Goldstein DJ, Mallinckrodt CH, Lu Y. Duloxetine in the treatment of major depressive disorder: a double-blind clinical trials. *J Clin Psychiatry* 2002; 36: 383-390.

[16] Rasch G. *Probalistic models for some intelligence and attainment tests.* Chicago: University of Chicago Press;1980.

[17] Bech P, Baastrup PC, de Bleeker E et al. Dimensionality, responsiveness and standarsization of the Bech-Rafaelsen Mania Scale in the ultra-short therapy with antipsychotics in patients with severe manic episodes. *Acta Psychiatr Scand* 2001; 104: 25-30.

[18] Rossi A, Daneluzzo E, Arduni L et al. A factor analysis of signs and symptoms of the manic episode with the Bech-Rafaelsen mania and melancholia scales. *J Affect Dis* 2001;64:267-270.

[19] Fava M, Evins AE, Dorer DJ et al. The problem of the placebo response in clinical trials for psychiatric disorders: culprits, possible remedies, and a novel study design approach. *Psychother Psychosom.* 2003; 72:115-127.

[20] Kendell RE. Clinical validity. In: Robins LN, Barrett JE, eds. *The validity of psychiatric diagnosis.* New York: Raven Press; 1979: 305-321 .

[21] Johnstone EC, Crow TJ, Frith CD, Owens DG . The Northwick Park "functional" psychosis study: diagnosis and treatment response. *Lancet* 1988; 2:119-125.

[22] Rasmussen A, Lunde M, Poulsen DL et al. A double-blind, placebo-controlled study in the prevention of depression in stroke patients. *Psychosom* 2003; 44: 216-221.

[23] Stage KB, Middelboe T, Pisinger C. Measurement of depression in patients with chronic obstructive pulmonary disease (COPD). *Nord J Psychiatry* 2003; 57: 297-301.

[24] Bech P. *Rating scales for psychopathology, health status and quality of life. A compendium on documentation in accordance with the DSM-III-R and WHO systems.* Berlin: Springer;1993.

[25] Kraepelin E. Psychiatrie. *Ein Lehrbuch für Studierende und Ärzte.* 8. Aufl. Leipzig: Barth; 1913.

[26] Maj M. Prognostic and treatment response implications of 'switching' and 'rapid cycling' in bipolar disorder. *Curr Opin Psychiatry* 2003; 16 (suppl 2): 79-83.

[27] Gouliaev G, Licht RW, Vestergaard P et al. Treatment of manic episodes: zuclopenthixol and clonazepam versus lithium and clonazepam. *Acta Psychiatr Scand* 1996; 93: 119-124.

[28] Emrich HM. Studies with oxcarbazepine in acute mania. *Int J Clin Psychopharmacol* 1990; 5: 83-88.

[29] Walton SA, Berk M, Brook S. Superiority of lithium over verapamil in mania: A randomized, controlled single-blind trial. *J Clin Psychiatry* 1996; 57: 543-546.

[30] Walton SA. Whatever happened to the calcium channel blockers. In: Maj M, Akiskal HS, López-Ibor JJ, Sartorius N, eds. *Bipolar disorders*. Chichester: John Wiley; 2002: 277-280.

[31] Hellewell JS. Oxcarbazepine (Trileptal) in the treatment of bipolar disorders: a review of efficacy and tolerability. *J Affect Disord* 2002; 72 (Suppl 1): S23-34.

[32] Small JG, Klapper MH, Kellams JJ et al. Electroconvulsive treatment compared with lithium in the management of manic states. *Arch Gen Psychiatry* 1988; 45: 727-32.

[33] Lauritzen L, Odgaard K, Clemmesen L et al. Relapse prevention of paroxetine in ECT treated patients with major depression. A comparison with imipramine and placebo in medium-term continuation therapy. *Acta Psychiatr Scand* 1996; 94: 241-251.

[34] Gjerris A, Bech P, Broen-Christensen C et al. Haloperidol plasma levels in relation to antimanic effect. In: Usdin E, Dahl SG, Gram LF et al., eds. *Clinical pharmacology in psychiatry*. London: McMillan 1980:227-232.

[35] Frank E, Kupfer DJ, Gerebtzoff et al. The development of study exit criteria for evaluating antimanic compounds. *J Clin Psychiatry* 2001;62:421-425.

[36] Sethi BB, Timari SC. Carbamazepine versus chlorpromazine in mania: a double-blind trial. In: Emrich HM, Okuma T. Müller AA, eds. *Anticonvulsants in affective disorders*. Amsterdam, Excerpta Medica 1984:167-176.

[37] Erfurth A, Kammeren C, Grunze H et al. An open label study of gabapentin in the treatment of acute mania. *J Psychiatr Res* 1998; 32:261-264.

[38] Bozikars VP, Petrikis P, Kourtis A et al. Treatment of acute mania with topiramate in hospitalized patietns. *Prog Neuropsychopharmacol Biol Psychiatry* 2002; 26:1203-1206.

[39] Fagiolini A, Frank E, Houch PR et al. Prevalence of obesity and weight change during treatment in patients with bipolar I disorder. *J Clin Psychiatry* 2002; 63: 528-533.

[40] Licht RW, Bysted M, Christensen H. Risperidone versus zuclopenthixol in mania. an open experimental trial with a historical control group. *Nord J Psychiatry*. 2000; 54 (suppl 43): 38.

[41] Müller-Siecheneder F, Müller MJ, Hillert A et al. Risperidone versus haloperidol and amitriptyline in the treatment of patients with a combined psychotic and depressive syndrome. *J Clin Psychopharmacol*. 1998; 18: 111-120.

[42] Spiker DG. Weiss JC, Dealy RS. The pharmacological treatment of delusional depression. *Am J Psychiatry*, 1985; 142: 430-436.

[43] Ghaemi SN, Cherry EL, Katzon JA et al. Does olanzapine have antidepressant properties? A retrospective preliminary study. *Bipol Disord*. 2000; 2: 196-199.

[44] Bender S, Olbrich HM, Fischer W et al. Antipsychotic efficacy of the antidepressant trimipramine: a randomized, double-blind comparison with the phenothiazine perazine. *Pharmacopsychiatry.* 2003; 36: 61-69.

[45] Sechter D, Peuskens J, Fleurot O et al. Amisulpride vs risperidone in chronic schizophrenia: results of a 6-month double-blind study. *Neuropsychopharmacology* 2002; 27:1071-1081.

[46] Rifkin A, Saraf K, Kane J et al. A comparison of trimipramine and imipramine. A controlled study. *J Clin Psychiatry.* 1980; 41:124-129.

[47] Danish University Antidepressant Group. Paroxetine: A selective serotonin reuptake inhibitor showing better tolerance, but weaker antidepressant effect than clomipramine in a controlled multicenter study. *J Affect Dis* 1990; 18: 289-299.

[48] Danish University Antidepressant Group. Citalopram: Clinical effect profile in comparison with clomipramine. A controlled multicenter study. *Psychopharmacology.* 1986; 90: 131-138.

[49] Øhrberg S, Christiansen PE, Severin B et al. Paroxetine and imipramine in the treatment of depressive patients in psychiatric practice *Acta Psychiatr Scand.* 1992; 86: 437-444.

[50] Fuglum E, Rosenberg C, Damsbo N et al. Screening and treating depressed patients. A comparison of two controlled citalopram trials across treatment settings: Hospitalized patients vs. patients treated by their family doctors. *Acta Psychiatr Scand.* 1996; 94: 18-25.

[51] Szegedi A, Wetzel H, Angerbach D et al. A double-blind study comparing paroxetine and maprotiline in depressed outpatients. *Pharmacopsychiatry.* 1997;30:97-105 .

[52] Anderson IM. SSRIs versus tricyclic antidepressants in depressed inpatients: a meta-analysis of efficacy and tolerability. *Depression and Anxiety.* 1998; 7 (suppl 1): 11-17.

[53] Ottevanger EA. Fluvoxamine and clomipramine in depressed and hospitalised patients: results from a randomised, double-blind study. *Encephale.*1995; 21:317-321.

[54] Zohar J, Keegstra H, Barrelet L. Fluvoxamine as effective as clomipramine against symptoms of severe depression: results from a multicentre, double-blind study. *Human Psychopharmacol.* 2003; 18: 113-119.

[55] Bech P. Clinical effects of selective serotonin reuptake inhibitors. In Dahl SG, Gram LF, eds. *Clinical Pharmacology in Psychiatry*. Berlin: Springer; 1989:81-93 .

[56] Schou M. Prophylactic and maintenance therapy in recurrent affective disorders. In Gallant DM, Simpson GM, eds. *Depression: behavioral, biochemical, diagnostic and treatment concepts*. New York: Spectrum Publication; 1976:309-334.

[57] Bech P, Eplov L, Gastpar M et al. WHO pilot study on the validity of imipramine platelet receptor binding sites as a biological marker of endogenous depression. A preliminary report. *Pharmacopsychiatry* 1988; 21:147-150.

[58] Pandey GH, Pandey VSC, Ren X et al. Serotonin receptors in platelets of bipolar and schizoaffective patients: Effect of lithium treatment. *Pharmacopsychiatry* 2003; 170:115-123.

[59] Göder R, Weber EH, Hesse AC et al. Lithium treatment for relapse prevention after electroconvulsive therapy in a patient with major depressive disorder and end stage renal disease. *Pharmacopsychiatry.* 2003; 36: 228.

[60] van Moffaert M, Bartholome F, Cosyns P. A controlled comparison of sertraline and fluoxetine in acute and continuation treatment of major depression. *Hum Psychopharmacol.* 1995; 10: 393-405.

[61] Goodwin FK, Jamison KR. *Manic-depressive illness*. New York: Oxford University Press;1999.

[62] Coxhead N, Silverstone T, Cookson J. Carbamazepine versus lithium in the prophylaxis of bipolar affective disorder. *Acta Psychiatr Scand.* 1992; 85: 114-118.

[63] Hartong EG, Moleman P, Hoogduin CA, et al. Prophylactic efficacy of lithium versus carbamazepine in treatment-naive bipolar patients. *J Clin Psychiatry*. 2003; 64: 144-151.

[64] Jensen HV, Plenge P, Mellerup ET et al. Lithium profylaxis of manic depressive disorder: daily lithium dosing schedule versus every second day. *Acta Psychiatr Scand.* 1995; 92: 69-71.

[65] Greil W. Novel mood stabilising strategies and 50 years of lithium. In: Maj M, Akiskol HS, Lopex-Ibor JJ, Sarorius N, eds. *Bipolar disorder*. Chicago: John Wiley; 2002:233-235.

[66] Müller-Oerlinghausen B. Arguments for the specificity of the antisuicidal effect of lithium. *Eur Arch Psychiatry Clin Neurosci*. 2001; 251 (suppl 2): 72-75.

[67] Baldessarini RJ, Torda L, Hansen J. Lithium treatment and suicide risk in major affective disorders: update and new findings. *J Clin Psychiatry*. 2003; 64 (suppl 5): 44-52.

[68] Goodwin FK, Firemn B, Simon GE. Suicide risk in bipolar disorder during treatment with lithium and divalproex. *JAMA* 2003; 290: 1467-1473.

[69] Bech P, Vendsborg PB, Rafaelsen OJ. Lithium maintenance treatment of manic-melancholic patients. *Acta Psychiatr Scand.* 1976; 53:70-81.

[70] Keck PE. The management of acute mania. *BMJ* 2003;327:1002-1003.

[71] Frank E, Kupfer DJ, Perel JM. Three year outcome for maintenance therapies in recurrent depression. *Arch Gen Psychiatr*. 1990; 47: 1093-1099.

[72] Kupfer, DJ, Frank E, Perel JM et al. Five year outcome for maintenance therapies in recurrent depression. *Arch Gen Psychiatr*. 1992; 49: 769-773.

[73] Frank E, Kupfer DJ, Perel JM et al. Comparison of full-dose versus half-dose pharmacotherapy in the maintenance treatment of recurrent depression. *J Affect Dis*. 1993; 27: 139-149.

[74] Terra JL, Montgomery SA. Fluvoxamine prevents recurrence of depression. Results of a long-term, double-blind, placebo-controlled study. *Int Clin Psychopharmacol*. 1998; 13: 55-62.

[75] Hochstrasser B, Isaksen PM, Koponen H et al. Prophylactic effect of citalopram in unipolar, recurrent depression: placebo-controlled study of maintenance therapy. *Brit J Psychiatry*. 2001; 178: 304-310.

[76] Bent-Hansen J, Lunde M, Klysner R et al. The validity of three depression rating scales in discriminating between citalopram and placebo in depression recurrence in the maintenance therapy of elderly unipolar patients with major depression. *Pharmacopsychiatry*. 2003; 36: 1-5.

[77] Klysner R, Bent-Hansen J, Hansen HL et al. The efficacy of citalopram in the prevention of recurrent depression in elderly patients: a placebo-controlled study on maintenance therapy. *Brit J Psychiatry*. 2002; 181: 29-35.

[78] ECNP Guidelines for investigating efficacy in bipolar disorder. *Euro. Neuropsychopharmacol.* 2001; 11: 79-88.

[79] Bauer M, Whybrow PC, Angst A et al. Guidelines for the treatment of unipolar depressive disorders. *World J Psychiatry* 2002;3:3-43.

[80] Gelenberg AJ, Frank E, Keller MB et al. Evaluating pharmacological treatments for bipolar disorder. In Prien RF, Robinson DS, eds. *Clinical evaluation of psychotropic drugs: principles and guidelines*. New York, Raven Press; 1994: 327-344.

[81] Möller H-J. Methodological aspects in the assessment of severity of depression by the Hamilton Depression Scale. *Eur Arch Psychiatry Clin Neurosci*. 2001; 25 (suppl 2): 13-20.

[82] McDowell I. Newell C. *Measuring health. A guide to rating scales and questionnaires*. New York: Oxford University Press; 1987 .

[83] Schou M, Juel-Nielsen N, Stromgren E et al. The treatment of manic psychoses by the administration of lithium salts. *J Neurol Neurosurg Psychiatry* 1954; 17: 250-260.

[84] Henry C, Sorbara F, Lacoste J et al. Antidepressant-induced mania in bipolar patients: identification of risk factors. *J Clin Psychiatry*. 2001; 62: 249-255.

[85] Fava GA. Long-term treatment with antidepressant drugs: the spectacular achievements of propaganda. *Psychother Psychosom*. 2002; 127-132.

[86] Martiny K, Lunde M, Simonsen C et al. Relapse prevention by citalopram in SAD patients responding to one week of light therapy. A placebo-controlled study. *Acta Psychiatr Scand* 2004;109:1-5.

[87] Aubry JM, Simon AE, Bertschy G. Possible induction of mania and hypomania by olanzapine and risperidone: a critical review of reported cases. *J Clin Psychiatry*. 2000; 61: 649-655.

[88] Prien RF, Caffey EM, Klett CJ. Prophylactic efficacy of lithium carbonate in manic-depressive illness. *Arch Gen Psychiatry*. 1973; 28: 337-341.

In: Focus on Bipolar Disorder Research
Editor: Malcomb R. Brown, pp. 153-166
ISBN 1-59454-059-4

Chapter 8

TREATMENT-RESISTANT DEPRESSION: PERSONALITY VERSUS BIPOLAR DISORDERS. BIBLIOGRAPHY REVIEW WITH A CLINICAL CASE REPORT

Martín Ruiz, María Carolina Vairo
Daniel Matusevich and Carlos Finkelsztein
Hospital Italiano of Buenos Aires, Argentina

ABSTRACT

Treatment-Resistant Depression has not been well defined elsewhere. Souery et al. define it as the failure of two adequate time and dose antidepressant treatments.

Nearly 40% of depressed patients do not improve with the first pharmacological treatment, even with adequate time, dose and compliance; 20% of patients with major depressive disorder do not improve even with a two year treatment, and 12% never improve.

Psychiatric comorbidities such as Personality Disorders, Anxiety Disorders, Substance Abuse Disorders and Somatomorf Disorders should be considered when evaluating a patient with resistant depression.

Often, patients who do not improve with an antidepressant treatment have a potential risk for bipolarity. The mania or hypomania switch rate is 70 times larger in depressed patients who do not improve with antidepressants; these people may have a hidden bipolar disorder with an apparent unipolar course.

In this study we first present a case report, and then we make a review between narcissistic personality disorder, hypertimic personality, bipolar disorder and resistant depression, discussing its therapeutic implications.

INTRODUCTION

There is no clear definition for treatment-resistant depression [84]. Souery et al. [94] describe it as the treatment failure after undergoing two different types of antidepressants in the right time and dosing.

About 40% of patients treated for depression do not respond to a first line drug treatment even when the length, the dose and the completion of the treatment are correct [45, 56, 66]; more than 20% of patients with a major depressive disorder do not recover after 2 years of treatment [49] and 12% never improve [50].

When facing a case of treatment-resistant depression other psychiatric comorbidities must be considered: personality disorders, anxiety disorders, alcohol or drugs abuse and somatoform disorders. [64].

Usually, patients who have not responded to antidepressant treatments run a potential risk of bipolarity [91]. The rate of maniac or hypo-maniac switch is 70 times greater in depressed patients who are refractory to antidepressants [16]; these patients may undergo a latent bipolar disorder with an apparent unipolar course [53].

The aim of this paper is to provide a literature review of the relationship among narcissistic personality disorder, hyperthymic personality, bipolarity and treatment-resistant depression starting from a clinical case report and discussing its therapeutic implications.

CLINICAL CASE REPORT

R. is a 53 year-old patient who insidiously developed a course of severe depression in 1997 after a prolonged clinical admission of 3 months in which she underwent surgical treatment for perforated diverticulitis that required a splenectomy as well as a non-permanent colostomy. One year later, at the beginning of 1998, a maternal aunt passed away and she entered the menopause period. R. was persistently depressed, did not work and laid in bed most of the day. Then, she started psychotherapy and medical treatment with 20mg of Paroxetin a day that was increased to 30 mg due to progressive worsening of symptoms .In June 1998, R. showed marked anhedony, psychomotor inhibition, hyporexia with 16 Kg. loss in the last three months, persistent insomnia, lack of self-appearance and personal hygiene, self-pity, guilty, hopelessness and death ideas, self-infliction menaces, persecutory and hypochondriac delusions that rendered her psychiatric admission. According to the admission medical history, her family recalled the following aspects of her personality: "Highly demanding with herself and with others, manipulative, she always had methods to convince others, changing, impulsive, react depending on the daily mood, she tended to shout if she got angry, she was always expecting recognition for what she did, she was proud, outstood her virtues, she was self-congratulating". Diagnosis was Severe Major Depressive Disorder with Psychotic Symptoms in Axis I and Narcissistic Personality Disorder in Axis II (according to DSM-IV); as stressants in Axis IV, her daughter's rhinoplasty and maternity leave of her therapist the week previous to admission were highlighted. She was treated with progressive doses of venlafaxin and risperidone up to 225 and 3 mg/day respectively. At the moment of discharge, 28 days later, R. did not present either psychotic productivity or suicidal ideation but remission of depressive symptoms was partial. She continued ambulatory treatment. In December 1998 risperidone was interrupted while the patient kept a partial response to the antidepressant. Three months later, venlafaxine was progressively interrupted and started treatment with desipramine reaching a dose of 240 mg/day in six weeks.

In June 2000 she changed her therapist, starting therapy with one of the authors of this paper. In the first interview the patient appears unattractive, hypoactive, with a severe depressed mood, with ruin and hopelessness ideas, death fantasies, without psychotic production and referring anhedony, willingness to stay in bed, normal feeding and sleeping habits and a relevant social and working dysfunctions. R. graduated from a University as an English teacher and is the founder of a recognized academy which she directed until the depression started. She has been married for 27 years, having 2 sons. The first one died at the age of two in 1978 when he suffered from acute leukemia rendering R. to psychotherapeutic treatment for three moths. R. is the unique daughter and her father died in April 2000. Her mother is alive and she suffered several depressive episodes that required ambulatory psychiatric treatment. R. has a maternal aunt who underwent depressive episodes and a cousin (from mother's family) Who had a suicide attempt without records available of an underlying psychopathology. R. suffers from bilateral glaucoma of open angle undergoing medical treatment. In 1994 she exposed herself to plastic surgery for facial lifting and rhinoplasty. Familial and individual interviews were performed supporting in first instance the same diagnosis of the psychiatric admission. Although R. appears cooperative, comes to every scheduled session and follows the indication of permanent family surrounding, it is remarkable her tendency to lead the conversation: she constantly refers to her successful past, her professional achievements, her "model" family and her sons brought up according to "her image and resemblance". She states: "...I was fully wished by my parents… I carried the national flag while at school, I had the best marks, I was a model daughter… my daughter, she is splendid like me when I was her age… I used to trust God but not anymore because he forgot about me… before I got depressed, world had no limits for me, everyone loved me."

The same drug therapy was kept inferring that the partial response to medication was sustained by the presence of a narcissistic personality disorder.

Psychotherapy tends to work on the different narcissistic aspects of R. However, along the therapy, the patient appears to be well predisposed to talk about issues like time going by, old age, body changes, children growing up and recognizing needs in others different to herself. It is also remarkable the lack of idealization/devaluation towards the therapist, her emphatic and little omnipotent attitude, her ability of integration between bad and good objects, the standing capacity to frustration and the lack of pathologic envy since they are all features opposed to the presence of a narcissistic personality disorder. The existence of attributes such as self-assurance, extroversion, and the constant need of stimuli, the persistence of depression, the anhedony and hopelessness lead to the reassment of the diagnosis: the treatment-resistant depression is secondary to the presence of hyperthymic features. Lithium carbonate is added to her medication with a dose of 450 mg/day keeping blood levels of 0.7 mEq/l. The patient starts to feel mood improvement; she is more active and cares for her self-appearance. Six months later, R. is euthymic, does not present depressive ideas and is back to work. (See Figure 1: Evolution of the clinical case.)

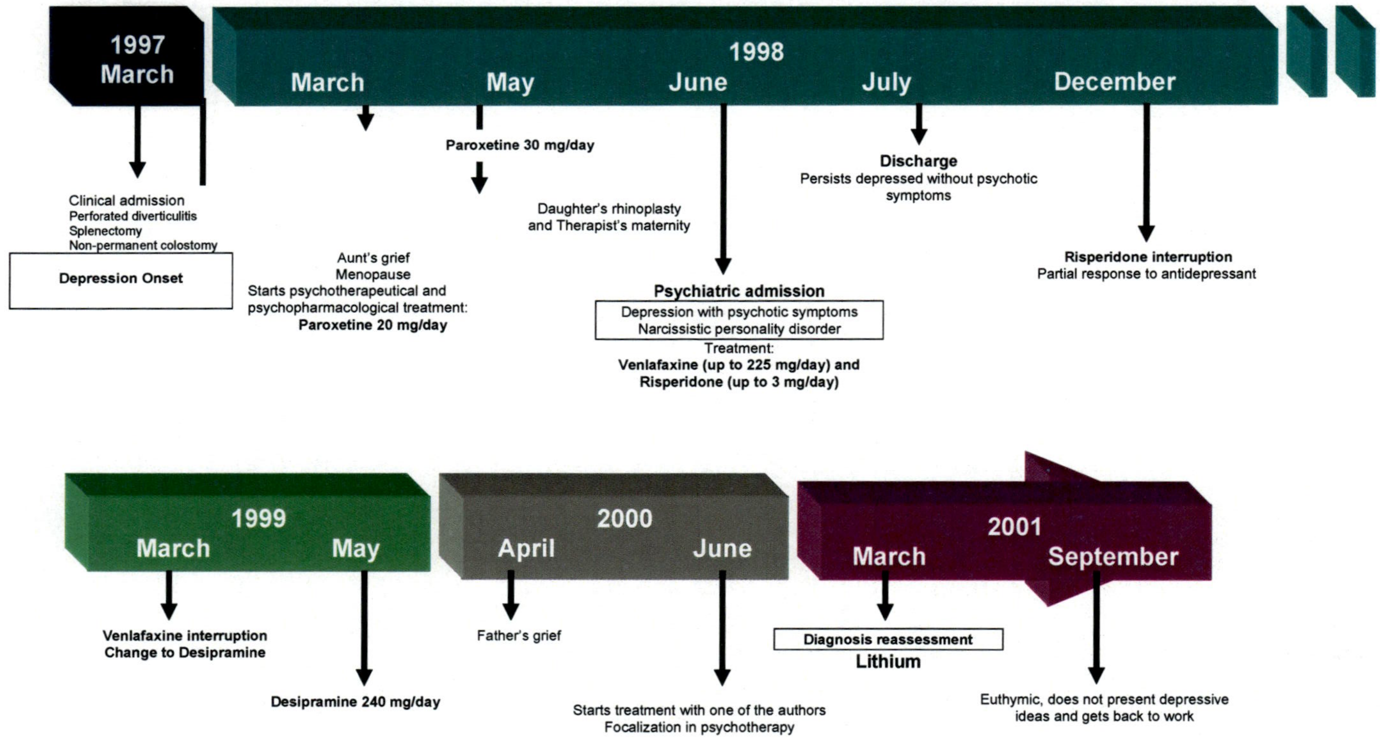

Figure 1. Evolution of clinical case report.

PERSONALITY DISORDER AND BIPOLAR DISORDER

There is a complex relation between personality and bipolar disorder in a theoretical background and from a diagnostic perspective. Being able to distinguish between persistent features of personality and changes that took place as a result of an affective disorder may be difficult since the affect is one of the ways in which personality is expressed. [9, 36, 38, 78].

Several studies have demonstrated that patients with bipolar disorders in remission show greater extroversion (sociability and impulsiveness) than those with unipolar disorders in remission [37, 54, 58]. Furthermore, the neurotic feature (mood changes, poor emotional adaptation, suspicion, social shyness and hypochondriasis, lack of social responsibility, of persistence and of relaxed posture) was observed in a higher degree in bipolar patients.

Specific studies found a high correlation among bipolar disorder and cluster B personality disorders from DSM-IV, mainly with borderline personality disorder [68, 98]. O′Connell et al. [67] studied 50 patients with bipolar disorder in euthymic state using the Personality Disorder Questionnaire and they found that 58% of patients met criteria for one or more personality disorders being the borderline and the histrionic disorders the most prevalent ones with 30% and 20% respectively. There is an important overlap of symptoms between bipolar and personality disorders when hypomania, cyclothymia and other slighter affective courses are considered. [4, 10, 36].

One feature that prevents the treatment of depression from being successful is the existence of an underlying personality disorder [79]. This concept is not new, Freud and Kraepelin speculated that personality was not only related to the etiology and the presentation of depression but also to the response of therapeutical interventions [39].

Many aspects of the studies relating features of depression with personality appear to be contradictory. On one hand, Fava et al. [30] reported that patients with early onset of depression have a higher rate of personality disorders than those with late onset depression but Skodol et al. [92] were not able to reproduce that data. On the other hand, it was observed that patients with depression together with personality disorders were more severely depressed at the beginning of treatment than those with depression alone [71, 77]. That association, however, was not found by other authors [24, 43, 85, 102].

Regarding the response to antidepressants, Peselow et al. [69, 70] state that those individuals who present a high autonomy (trying to maximize the control of the surrounding environment) and low sociotropic traits (those who worry about others rejection) have a better response to antidepressants than those with the opposite features. It is commonly stated that patients with personality disorders usually respond very slowly to antidepressants [59, 63, 82] though Mulder et al. [57] found that the presence of a co-morbid disorder in Axis II would not worsen the results of a major depression treatment.

NARCISSISTIC DISORDER, HYPERTHYMIA AND BIPOLARITY

Many studies reported that narcissistic personality disorders are more frequent among bipolar patients than in the general psychiatric population (2 to 16%) [33, 51, 68, 72, 98]; furthermore, it is one of the most frequent diagnosis of Axis II in bipolar patients [96] and the bipolar disorder is the third comorbidity disorder of Axis I in narcissistic patients (5 to 11%) after depression and substance abuse [80].

Gabbard [32] declares a characteristic feature of the narcissistic personality is the impairment to love. These people consider those who surround them as objects to be used without being able to recognize their needs. The other is not seen as a separate person but as a source of gratitude to their own ego. They are typically envious and sensible to other's critics. During transference they act as if they were facing a big audience, they are boring, they keep talking about their own achievements and they care so little for other's needs that they usually do not allow the therapist to participate in the conversation. When confronted to their inability to recognize other's needs they feel humiliated or painfully exposed.

Despite the fact that mania and pathological narcissism are different from a conceptual and phenomenological point of view, conductive and affective manifestations are similar in some aspects. The features that differentiate narcissistic patients from maniacs are the need to be admired, the envy to the others and the fact that narcissists tend to be more contemptuous and neglectful than maniac patients [1].

Akiskal [5]suggests that a temperamental deregulation would be the substrate for an affective disorder to develop. According to this model, temperamental dispositions, including cyclothymia, dysthymia and hyperthyimia would represent the first observable phenotype that would indicate an underlying bipolar genotype. Cyclothymic temperament is often mistaken with the borderline disorder and hyperthymic temperament with the narcissistic disorder or with a compulsive personality [8]. According to this author, the presence of narcissistic features would be of great clinical value to include a depressed patient in the category of hyperthymic depressions [6]. These individuals who are clinically depressed and have no previous history of hypomaniac episodes but are ambitious, energetic, emphatic, extroverted, merry, optimistic, friendly and hyperactive (all qualities that helped them go forward in life and reach success) would have hyperthymic or hypomanic temperament and would represent 4 to 8 % of general population [6]. Temperament attributes are not transient and they are, in contrary, part of the normal functioning of the individual. In these patients, depression generally appears with hypersomnia and psychomotor inhibition. However, elements of temperament such as accelerated thinking and increase in sexual activity also rise in depression [8]. Akiskal calls hyperthymic depression or bipolar disorder kind IV to the depressive course that takes place late in life and that is overlapped with this temperament [2, 8].

From Akiskal`s stand point, affective conditions and personality attributes are clearly superimposed and that would lead to many kinds of affective disorders [7].

DSM-IV ignores attributes of temperament and family history of bipolarity in major depression though it should be kept in mind that only 15% of hyperthymic patients have family history of bipolarity [6].

It is estimated that patients with hyperthymic temperament and major depression are about 10 to 20% of those who are normally diagnosed as unipolars [6].

Unipolar Depression and Bipolar Depression

The differentiation between bipolar disorder and unipolar depressive disorder has been a key in the psychiatric classification since 1960.

The prevalence of depression along life is 10 to 17% whereas for bipolar disorder is 0.4 to 1.7% [6]. Approximately 10 to 20% of patients with unipolar depression change their diagnosis to bipolar disease during time [14, 52, 76, 88, 93].

A Family history of bipolar disorder, with an onset of disease in adolescence or early adulthood and the acute onset of symptoms with psychotic or catatonic features, have been reported as clinical predictors of bipolarity [11, 12, 25, 97, 99, 100]. However, Coryell et al. [26] asserts that these clinical attributes are of low sensitivity and points to the long lasting depression episodes and onset in youth as the main predictors.

Unipolar patients have a slower course of disease tending to remain more stable. Bipolars, instead, have a variable course with lots of episodes and admissions [22, 101]; more than three depressive episodes and a seasonal pattern should lead to think bipolarity. [3].

Anergy, hypersomnia and hyperphagia are more frequently seen in bipolar depression episodes and they are more common after delivery status. Unipolar depressions appear with greater anxiety, psychomotor irritation, irritability and greater associated physical symptoms [6, 100]. Winokur et al. [100] found that patients with unipolar disease present more frequently and they are prone to remain chronically ill.

Akiskal [3] strongly criticizes DSM-IV since it assumes that clinical presentation and onset of bipolar and unipolar depressions are similar and does not take into account family history for diagnosis. Faeda et al. [31] suggest to exhaustively explore the individual and family history of bipolar disorder in treatment-resistant depressed patients.

Lithium and Treatment-Resistant Depression

Combining Lithium with antidepressants has been recommended as the first line treatment for patients with refractory depression. [28, 46, 48, 64, 87, 89]. Although augmentation treatment with lithium in refractory depression is widely known, it is only used by one third of psychiatrists in the USA [65], Canada [23] and Great Britain [90].

Augmentation with lithium was the subject of research in many double-blind placebo controlled trials [18, 19, 35, 41, 44, 47, 86, 95, 103]. Although some studies did not find improvements with augmentation [19, 44, 103], recent studies have shown a clear benefit [18, 41, 47]. One metha-analysis that included nine double-blind placebo controlled essays showed strong evidence that augmentation with lithium has a statistically significant positive effect [17]. However, it is important to highlight that almost half of the patients do not improve with augmentation [15, 20, 45, 81]. Nelson [61] states that augmentation with lithium could be more effective in those patients having a partial response rather than in those who have a poor response in which he does not recommend its use.

Three trials that combined lithium with tryciclic antidepressants from the beginning of treatment found that this combination may act faster than the antidepressant alone but is not necessarily more effective [21, 29, 55].

At least two studies [42, 75] found that the combination of lithium with tryciclic antidepressants had no benefits over lithium alone in bipolar patients, while the same combination is not more effective either, comparing it with antidepressants alone in unipolar patients.

Price et al. [74] declared that melancholic patients have a better response to lithium augmentation (50%) than the non-melancholic patients (23%). On the other side, Rybakobski and Matkobsky [83] found a greater response to augmentation in moderate depressions without being able to find any difference between psychotic and non-psychotic depressions, unique or relapsing depression, acute or insidious onset or between presence or absence of family history. However, De Montigny et al. [27] did not find a correlation between the severity of depression and the magnitude of response to lithium augmentation.

Few predictors of the response to lithium could be demonstrated. Greater utility has been called in patients with probable bipolar disorders, patients with hypomania history or patients with a first-degree relative with bipolar disorder [13, 34, 40, 60-62, 73, 83]. Bschor et al. [20], in a retrospective study of patients with tryciclic antidepressants refractory depression found that patients who respond to lithium are severely depressed, they have an ongoing depression episode of short duration and less frequently have co-morbid personality disorders.

Akiskal [6] supports the idea of heterogeneity among affective disorders stating the existence of soft bipolar patients; he explains, that way, that the favorable response to lithium (or to combination) in apparently unipolar depressions is because these patients belong to the hyperthymic group.

Discussion

Though there is no certainty that a treatment-resistant depression is due to the existence of an underlying personality disorder, it is frequently observed in the every-day practice. These resistant patients are treated with different classes of antidepressants and a partial response is the best they can get. In the clinical case report it was emphasized the treatment of the personality disorder was thought to be the cause that interfered in the favorable evolution of the depression. We believe that it is a common mistake not to obtain complete medical histories which are essential to get positive results. Moreover, when we face a treatment-resistant depression, pressed by the immediate results we do not give enough time to the patient.

To distinguish between a narcissistic personality disorder and a hyperthimic personality may be a hard task if we do not consider the transferential aspects that are played in the patient-therapist interaction since they share a lot of features and in a superficial layer they behave the same way.

It is also imperative to look for bipolar attributes when facing a first episode of an apparent unipolar depression. The characteristics of the depression as well as the individual and familiar history may contribute with relevant data that can help the patient to get an appropriate treatment.

Despite lithium augmentation improving almost 50% of treatment-resistant depression, we must properly identify the patient before adding a non-harmless medication. There are no proven predictors of lithium response though some factors are mentioned such as probable bipolarity, personal history of hypomania, familiar history of bipolarity, severe depression and lesser frequency of comorbid personality disorders. In our clinical case report we outline the severity of depression (with psychotic symptoms), the family history of relapsing depressions and over all the hyperthymic features of personality. Therapy success after lithium augmentation strongly suggests bipolarity in our patient.

Since undergoing an affective disorder may affect self-image, personality attributes, emotional expression and behavior, a prospective study where personality features are identified prior to an affective episode might bring clearer information about the relationship between a personality disorder and bipolarity.

REFERENCES

Akhtar S. Narcissistic personality disorder: Descriptive features and differential diagnosis. *Psychiatr Clin North Am* 1989; 12: 505-530.

Akiskal HS. Delineating irritable-choleric and hyperthymic temperaments as variants of cyclothymia. *J Pers Disord* 1992; 6: 326-342.

_____ . The Prevalent Clinical Spectrum of Bipolar Disorders: Beyond DSM-IV. *J Clin Psychopharmacol* 1996; 16 Suppl 1: 4-14.

_____ . Characterologic manifestations of affective disorders. *Integrative Psychiatry* 1984: 83-88.

_____ . Developmental Pathways to Bipolarity: Are Juvenile-Onset Depressions Pre-Bipolar? *J Am Acad Child Adolesc Psychiatry* 1995; 34: 754-763.

_____ . Mood disorders: clinical features. En *Comprehensive Textbook of Psychiatry / VII.* Eds Kaplan HI, Sadock BJ. Baltimore, MD: Lippincott, Williams & Wilkins 2000; vol I, cap 14.6: 1338-1377.

Akiskal HS, Akiskal K. Cyclothymic, hyperthymic, and depressive temperaments. En Psychiatry Update: American Psychiatric Association Annual Review, vol 5. Eds. Frances AJ, Hales RE., *American Psychiatric Press*; Washington 1986.

Akiskal HS, Pinto O. The Evolving Bipolar Spectrum: Prototypes I, II, III, and IV. *Psychiatr Clin North Am* 1992; 2: 518-533.

Akiskal HS, Hirschfeld RM, Yerevanian BI. The relationship of personality to affective disorders: a critical review. *Arch Gen Psychiatry* 1983; 40: 801-810.

Akiskal HS, Khani MK, Scott-Strauss A. Cyclothymic temperamental disorders. *Psychiatr Clin North Am* 1979; 2: 527-554.

Akiskal HS, Maser JD, Zeller PJ, Endicott J et al. Switching from "Unipolar" to Bipolar II: An 11-year Prospective Study of Clinical and Temperamental Predictors in 559 Patients. *Arch Gen Psychiatry* 1995; 52: 114-123.

Akiskal Hs, Walker P, Puzantian VR, King D et al. Bipolar outcome in the course of depressive illness: phenomenologic, familiar, and pharmacologic predictors. *J Affect Disord* 1983; 5: 115-128.

Alvarez, E, Pérez-Sola, V, Pérez-Blanco J, Queraltó JM et al. Predicting outcome of lithium added to antidepressants in resistant depression. *J Affect Disord* 1997; 42: 179-186.

Angst J, Felder W, Frey R, Stassen HH. The course of affective diosrders, I: change of diagnosis of monopolar, unipolar, and bipolar illness. *Arch Psychiatr Nervenkr* 1978; 226: 57-64.

Austin MP, Souza FG, Goodwin GM. Lithium augmentation in antidepressant-resistant patients: A quantitative analysis. *Br J Psychiatry* 1991; 159: 510-514.

Bauer M, Bschor T, Kunz D, Berghofer A et al. Double-blind, placebo-controlled trial of the use of lithium to augment antidepressant medication in continuation treatment of unipolar major depression. *Am J Psychiatry* 2000; 157: 1429-1435.

Bauer M, Döpfmer S. Lithium Augmentation in Treatment-Resistant Depression: Meta-analysis of Placebo-Controlled Studies. *J Clin Psychopharmacol* 1999; 19: 427-434.

Baumann P, Nil R, Souche A et al. A double-blind, placebo-controlled study of citalopram with and without lithium in the treatment of therapyresistant depressive patients: a clinical, pharmacokinetic and pharmacogenetic investigation. *J Clin Psychopharmacol* 1996; 16: 307-314.

Browne M, Lapierre YD, Hrdina PD, Horn E. Lithium as an adjunct in the treatment of major depression. *Int Clin Psychopharmacol* 1990; 5: 103-110.

Bschor T, Canata B, Muller-Oerlinghausen B, Bauer M. Predictors of response to lithium augmentation in tricyclic antidepressant-resistant depression. *J Affect Disord* 2001; 64: 261-265.

Cappiello AC, McDougle CJ, Delgado PL. Lithium plus desipramine versus desipramine alone in the treatment of severe major depression: a preliminary study. *Int Clin Psychopharmacol* 1998; 13: 191-198.

Cassano G, Akiskal HS, Musetti L, Perugi G et al. Psychopathology, temperament and past course in primary major depressions, II: towards a definition of bipolarity with a new semistructured interview for depression. *Psychopathology* 1989; 22: 278-288.

Chaimowitz GA, Links PS, Padgett RW, Carr AC. Treatment-resistant depression: a survey of practice habits of Canadian psychiatrists. *Can J Psychiatry* 1991; 36: 353-356.

Charney DS, Nelson JC, Quinlan DM. Personality traits and disorder in depression. *Am J Psychiatry* 1981; 138: 1601-1604.

Coryell W, Endicott J, Andreasen N, Keller M. Bipolar I, bipolar II, and nonbipolar major depression among the relatives of affectively ill probands. *Am J Psychiatry* 1985; 144: 817-821.

Coryell W, Endicott J, Maser JD, Keller MB et al. Long-term stability of polarity distinctions in the affective disorders. *Am. J. Psychiatry* 1995 152: 385-390.

De Montigny C, Cournoyer G, Morissette R, Langlois R et al. Lithium carbonate addition in tricyclic antidepressant-resistant unipolar depression. *Arch Gen Psychiatry* 1983; 40: 1327-1334.

De Montigny C, Grunberg F, Mayer A et al. Lithium induces rapid relief of depression in tricyclic antidepressant drug non-responders. *Br J Psychiatry* 1981; 138: 252-256.

Ebert D, Jaspert A, Murata H et al. Initial lithium augmentation improves the antidepressant effects of standard TCA treatment in non-resistant depressed patients. *Psychopharmacol* 1995; 118: 223-225.

Fava M, Alpert JE, Borus JS, Nierenberg AA et al. Patterns of personality disorder comorbidity in early-onset versus late-onset major depression. *Am J Psychiatry* 1996; 153: 1308-1312.

Faedda GL, Tondo L, Baldessarini RJ. Lithium Discontinuation: Uncovering Latent Bipolar Disorder? *Am J Psychiatry* 2001; 158: 1337-1338.

Gabbard GO. Cluster B Personality Disorders: Narcissistic. En *Psychodynamic Psychiatry in Clinical Practice.* 3rd Ed, American Psychiatric Press; Washington 2000; Cap. 16: 463-489.

Gunderson J, Ronningstam E, Smith L. Narcissistic personality disorder: A review of data on DSM-III-R descriptions. *J Pers Disord* 1991; 5: 167-177.

Heit S, Nemeroff CB. Lithium augmentation of antidepressants in treatment-refractory depression. *J Clin Psychiatry* 1998; 59: 28-35.

Heninger GR, Charney DS, Sternberg DE. Lithium carbonate augmentation of antidepressant treatment – an effective prescription for treatment of refractory depression. *Arch Gen Psychiatry* 1983; 40: 1335-1342.

Hilty DM, Brady KT, Hales RE. A Review of Bipolar Disorder Among Adults. *Psychiatr Serv* 1999; 50 201-213.

Hirschfeld RMA, Klerman GL. Personality attributes and affective disorders. *Am J Psychiatry* 1979; 136: 67-70.

Hirschfeld RMA, Klerman GL, Clayton PJ, Keller MB et al. Assessing personality: the effects of the depressive state in trait measurement. *Am J Psychiatry* 1983; 140: 695-699.

Ilardi S, Craighead W. Personality pathology and response to somatic treatments for major depression: a critical review. *Depression* 1995; 2: 200-217.

Joffe RT, Levitt AJ, Bagby RM, MacDonald C et al. Predictors of response to lithium and triiodothyronine augmentation of antidepressants in tricyclic non-responders. *Br J Psychiatry* 1993; 163: 574-578.

_____ . A placebo-controlled comparison of lithium and triiodothyronine augmentation of tricyclic antidepressants in unipolar refractory depression. *Arch Gen Psychiatry* 1993; 50: 387-393.

Johnstone EC, Owens DG, Lambert MT, Crow TJ et al. Combination tricyclic antidepressant and lithium maintenance medication in unipolar and bipolar depressed patients. *J Affect Disord* 1990; 20: 225-233.

Joyce PR, Mulder RT, Cloninger CR. Temperament predicts clomipramine and desipramine response in majoe depression. *J Affect Disord* 1994; 30: 35-46.

Kantor D, McNevin S, Leichner P et al. The benefit of lithium carbonate adjunct in refractory depression – fact or fiction. *Can J Psychiatry* 1986; 31: 416-418.

Katona CL. Refractory depression: A review with particular reference to the use of lithium augmentation. *Eur Neuropsychopharmacol* 1995; Suppl: 109-113.

Katona CL. Lithium augmentation in refractory depression. *Psychiatr Dev*;1988 2: 153-171.

Katona CL, Abou-Salch MT, Harrison DA, Nairac BA et al. Placebo-controlled trial of lithium augmentation of fluoxetine and lofepramine. *Br J Psychiatry* 1995; 166: 80-86.

Kaplan & Sadock's. *Pocket Handbook of Psychiatric Drug Treatment.* Eds. Sadock BJ, Sadock VA, Lippincott Williams & Wilkuns 3 era edicion Philadelphia 2001; 19: 136-147.

Keller MB, Klerman GL, Lavori PW et al. Long-term outcome of episodes of major depression. *JAMA* 1984; 252: 788-792.

Keller MB, Lavori PW, Mueller TL et al. Time to recovery, chronicity, and levels of psychopathology in major depression. A 5-year prospective follow-up of 431 subjects. *Arch Gen Psychiatry* 1992; 49: 809-816.

Kutcher H, Marton P, Korenblum M. Adolescent bipolar illness and personality disorder. *J Am Acad Child Adolesc Psychiatry* 1990; 29: 355-358.

Lee AS, Murray RM. The long-term outcome of Maudsley depressives. *Br J Psychiatry* 1988; 153: 741-751.

Lehmann HE, Fenton FR, Deutsch M, Feldman S, Engelsmann F. An 11-year follow-up study of 110 depressed patients. *Acta Psychiatr Scand* 1988; 78: 57-65.

Liebowitz MR, Stallone F, Dunner DL, Fieve RR. Personality features of patients with primary affective disorders. *Acta Psychiatr Scand* 1979; 60: 214-224.

Lingaerde O, Edlund AH, Gormsen CA et al. The effect of lithium carbonate in combination with tricyclic antidepressants in endogenous depression. *Acta Psychiatr Scand* 1974; 50: 233-242.

Moller HJ, Fischer G, Zerssen D. Prediction of therapeutic response in acute treatment with antidepressants. Results of an empirical study involving 159 endogenous depressive patients. *Eur Arch Psychiatr Neurol Sci* 1987; 236: 349-357.

Mulder RT. Personality pathology and treatment outcome in major depression: a review. *Am J Psychiatry* 2002; 159: 359-371.

Murray LG, Blackburn IM. Personality differences in patients with depressive illness and anxiety neurosis. *Acta Psychiatr Scand* 1974; 50: 183-191.

Nelsen MR, Dunner DL. Treatment resistant in unipolar depression and other disorders: Diagnostic concerns and treatment possibilities. *Psychiatr Clin North Am*; 1993 16: 541-566.

Nelson JC. Augmentation strategies in depression 2000. *J Clin Psychiatry* 2000; 61: 13-23.

Nelson JC. Treatment of antidepressant nonresponders: Augmentation or switch?. *J Clin Psychiatry* 1998; 59: 35-44.

Nelson JC, Mazure CM. Lithium augmentation in psychotic depression refractory to combined drug treatment. *Am J Psychiatry* 1986; 143: 363-366.

Nelson JC, Mazure CM, Jatlow PI. Characteristics of desipramine-refractory depression. *J Clin Psychiatry* 1994; 55: 12-19.

Nemeroff CB. Augmentation strategies in patients with refractory depression. *Depress Anxiety* 1996/1997; 4: 169-181.

Nierenberg AA. Treatment choice after one antidepressant fails: a survey of Northeastern psychiatrists. *J Clin Psychiatry* 1991; 52: 383-385.

Nierenberg AA, Amsterdam JD. Treatment-resistant depression: Definition and treatment approaches. *J Clin Psychiatry* 1990; 51 Suppl 6: 39-47.

O' Connell RA, Mayo JA, Sciutto MS. PDQ-R personality disorders in bipolar patients. *J Affect Disord* 1991; 23: 217-221.

Peselow ED, Sanfilipo MP, Fieve RR. Relationship Between Hypomania and Personality Disorders Before and After Successful Treatment. *Am J Psychiatry* 1995; 152: 232-238.

Peselow ED, Sanfilipo MP, Fieve RR, Gulbenkian G. Personality traits during depression and following clinical treatment. *Br J Psychiatry* 1994; 146: 349-354.

Peselow ED, Robins CJ, Sanfilipo MP, Block P et al. Sociotropy and autonomy: relationship on antidepressant drug treatment response and endogenous-nonendogenous dichotomy. *J Abnorm Psychol* 1992; 101: 479-486.

Pfohl B, Stangl D, Zimmerman M. The implications of DSM-III personality disorders for patients with major depression. *J Affect Disord* 1984; 7: 309-318.

Pica S, Edwards J, Jackson H, Bell R et al. Personality disorders in recent onset bipolar disorder. *Compr Psychiatry* 1990; 31: 499-510.

Post RM. *Mood disorders: Treatment of bipolar disorders. En Comprehensive Textbook of Psychiatry / VII.* Eds Kaplan HI, Sadock BJ. Baltimore, MD: Lippincott, Williams & Wilkins 2000; vol I, cap 14.8: 1385-1430.

Price LH, Conwell Y, Nelson JC. Lithium augmentation of combined neuroleptic-tricyclic treatment in delusional depression. *Am J Psychiatry* 1983; 140: 318-322.

Prien RF, Kupfer DJ, Mansky PA, Small JG et al. Drug therapy in the prevention of recurrences in unipolar and bipolar affective disorders. *Arch Gen Psychiatry* 1984; 41: 1096-1104.

Rao AV, Nammalvar N. The course and outcome in depressive illness: a follow-up study of 122 cases in Madurai, India. *Br J Psychiatry* 1977; 130: 392-396.

Reich J. Effect of DSM-III personality disorders on outcome of tricyclic antidepressant-treated nonpsychotic outpatients with major or minor depressive disorder. *Psychiatry Res* 1990; 32: 175-181.

Reich J, Noyes R Jr, Hirschfeld R, Coryell W, O' Gorman T. State and personality in depressed and panic patients. *Am J Psychiatry* 1987; 144: 181-187.

Reich J, Green A. Effect of personality disorders on outcome of treatment. *J Nerv Ment Dis* 1991; 179: 74-82.

Ronningstam E, Gunderson J. Identifying criteria for narcissistic personality disorder. *Am J Psychiatry* 1990; 147: 918-922.

Rouillon F, Gorwood P. The use of lithium to augment antidepressant medication. *J Clin Psychiatry* 1998; 59 Suppl 5: 32-39.

Rush AJ. *Mood disorders: Treatment of depression. En Comprehensive Textbook of Psychiatry / VII.* Eds Kaplan HI, Sadock BJ. Baltimore, MD: Lippincott, Williams & Wilkins 2000; vol I, cap 14.7: 1377-1385.

Rybakowski J, Matkowski K. Adding lithium to antidepressant therapy: factors related to therapeutic potentiation. *Eur Neuropsychopharmacol* 1992 2: 161-165.

Sackheim HA. The Definition and Meaning of Treatment-Resistant Depression. *J Clin Psychiatry* 2001; 62 suppl 16: 10-17.

Sato T, Sakado K, Sato S. Is there any specific personality disorder or personality disorder cluster that worsens the short-term treatment outcome of major depression? *Acta Psychiatr Scand* 1993; 88: 342-349.

Schopf J, Baumann P, Lemarchand T, Rey M. Treatment of endogenous depressions resistant to tricyclic antidepressants or related drugs by lithium addition. Results of a placebo-controlled double-blind study. *Pharmacopsychiatry* 1989; 22: 183-187.

Schou M, Mult HC. Forty Years of Lithium Treatment. *Arch Gen Psychiatry* 1997; 54: 9-13.

Shapiro RW, Keller MB. Initial 6-month follow-up of patients with major depressive disorder: a preliminary report from the NIMH collaborative study of the psychobiology of depression. *J Affect Disord* 1981; 3: 205-220.

Shelton RC. Treatment options for refractory depression. *J Clin Psychiatry* 1999; 60 Suppl 4: 57-61.

Shergill SS, Katona CL. Pharmacological choices after one antidepressant fails: a survey of UK psychiatrists. *J Affect Disord* 1997; 43: 19-25.

Shergill SS, Robertson MM, Stein G, Bernadt M, Katona CL. Outcome in refractory depression. *J Affect Disord* 1999; 54: 287-294.

Skodol AE, Stout RL, McGlashan TH, Grilo CM et al. Co-occurrence of mood and personality disorders: a report from the Collaborative Longitudinal Personality Disorders Study. *Depress Anxiety* 1999; 10: 175-182.

Solomon DA, Keller MB, Leon AC, Mueller TI et al. Recovery from major depression: a 10-year prospective follow-up across multiple episodes. *Arch Gen Psychiatry* 1997; 54: 1001-1006.

Souery D, Amsterdam J, De Montigny C et al. Treatment resistant depression: methodological overview and operational criteria. *Eur Neuropsychopharmacol* 1999; 9: 83-91.

Stein G, Bernadt M. Lithium augmentation therapy in tricyclic-resistant depression: a controlled trial using lithium in low and normal doses. *Br J Psychiatry* 1993; 162: 634-640.

Stormberg D, Ronningstam E, Gunderson J, Tohen M. Brief Communication: Pathological Narcissism In Bipolar Disorder Patients. *J Pers Disord* 1998; 12: 179-185.

Strober M, Carlson G. Bipolar illness in adolescents with major depression: clinical, genetic, and psychopharmacologic predictors in a three- to four- year prospective follow-up investigation. *Arch Gen Psychiatry* 1982; 39: 549-555.

Turley B, Bates G, Edwards J, Jackson H. MCMI-II personality disorders in recent-onset bipolar disorders. *J Clin Psychol* 1992; 48: 320-329.

Winokur G. The Iowa 500: heterogeneity and course in manic-depressive illness (bipolar). *Compr Psychiatry* 1975; 16: 125-131.

Winokur G, Coryell W, Endicott J, Akiskal HS. Further Distinctions Between Manic-Depressive Illness (Bipolar Disorder) and Primary Depressive Disorder (Unipolar Depression). *Am J Psychiatry* 1993; 150: 1176-1181.

Winokur G, Coryell W, Keller M, Endicott J, Akiskal HS. A Prospective Follow-up of Patients With Bipolar and Primary Unipolar Affective Disorder. *Arch Gen Psychiatry* 1993; 50: 457-465.

Zimmerman M, Coryell W, Pfohl B, Corenthal C et al. ECT response in depressed patients with and without a DSM-III personality disorder. *Am J Psychiatry* 1986; 143: 1030-1032.

Zusky PM, Biederman J, Rosenbaum JF et al. Adjunct low dose lithium carbonate in treatment-resistant depression: a placebo-controlled study. *J Clin Psychopharmacol* 1988; 8: 120-124.

In: Focus on Bipolar Disorder Research
Editor: Malcomb R. Brown, pp. 167-194
ISBN 1-59454-059-4

Chapter 9

Late-Life Bipolar Disorder

Martha Sajatovic
Case University School of Medicine and
University Hospitals of Cleveland, Cleveland, Ohio
Subramoniam Madhusoodanan
St John's Episcopal Hospital, Far Rockaway, New York,
State University of New York, Health Science Center at Brooklyn, New York
Helen C. Kales
Section of Geriatric Psychiatry, University of Michigan, Ann Arbor, Michigan USA, and
Geriatric Psychiatry Clinic, VA National Serious Mental Illness Treatment Research and
Evaluation Center (SMITREC) Geriatric Research Education and Clinical Center,
Department of Veterans Affairs Ann Arbor Healthcare System, Ann Arbor, Michigan
Frederic C. Blow
Department of Psychiatry,
University of Michigan and Director, VA National Serious Mental Illness Treatment
Research and Evaluation Center (SMITREC),
Department of Veterans Affairs Ann Arbor Healthcare System, Ann Arbor, Michigan

Abstract

Bipolar Disorder among older adults is a problem that has gained recognition due to changes in population demographics and growing sophistication in the assessment and diagnosis of bipolar illness. Among older adults, bipolar illness may first manifest in young adulthood persisting into late life, or may be of more recent, later-life onset. Most, but not all research studies refer to "late-onset" bipolar illness as that which begins at age 50 or older. It has been proposed that patients with late-onset manic symptoms may have a disease process that is initiated by organic, particularly neurologic factors, whereas genetic factors may be more important in the genesis of early-onset mania.

Understudied issues in the area of late-life bipolar disorder include a clear definition of early vs. late-onset illness, an adequate understanding of illness presentation and course among older adults with bipolar illness, as well as a clear consensus as to what constitutes best treatments. Treatments for late-life bipolar disorder include pharmacologic as well as psychosocial interventions. There are very few published, controlled studies on drug treatments of bipolar disorder in older adults. The limited literature suggests that lithium, a mainstay of treatment in younger bipolar populations, may have limited usefulness due to poor tolerability in older populations and possibly less efficacy in secondary manic states. Finally, there are aging–related modifiers that affect treatment decisions for late-life bipolar illness including medical comorbidity, polypharmacy and access to care.

INTRODUCTION

Bipolar Disorder among older adults is a problem that has gained recognition due to changes in population demographics and growing sophistication in the assessment and diagnosis of bipolar illness. In the United States, it is estimated that by the year 2010, 40% of the population is expected to be 45 years of age or older (U. S. Bureau of the Census, 1996). This reflects a general aging trend in the population, and it is critical that health care providers, health care administrators and program planners are aware of the impact of a greater proportion of older adults in the population.

The Depression and Bipolar Support Alliance (DBSA) recently convened a Consensus Development Panel to review progress made during the past decade in late-life mood disorder, and to identify unmet needs in health care delivery and research. This Panel, composed of experts in late-life mood disorders, primary care, geriatrics, mental health and aging policy research and advocacy issued the conclusion, that despite the many advances made in safe and efficacious treatments, mood disorders remain a significant health care issue for the elderly (Charney 2003). Mood disorders in older adults are associated with functional decline, disability, reduced quality of life, increased mortality, substantial caregiver burden and increased health services utilization (Bartels 2000, Angst 2002, Charney 2003). Furthermore, the expert panel noted a critical need for improvements in diagnosis, treatment and delivery of services for older adults with mood disorders. In the area of bipolar disorder in later life, there is a paucity of controlled-treatment data (Cassano 2000, Sajatovic 2002). Therefore, clinicians have little evidence upon which to base treatment decisions beyond controlled trials involving mixed-aged participants or young adult participants, and uncontrolled clinical studies and case reports involving older patients (Colenda 2002). This chapter reviews the prevalence of bipolar disorder in later life, criteria and characteristics of late-life bipolar disorder, treatment guidelines, health resource use, complicating factors in management, and treatments for late-life bipolar disorder. Finally, future directions for research are summarized based upon current gaps in the literature on late-life bipolar disorder.

PREVALENCE OF BIPOLAR DISORDER

Bipolar Disorder I occurs in an estimated 0.4-1.6% of the general population, while Bipolar II occurs in an estimated 0.5% of the general population (Evans 2000, Bourdon 1992, American Psychiatric Association 1999, Regier 1984). In patients over 65 years of age, prevalence rates of bipolar disorder range from 0.1% to 0.4% (Van Gerpen 1999). It has been suggested that current prevalence estimates for bipolar disorder among older adults dwelling in the community may be artificially low as elderly patients tend to under-report psychiatric symptoms, may underutilize mental health systems or may be treated in non-hospital/non-clinic settings such as nursing homes where their mental disorders may remain undetected by surveys or standard assessment methods (McDonald 2000).

While it is generally believed that the incidence of mania declines with age (McDonald 2000, Loranger 1978, Mendlewicz 1972), there are contrasting reports that there is an increased incidence of new –onset mania among older adults (Goodwin 1984).

In clinical samples, numbers of older adults with bipolar disorder may vary depending on sample type or sample selection. Data from the Veterans Health Administration (VHA), which has a relatively high proportion of older adults utilizing mental health care services, indicate that nearly 25% of individuals with bipolar disorder (n = 16,330) are age 60 or older, and over 10% are age 70 and older (n = 8,148) (Sajatovic 2004).

It has been reported that 10% of all patients with bipolar disorder develop their illness after the age of 50, and 5%-12% of geriatric psychiatry admissions are for bipolar disorder (Yassa 1988, Van Gerpen 1999). Almeida and Fenner (2002) recently reported on the evaluation of a mental health service use registry involving over 6,000 individuals whose primary or secondary clinical diagnosis was bipolar disorder. In this report, most patients had an onset of illness between 15 and 45 years of age, but approximately 8% of individuals were aged 65 years or over at their time of first contact with mental health services. Interestingly, in this report, the relative frequency of late-onset bipolar disorder increased from 1% in 1980 to 11% in 1998 (Almeida 2002).

CRITERIA AND CHARACTERISTICS OF LATE-ONSET BIPOLAR DISORDER

Among older adults, bipolar illness may be that which has first manifested in young adulthood and persists into late life, or that which is of more recent, later-life onset. In some cases, occurrence of a first manic episode late in life may reflect a change in mood disorder polarity. Among elderly individuals with bipolar illness, depression precedes mania by an average of 20 years (Young 1992, Alexopoulos 1988). The National Institute of Mental Health (NIMH) Epidemiologic Catchment Area study found the median age of onset for bipolar disorder to be 19 years of age (Burke 1990), however it has been documented that bipolar disorder may first manifest as late as the eight or ninth decade of life (Sibisi 1990, Spicer 1973). Most, but not all research studies refer to "late-onset" bipolar illness as that which begins at age 50 or older.

Some researchers have suggested that late-onset mania is a distinct subtype of bipolar disorder associated with medical and neurological disorder. Goodwin and Jamison (1990) noted that individuals with late-onset bipolar disorder were: 1) less likely to have a positive family history of mood disorders; and 2) more likely to have concurrent medical and neurologic disorders when compared to cases of early onset mania. In terms of family history, Moorhead and colleagues (2003) found in a retrospective record review of 277 patients with bipolar disorder that age at first admission in those with a negative family psychiatric history was significantly older, with a skewed age distribution. This non-familial group contained significantly more individuals with a first admission at age 50 years and older. The authors concluded that patients with bipolar –I disorder whose age at first admission is 50 years or above may belong to a different etiological sub-group (Moorhead 2003). With regard to medical and neurological comorbidity, Cassidy and Carroll (2002) reported that late-onset mania occurred in 6.3% of retrospectively reviewed cases of mania from a mixed-age sample, and was associated with vascular risks/vascular disorder including smoking, hypertension, diabetes, coronary artery disease and atrial fibrillation. Beyond an association of mania with vascular risk factors, such illness may also be associated with brain changes; Rabins and colleagues (2000) have demonstrated that MRI assessments of elderly patients with unipolar and bipolar affective disorders are similar—left sylvian fissure and left and right temporal sulcal enlargement and bilateral cortical atrophy, which differs from normal elderly controls and elderly patients with schizophrenia.

With respect to symptom presentation, it has been suggested that individuals with late-onset bipolar mania have a manic presentation that is milder compared to that seen in younger individuals (Cassano 2000). However, there may be a tendency towards irritable behavioral characteristics (James 1977). Additionally, older adults with bipolar illness may present with mixed manic dysphoric or agitated states. Cognitive symptoms may mimic a dementia.

There is limited information on the course of late-life bipolar disorder, though it has been reported that such patients may exhibit chronicity (Ameblas 1987, Angst 1980), treatment resistance (Young and Falk 1989) and higher mortality rates (James, 1977, Shulman and Tohen 1994, Dhingra and Rabins 1991). With respect to mortality findings, Angst and colleagues (2002) reported on a group of over 400 hospitalized patients with affective disorders followed prospectively for 22 years or more. In this study, individuals with bipolar disorder had elevated mortality rates due to suicide and cardiovascular disease. In contrast to some reports that suggest that suicide risk occurs primarily early in the course of affective illness/around the time of hospital discharge, the study by Angst et al. (2002) demonstrated a persistent high suicide risk over decades for some individuals.

Secondary Mania

Secondary mania, described by Krauthammer and Klerman in 1978, refers to mania secondary to specific organic factors (Krauthammer 1978). Secondary mania is distinctly more common in older adults compared to younger individuals and is often due to central nervous system pathology, particularly right- sided lesions (Goodwin 1990). Secondary mania is noted to be particularly challenging to treat, as individuals with secondary mania are often refractory or poorly tolerant of lithium and may have complicating medical disorders (Evans 1995). Valproate and carbamazepine are widely prescribed medications in secondary mania due to generally better tolerability and efficacy in this population (McDonald 2000). In medical settings, bipolar disorder may not be accurately identified in older adults with both mania and organic brain syndromes (McDonald 1996). Finally, there has been very limited systematic research in the area of mood disorder associated with specific organic factors, and much of the available data is derived from single case reports, case series and small retrospective studies (Evans 1995). Some research suggests, that as in late-onset depression, there is evidence of subtle vascular disease in those with late-onset mania (Krishnan 2002). Vascular changes found include deep white matter and subcortical ischemic changes found on MRI (McDonald 1999).

Treatment Guidelines in Late-Life Bipolar Disorder

Currently available treatment guidelines generally do not provide specific recommendations for the treatment of older adults with bipolar illness (Van Gerpen 1999, American Psychiatric Association 2002). Common clinical practice has been to treat geriatric bipolar patients extrapolating from the treatment of younger individuals, making adjustments as needed in drug treatment based upon individual tolerability/adverse events (Van Gerpen 1999). However, given current demographic trends, and the growing proportion of older adults in the population, the development of more specialized guidelines may potentially improve health care and health outcomes for geriatric patients with mood disorders. Issues most relevant to older adults with bipolar disorder include clarification regarding possible differences in early vs. late-onset illness, variation in drug treatment response, drug tolerability related to the aging process, and the interface between medical comorbidity and symptom presentation. Finally, there may be age-related modifiers of response to commonly utilized psychotherapeutic interventions, an area that has received particularly limited attention by the research community. For example, it has been noted that both younger and older patients with bipolar disorder have decreased social support compared to individuals without bipolar disorder (Beyer 2003). Many psychotherapeutic interventions in bipolar disorder involve family members or the support of significant other individuals (Sajatovic, 2004). Young and middle-aged patients with impaired social support are more likely to be treatment- resistant and have increased hospitalization rates (Beyer 2003), however, the role of social support vis- a- vis psychotherapeutic interventions and treatments outcomes are not well understood in older populations.

The absence of evidence- and guideline-based treatment in late-life bipolar disorder is perhaps most clearly illustrated in providers' shift from prescribing lithium to valproic acid for older patients over the last decade. Shulman and colleagues (2003) recently analyzed this issue using data from a comprehensive Canadian drug benefits program during the time period from 1993 to 2001. Among older patients, the number of new valproate users surpassed new lithium users in 1997, with a steady decline in new lithium users and a steady increase in new valproate users between 1993 and 2000 (Shulman 2003). Given the use of valprote in behavioral disturbance found in dementia, the authors also performed an analysis excluding those with dementia and found that the trend was still similar. The authors questioned the relatively rapid shift in prescription patterns in the absence of evidence-based data, and suggested that before the use of lithium is abandoned, adequate evidence that valproate offers a comparable or superior efficacy, effectiveness and safety profile is needed (Shulman 2003).

Health Resource Use in Late-Life Bipolar Disorder

There is a paucity of studies examining health resource use in late-life bipolar disorder. As Bartels (2000) has noted, data suggest that late-life bipolar disorder may be persistent, chronic and refractory to treatment; thus, it is likely that the use of health care resources among elderly individuals with bipolar disorder may be substantial, even compared to older individuals with other serious mental disorders. Further, an understanding of the health resource needs of such patients can inform the development of appropriate treatment interventions.

Sajatovic et al. (1996) compared elderly veterans with bipolar disorder to those with schizophrenia and found substantial use of inpatient and pharmacy services by both groups, although older individuals with schizophrenia used significantly more inpatient hospital days. Bartels and colleagues (2000) examined mental health service use in elderly patients with bipolar disorder in comparison with elderly patients with unipolar major depression. These investigators found that bipolar elderly patients used almost four times the total amount of mental health services and were four times more likely to have had a psychiatric hospitalization in the previous 6 months as compared with elderly patients with depression. Older patients with bipolar disorder also had greater total symptom severity and impairment of community-living skills. A strength of the latter study was the identification of a bipolar sample that included those with primarily early-onset disease which allowed confirmation that a clinically significant subgroup of older patients with bipolar illness do not "burn out" with age (Bartels 2000).

There are few studies comparing older and younger patients with bipolar disorder. A recent VA study (Sajatovic 2004) found that older veterans (age 60 and older) with bipolar diagnoses compared to younger veterans with bipolar disorder had significantly longer hospital stays. In addition, older veterans with bipolar disorder had over twice the utilization of outpatient mental health visits as the youngest group of veterans (age less than 30).

Further research is needed into the services outcomes of both early- and late-onset mania. McDonald (1996) has noted that late-onset mania may be associated with poor recognition of mood symptoms by providers, resulting in increased caregiver burden, premature nursing home placement, and a more rapid functional decline. Similar to health services research studies of late-life depression, further studies on outcomes and health resource use in late-life bipolar disorder could help to answer the following questions: 1) does late-onset mania signal the development of an emerging dementia in a significant number of patients? ; 2) what are the patterns of nursing home utilization for older patients with early- and late-onset bipolar disorder?; 3) in addition to neurological diseases, what are the most common medical comorbidities associated with late-life bipolar disorder and how does bipolar illness affect the course of such comorbidities in terms of treatment adherence?; and 4) how prevalent is the treatment of late-life bipolar disorder in primary care settings and to what extent is such treatment guideline-concordant?

Complicating Factors: Medical Comorbidity, Psychiatric Comorbidity, Polypharmacy and Access to Care

Medical comorbidity is a key consideration among older patients with bipolar disorder, complicating both diagnosis and treatment. In terms of diagnosis, symptoms of bipolar disorder may overlap symptoms of delirium, dementia, medical illnesses and medication side effects (McDonald 2000). Treatment is also affected by medical comorbidity in terms of choice of medications. For example, lithium use may be precluded by renal disease or valproic acid use may be contraindicated due to liver problems or hematologic issues.

With regard to specific comorbidities, studies of mania have demonstrated a clear association with a heterogeneous group of neurological disorders (Shulman 1992), with cerebrovascular disease emerging as the most common medical condition to be associated with mania (Shulman 2002). It has also been suggested that individuals with bipolar disorder develop dementia at a much higher rate than older individuals without bipolar illness (Dhingra and Rabins 1991). Thus, just as a subtype of depression, "vascular depression", has been proposed based on the association of late-life depression with vascular disease and risk factors as well as MRI changes (Alexopoulos 1997), there might be a vascular subtype of mania (Steffens and Krishnan 1998). Further research is needed regarding the latter hypothesis.

Many older patients with bipolar disorder have concurrent mental health and substance abuse comorbidities. Unfortunately, the impact of these comorbidities on treatment outcomes and costs have not been studied specifically for older adults with bipolar disorder. Nonetheless, among patients of all ages diagnosed with bipolar disorder, McElroy and colleagues (2001) reported that 65% of those with bipolar disorder meet DSM-IV criteria for at least one additional comorbid lifetime axis I disorder. In particular, comorbid substance abuse and anxiety disorders are problematic and common among individuals with BPD (McElroy 2001), resulting in complex treatment needs and poor treatment outcomes. Comorbid PTSD among those with bipolar disorder appears to represent a truly separate disorder (Strakowski 1998, Blow 2004), yet little is known about the relationship of this comorbidity to treatment outcomes.

Cost and resource utilization studies examining the impact of comorbid mental health and substance abuse among those with bipolar disorder have been limited. While it has been reported that in VA and large state mental health systems the cost of care for patients with bipolar disorder is higher for those with comorbid disorders on an outpatient basis compared to other psychiatric outpatients, there may be less of a difference between bipolar disorder inpatients with comorbid diagnoses and other psychiatric patients (Hoff 1998, Hoff 1999, Dickey 1996, Bradley 1996). In private health care systems, patients with bipolar disorder and a primary substance abuse diagnosis are reported to have lower rates of use of all types of care compared to individuals with primary substance use disorder and no psychiatric comorbidity (Lyons 1989, Pirzada 1997). Research is urgently needed focused on optimizing treatment service delivery for patients with bipolar disorder in late life with comorbid mental health and substance abuse diagnoses, who have unique treatment needs that can have a substantial impact on treatment outcomes.

Another issue complicating the treatment and management of late-life bipolar illness and closely related to medical comorbidity is polypharmacy, or the number of total medications prescribed to older patients. Surveys of medication use in the elderly show that older adults use an average of 7 drugs each day (Cloyd 1994). Multi-drug regimens are independently associated with adverse drug reactions (ADRs) (Onder, 2002) and the incidence and severity of ADRs increase with age (Pollock, 1999).

In addition, adherence to psychotropic regimens is a major issue with bipolar patients of any age. Although there is a paucity of research on adherence in older individuals with bipolar illness, given that non-adherence rates climb with the total number of drugs prescribed (Salzman 1995), it is likely that non-adherence may be even more significant in those with late-life bipolar disease.

In terms of access to care, many older adults have age-related psychosocial problems that potentially complicate treatment in "real-world" settings. These include the need to see multiple medical providers, transportation issues, lack of social supports needed to assist with care and inadequate prescription drug coverage. The latter, along with inadequate insurance coverage are critical barriers to effective care (Charney 2003), especially for the vulnerable population of older patients with bipolar disorder.

TREATMENTS FOR LATE LIFE BIPOLAR DISORDER

General Medication Treatment Issues

Pharmacological treatment of older adults with bipolar disorder requires careful consideration of general aging-related modifiers including variations in drug absorption, distribution, metabolism, and CNS activity. Elderly individuals generally require modified (lower) dosing of psychotropic medications and are more prone to medication-induced adverse effects. In addition to reduced overall dosage, the speed of drug titration regimens also must be modified -- "slow and low", to minimize medication adverse effects.

The majority of psychotropic medications are administered orally. Possible aging-related changes in absorption may be related to impaired gastric acid secretion, a reduced rate of gastric emptying, and reduced intestinal absorptive surface. The amount of adipose tissue increases with aging, and may contribute to an increased volume of distribution (Greenblatt 1986). For most psychotropic medications, drug metabolism occurs primarily in the liver, with lithium being a notable exception. Generally the metabolic capacity of the liver declines with advancing age, and liver volume declines by approximately one-third between the third and tenth decade of life in both men and women (Bernus 1997). Phase I hepatic enzyme groups (P-450) show decreased rates of function, thus altering rates of elimination and extending elimination half-life (Willmore 2000). Kidney functioning decreases with age as well--the glomerular filtration rate in healthy elderly individuals has been reported to be in the range of 40-70% compared to young patients (Friedman 1972). Impaired renal function is a particularly relevant issue for drugs which are substantially excreted unchanged in the urine such as lithium (Dawling 1989).

While the above are general issues concerning psychotropic treatment in the elderly, it must be remembered that chronological age is not absolutely indicative of biological status, and thus, prescribing decisions should be based upon an individual's medical status and previous medication history. There is tremendous variability among elderly patients, and acute medical conditions may suddenly precipitate a crisis. An example of this is the elderly individual with bipolar illness, maintained for many years on a stable and therapeutic dose of lithium, who rapidly develops lithium toxicity in the context of flu symptoms and dehydration. Education of patients and families regarding appropriate monitoring and management of medications with a narrow therapeutic window will minimize potential of such emergent conditions.

Medication Treatments

Lithium

In younger populations lithium is a first-line treatment for bipolar mania (Goldberg, 2000, Poolsup 2000), and it has been reported that 50% or more of general populations with bipolar disorder receive lithium (Ahmed 2001, Levine 2000). However, in the elderly, lithium therapy may be problematic due to impaired tolerability, particularly in medically compromised individuals (Tueth 1998, McDonald 2000). Unfortunately, there are no published, randomized placebo-controlled trials of lithium in older adults. Thus, clinical recommendations are based on extrapolation from pharmacokinetic studies in healthy elderly individuals, anecdotal reports from mixed-age patient populations and clinical experience in geriatric psychiatry (Sproule 2000).

Although the absorption of lithium is generally unchanged by the aging process, the volume of distribution and renal clearance of lithium is substantially different in older adults compared to younger individuals (Foster 1992). A decrease in skeletal muscle mass and decrease in total body water occurs with aging, along with increased adipose tissue. Together, these changes lead to a decreased volume of distribution in the elderly (Foster 1992). Elimination half-life of lithium in older adults ranges from 28-36 hours, compared to approximately 24 hours in younger individuals (Chapron 1988, Shulman et al. 1987).

There are clinically significant pharmacokinetic drug interactions associated with lithium and other drugs commonly used in the elderly, such as thiazide diuretics, non-steroidal anti-inflammatory medications and ACE inhibitors. All of these agents may increase serum lithium concentrations (Sproule 2000). In patients with hypertension, congestive heart failure or renal dysfunction, reduced lithium clearance may be expected (Sproule 2000). Not surprisingly, the frequency of acute lithium toxicity in the elderly has been reported to range from 11-23% (Foster 1992). Lithium-associated adverse effects particularly relevant to the elderly include renal impairment and urinary frequency, cognitive impairment, ataxia/incoordination, tremor, increase in fasting blood glucose, weight gain, peripheral edema, and the worsening of chronic skin conditions and arthritis (Jefferson et al. 1987, McDonald 2000).

Eastham (1998) has noted that elderly patients with bipolar disorder typically require lithium dosages that are 25-50% lower than those used in younger individuals. It is known that neurotoxicity occurs in the elderly at concentrations considered "therapeutic" in younger-adult populations (Sproule 2000), and thus, determination of appropriate serum levels in the elderly is largely determined by medical status and frailty as well as chronological age. Close monitoring is known to improve outcome and minimize risk (Fielding 1999).

Chen (1999) has suggested that among older adults with classic mania and minimal neurologic pathology, lithium may be more efficacious than anticonvulsant medication, while older individuals with mixed mania appear to do equally well on lithium or valproate. In contrast, individuals with secondary mania appear to generally have a poor response to lithium (Evans 1995, McDonald 1996). Still, controlled trials are needed to clarify the role of lithium with respect to efficacy and tolerability in geriatric mania.

Anticonvulsant Drugs

As is the case with lithium therapy, there are currently no published, controlled trials with anticonvulsant compounds that specifically focus on late-life bipolar disorder. Clinical evidence for use in late-life bipolar disorder is thus generally compiled from bipolar studies in mixed-age populations, studies in older adults with seizure disorders, behavioral complications of dementia, and psychotic conditions other than bipolar disorder. However, the popularity of the anticonvulsant compound valproate has surpassed that of lithium in some clinical settings in spite of an absence of evidence-based data (Shulman 2003). A retrospective review by Sanderson (1998) analyzed the comparative efficacy of selected mood stabilizers including valproate, carbamazepine and lithium in 72 elderly patients with bipolar disorder treated on an inpatient psychiatric unit. Sanderson (1998) noted that while a major trend for the more frequent use of valproate was apparent, valproate use did not lead to significant changes in length of hospital stay or in functional outcome measures as compared to lithium and carbamazepine.

Valproate is used extensively for late-life bipolar disorder (Sajatovic 2004, Shulman 2003). Elderly patients (age range 68-89 years) have a reduced capacity to eliminate valproate compared to younger adults (age range: 22-26 years) (Depakote Tablet Product Information, 2001). Thus dosing should be started lower, and titrated more slowly in geriatric patients (Leppik, 2001). Uncontrolled trials in late-life bipolar disorder have suggested that valproate is safe and effective in older individuals with medical conditions, and that valproate augmentation of lithium may enable a greater safety range in the use of lithium in elderly patients (McFarland 1990, Puryear 1995, Schneider 1998, Mordecai 1999). Optimal dosing of valproate in late-life bipolar disorder has not been established with prospective trials. However, a small case series of elderly manic patients treated with valproate found that serum concentrations ranged from 50-75 mg/L at dosages of 1,000-1,500 mg/day.

With respect to practical issues of dosing/medication ingestion in the elderly, divalproex sodium is available in a sprinkle formulation (Fuller 2002) and a more recently introduced extended release formulation. Both of these alternative formulations offer potential benefits in elderly populations where pill swallowing may be a barrier to effective treatment.

The most common adverse effects associated with valproate are nausea, gastrointestinal symptoms, somnolence, and weight gain (Depakote Tablet Product Information, 2001). Hair thinning, thrombocytopenia, and dose-related elevations in selected liver enzymes may occur less commonly. Pancreatitis as well as serious hepatotoxicity are rare occurrences, and these risks appears lessened with increased age (Bowden 2003).

Lamotrigine is an anticonvulsant medication which has received US FDA approval for a bipolar indication based upon results of multiple controlled trials in mixed-age patients (Leadbetter 2002,Calabrese 1999, Calabrese 2000). Lamotrigine appears to have efficacy in acute bipolar depression as well as efficacy in preventing mood relapse overall and depressive relapse in particular. However, lamotrigine has not been well studied in geriatric populations, and there are no published, controlled trials. A recent small, open label trial by Robillard and Conn (2002) involved lamotrigine therapy for 5 elderly women with bipolar disorder (average age 71.5 years, range 65-85). Lamotrigine was well tolerated in this group of older bipolar women, although one patient developed dose-dependent coarse hand tremor on lamotrigine therapy. Symptom remission, defined as a 50% or greater improvement in Hamilton Depression Rating Scale (HDRS) score, occurred in 3 out of 5 patients by six weeks of treatment.

In younger populations, adverse effects associated with lamotrigine are primarily headache and nausea (Calabrese 1999, Calabrese 2000). In a study comparing lamotrigine and carbamazepine in elderly patients with epilepsy, lamotrigine was the better tolerated of the two compounds (Brodie 1999). Dosing in mixed-age populations ranges from 50-200 mg/day. The dose of lamotrigine should be halved if given concurrently with valproate, which inhibits the metabolism of lamotrigine (Calabrese 2002). Dose titration commonly requires several weeks in younger populations in order to minimize potential hypersensitivity reactions/rash (Leadbetter 2002), and slow, incremental dosing appears prudent in older populations as well (Robillard 2002). Serious skin rash (Stevens Johnson Syndrome) has been reported with lamotrigine (Lamictal Product Information). The incidence of rash with lamotrigine may be increased with high initial dosing, more rapid dose titration or with concomitant use of valproate (Messenheimer 1998, Lamictal Product Information).

Carbamazepine is widely used in clinical settings for the treatment of bipolar disorder in spite of the fact that recent studies in mixed populations suggest that carbamazepine is inferior to both lithium in the long-term treatment of classic bipolar illness and to valproate in acute mania (Greil 1998,Vasudev 2000, Bowden 2003). However, it has been suggested that carbamazepine may offer some advantage in individuals with atypical bipolar disorder (Greil 1998), and may be of particular relevance in older adult populations where bipolar symptoms secondary to neurological illness are a greater concern (Evans, 1995).

Battino and colleagues (2003) recently found that carbamazepine apparent oral clearance (CL/F) is decreased in an age-dependent manner in older patients, presumably because of a reduction in the rate of CYP 3A4- mediated drug metabolism. Compared to corresponding controls, mean carbamazepine CL/F values are 23% lower in elderly patients receiving carbamazepine monotherapy. As in younger patients, carbamazepine metabolism is auto-induced in the elderly (Battino 2003, Leppik 2001), however metabolic rates still remain considerably below younger patients (Battino 2003).

Carbamazepine may cause drowsiness, dizziness, lightheadedness, nausea and ataxia (Leppik 2001, McDonald 2000). Cognitive impairments may occur as well, and are of special concern in the elderly (Hirsch 2003). Hyponatremia secondary to syndrome of inappropriate antidiuretic hormone secretion (SIADH), skin rashes and blood dyscrasias are additional uncommon possible side effects (Leppik 2001, Cates 1998).

Other novel anticonvulsants including oxcarbazepine, gabapentin, topiramate and zonisamide have been reported to be of benefit in mixed-age populations (Keck 2002, Chengappa 2001,Calabrese 2001, Kanba 1994, Evins 2003), however minimal data is available on these agents in late-life bipolar disorder. In some instances, compounds that have not showed promise in controlled trials with mixed-age populations could potentially be of benefit to some special populations with bipolar disorder, such as the elderly or treatment-refractory individuals. Sethi and colleagues (2003) recently reported on a small case series (N=7) in which gapapentin appeared effective in geriatric mania with excellent tolerability, while Madhusoodanan (2002) recently published a case report of topiramate as adjunctive therapy in an elderly patient with treatment-refractory bipolar disorder. Controlled trials in geriatric bipolar populations are needed to answer more fully questions regarding the potential usefulness of other novel anticonvulsants for the treatment of late-life bipolar disorder.

Antipsychotic Medications

Conventional Antipsychotics

Although conventional antipsychotics have been used as monotherapy and adjunctive therapy in bipolar mania, their use has been limited in the elderly because of side effects which increase morbidity in geriatric patients. These side effects include extrapyramidal, cardiovascular, anticholinergic and tardive dyskinetic symptoms. Conventional antipsychotics also have been reported to cause depression in patients with bipolar disorder (Sachs 2000, Sernyak 1994). The risk of tardive dyskinesia is higher in patients with bipolar disorder compared to schizophrenia (Hunt 1991, Murkherjee 1986), and the incidence of both extrapyramidal symptoms (EPS) and tardive dyskinesia (TD) increases with age (Kane 1995). Antipsychotic-induced parkinsonism has been noted in over 60% of elderly patients receiving conventional antipsychotics (Hoffman 1991). The incidence of new onset TD among elderly patients treated with conventional antipsychotics is reported to range from 31% (Woerner, 1998) to 37% (Jeste, 1999). Thus EPS may be a particularly problematic issue for older individuals with bipolar disorder.

However, conventional antipsychotics remain an effective treatment for acute mania. A recent mixed-age comparison study of olanzapine vs haloperidol indicated that both drugs did not differ in achieving overall remission of bipolar mania (Tohen et al. 2003). Conventional agents may still have a role in the treatment of geriatric patients with bipolar disorder who are unable or unwilling to take atypical antipsychotic agents.

Atypical Antipsychotics

Atypical antipsychotics are a welcome addition to the treatment options for elderly patients with bipolar disorder. The antipsychotic agents which are currently approved by the U.S. Food and Drug Administration (FDA) for short-term therapy of bipolar I mania are olanzapine, risperidone, quetiapine, ziprasidone and aripiprazole.

Published, controlled studies of atypical antipsychotics in geriatric mania are limited. Olanzapine, risperidone, quetiapine, ziprasidone and aripiprazole have been found to be effective and safe in controlled double-blind studies in mixed-age samples as monotherapy and or adjunct therapy (Hirschfeld 2003, Segal 2003). As with data on mood stabilizing medications, much of the information about atypical antipsychotic agents in geriatric bipolar disorder has to be extrapolated from mixed population studies and elderly samples with schizophrenia or schizoaffective disorder and dementia. More controlled double blind studies and head to head comparison studies are needed to establish the efficacy and safety of atypical antipsychotics in elderly patients with bipolar disorder.

Clozapine

Use of clozapine in geriatric bipolar disorder is limited to treatment-refractory conditions in view of the risk for serious side effects such as agranulocytosis. Alvir et al. (1993) report that older age is associated with an increased risk for agranulocytosis. Women may also be at a greater risk for leukopenia. Side effects of particular concern in the elderly include sedation, postural hypotension, anticholinergic side effects, and increased risk for seizures. Side effects can lead to delirium and/or falls. Metabolic side effects such as weight gain, hypertriglyceridemia and hyperglycemia also may occur. Hyperglycemia has been noted to occur in over 50% of individuals receiving long-term clozapine treatment, and the elevated risk of developing diabetes may continue as long as the treatment (Henderson 2000). The potential for serious complications such as diabetic ketoacidosis should be monitored during clozapine treatment. There is also a recent FDA black box warning regarding the incidence of myocarditis associated with clozapine.

Open- label studies with clozapine in mixed-age samples with bipolar disorder suggest marked symptom improvement when used as monotherapy or augmentation therapy (Hirschfeld 2003). Open label studies in bipolar disorder in adults also suggest that clozapine has greater antimanic than antidepressant properties and has shown promise as an antimanic drug for patients who do not respond to first-line agents (Frye 1998).

There are case reports regarding clozapine use in elderly bipolar patients. (Schulman 1997). Sajatovic et al. (1998) noted improvement, in an open label trial of 329 older adults with treatment-refractory serious mental illness (mean age 63.4 years), with patients 55-64 years of age showing better response that those 65 years or older. In spite of the potential adverse effects, clozapine does have a role in the treatment of bipolar disorder in the elderly when older patients are refractory to other medications, have severe extrapyramidal side effects, or have tardive dyskinesia. The recommended starting dose of clozapine in the elderly is 6.25mg/day with slow titration and a maximum dose of 400mg/day.

Risperidone

Risperidone has recently been approved by the FDA for treatment of bipolar disorder. Hirschfeld (2003) has recently reviewed the role of risperidone for the treatment of bipolar disorder and notes overall good tolerability and efficacy (Hirschfeld 2003). A long- acting, injectable formulation of risperidone has been approved by the FDA, and a rapidly dissolving oral preparation has also been recently introduced.

There are case reports and retrospective studies indicating improvement with risperidone in elderly bipolar patients (Madhusoodanan 1995, Madhusoodanan 1999). A prospective nine month longitudinal study compared the cumulative incidence of TD with risperidone and haloperidol in older patients with a variety of conditions, including mood disorders (Jeste 1999). Patients treated with haloperidol were significantly more likely to develop TD than patients treated with risperidone ($p<0.05$), as suggested by lifetable analysis.

The recommended starting dose of risperidone in the elderly is 0.5mg once or twice a day. The dose may be titrated slowly up to a target dose of 1 to 3 mg/day. The long- acting injectable form of risperidone has been found to be safe and effective in a 12- month open label trial in symptomatically stable schizophrenia patients (mean age 48.3+1.6 range 18-74). The initial dose of long acting risperidone is 25mg IM every two weeks for adults with schizophrenia.

A recent international double-blind study examined the use risperidone and olanzapine in elderly patients (mean age 71.1) with schizophrenia or schizoaffective disorder. In this study, Jeste et al. (2003) found that elderly patients with chronic schizophrenia or schizoaffective disorder receiving appropriate doses of risperidone (2mg/day median dose) or olanzapine (10mg/day median dose), over an 8 week period experienced significant reductions in severity of psychotic and extrapyramidal symptoms, with a relatively low risk of side effects.

There are no published, double-blind, controlled studies of risperidone in geriatric bipolar disorder. Advantages of risperidone in the elderly include minimal anticholinergic and sedative effects (Davidson 2000). Side effects of concern in the elderly include dose-dependant EPS, postural hypotension (Madhusoodanan 2002) and increased risk for cerebrovascular events in elderly patients with dementia (Risperidone Product information 2002).

Olanzapine

Olanzapine is an atypical antipsychotic agent, approved by the FDA for use in bipolar disorder. Hirschfeld (2003) and Mollen and Nasrallah (2003) have reviewed several double-blind studies of olanzapine in adults as monotherapy for mania, comparative study with divalproex in acute mania, combination therapy with lithium or valproate and in depression in bipolar disorder. In mixed-age samples, olanzapine has been found to be superior to placebo, superior or equally efficacious as divalproex and demonstrated superior efficacy when added to lithium or valproate (Hirschfeld 2003, Mollen and Nasrallah 2003). Patients treated with combined therapy experienced more adverse events which included somnolence, dry mouth, weight gain, increased appetite, tremor, asthenia, depression, headache, dizziness, diarrhea, nervousness and thirst.

There are no published double-blind controlled studies of olanzapine in geriatric bipolar disorder. In a subset analysis of 8 elderly patients (age range 61-67 years) from a double-blind placebo controlled study of a group of 139 patients with bipolar disorder, Street et al. (2000) reported improvement with olanzapine and worsening with placebo. The mean modal dose was 16mg/day. Bayer et al. (2001) reported on a within- group treatment response of older adults (age > 50 years) with acute mania treated with placebo, divalproex or olanzapine in the olanzapine clinical trials database. Among 94 older adults (mean age 57.1 years range 50.1-74.8 years) participating in a 3- week treatment period, these were 47 individuals treated with olanzapine, 31 treated with divalproex, and 16 who received placebo. In this report, patients treated with olanzapine or divalproex but not placebo, demonstrated improvement as indexed by the Young Mania Rating Scale (YMRS). Safety findings were comparable with previously published reports of both agents.

The recommended dose of olanzapine in elderly patients with bipolar disorders is in the range of 5.0 –10mg/day. A rapidly dissolving oral preparation of olanzapine as well as a short-acting intramuscular preparation are also available. Advantages of olanzapine in the elderly include the low incidence of EPS.

Areas of concern include the potential for sedation, weight gain and diabetes mellitus. Recently 25 deaths have been reported in association with olanzapine-induced ketoacidosis primarily in younger patients. (Koller et al. 2002, Meatherall and Younes 2002, Torney and Swalwell 2003).

Quetiapine

Quetiapine is an atypical antipsychotic medication with an FDA indication for the treatment of bipolar mania. Quetiapine has been found to be effective and safe as adjunctive therapy to mood stabilizers for the treatment of acute mania in adults in a 3-week double blind, placebo controlled trial (Sachs 2002). Adverse events included somnolence, headaches, dry mouth, asthenia, orthostatic hypotension, and dizziness.

Quetiapine is reported to have beneficial effects in elderly bipolar patients in case reports (Madhusoodanan 2000, Sicuro 2003) and open-label studies (Tarriot 2000) and may offer some advantages in the treatment of elderly patients with mood disorders particularly with respect to low potential for EPS (Yeung 1999, Jeste 1999, Tarriot 1999, McManus 1999). Quetiapine has been associated with minimal EPS in a 52 -week open label trial in older adults with psychosis secondary to various conditions including bipolar disorder (McManus 1999, Tarriot 2000).

The starting dose of quetiapine is 25mg once or twice daily, titrated in increments of 25mg once or twice daily to initial target dose of 100mg/day. Further dosage increment of 50mg every one to three days up to 800mg can be made. Higher doses are being increasingly used in older adults (Madhusoodanan 2000, Sicuro 2003.) In a case series of 8 elderly patients (mean age 67.6 years) Sicuro (2003) reported that quetiapine treatment was efficacious (mean dose 312.5mg/day range 50-600mg/day), and well tolerated.

Advantages of quetiapine include minimal EPS and anticholinergic side effects. Side effects of concern with quetiapine in the elderly include sedation, dizziness and postural hypotension.

Ziprasidone

Ziprasidone is an atypical antipsychotic with an FDA indication for bipolar mania which is currently available as an oral and an intramuscular preparation. Studies of intramuscular administered ziprasidone for treatment of agitation included mixed cohorts of patients including individuals with bipolar mania. Results of these studies, although not being specific for patients with bipolar disorder or the elderly, suggest that 10mg of intramuscular ziprasidone is likely to be an efficacious and well tolerated for treating manic agitation in many patients, and may be superior to intramuscular haloperidol. A number of studies have reported no significant QTc prolongation associated with ziprasidone (Brook 2000, Lesem 2001, Daniel 2001). While the potential for QTc prolongation is a concern for the elderly who are already at higher risk in view of advanced age and comorbidities (Pfizer Inc 2000), there are early reports of good tolerability of ziprasidone therapy for elderly patients with various psychiatric diagnosis (Berkowitz 2003, Etemad 2003, Loebel 2003).

In a double-blind placebo controlled trial of 202 patients with bipolar I disorder treated with ziprasidone (80-160mg/day) or placebo, ziprasidone was superior to placebo in improving manic symptoms and global illness severity. The sample included 23% in the 45-64 age group and 3.6% in the $\geq$ 65 age group. Rapid improvement in mania (within 2 days) was observed with ziprasidone but not with placebo. There was no significant QTc prolongation, and ziprasidone was well tolerated. Adverse events included somnolence, headache, EPS, dizziness, akathesia, nausea, tremor, abnormal vision, asthenia, constipation, dry mouth and dystonia (reported in $\geq$ 5% of ziprasidone treated patients (Segal et al. 2003.)

The usual dosage range of ziprasidone in adults is 20mg bid to 80mg bid (Fuller 2002). Dosage in the elderly appears to be in the same range as for younger adults. Advantages of ziprasidone include availability of a paranteral form which may be beneficial in acute mania, and minimal EPS, anticholinergic, sedative or weight-gain related side effects. An area of concern is the potential for prolongation of QTc interval and resultant complications in the elderly who are vulnerable due to age, comorbidities and concomitant medications (Geodon Prescribing Information 2003).

Aripiprazole

Aripiprazole is the most recent atypical antipsychotic marketed in the US. Aripiprazole has an FDA indication for treatment of bipolar mania. There are no published reports of aripiprazole use in elderly bipolar patients. A double- blind, 3-week study of aripiprazole in adults with bipolar mania showed that aripiprazole was superior to placebo by day 4 of treatment. A second study showed comparable efficacy with haloperidol at week 3, and significantly better response compared to haloperidol at week 12 (Keck et al. 2002, Bourin 2003). The most common adverse events were akathesia, dyspepsia and constipation. Preliminary reports on use in elderly patients with dementia suggest that aripiprazole at a mean dose of 10mg/day is well tolerated (DeDyn et al. 2003). The most common adverse events (aripiprazole compared to placebo) reported in clinical trials include UTI (8% vs 12%), accidental injury (8% vs 5%), somnolence (8% vs 1%), bronchitis (6% vs 3%) and EPS related events (5% vs 4%).

The dosage range of aripiprazole for general populations is 10-30 mg/day (Abilify Product Information 2002). Initial starting dose of aripiprazole in most elderly patients is 5-10 mg/day. Advantages of aripiprazole include minimal EPS, anticholinegic, sedative, metabolic, hematologic or QTc prolongation related side effects. However, further data are needed in geriatric population to make definitive conclusions.

Antidepressants

The role of antidepressants in bipolar depression is complicated by their tendency to induce "switching" into mania. According to the Expert Consensus Guidelines (Sachs et al. 2000) on treatment of bipolar disorder, a general preference for management of mild depression is for use of a mood stabilizer alone. However, patients with moderate or severe acute bipolar depression and those who do not respond to mood stabilizers alone, require effective antidepressant treatment. (Moller et al. 2000, Grunze et al. 2002).

For elderly patients, newer antidepressants such as selective serotonin reuptake inhibitors (SSRI's), buproprian and venlafaxine are recommended because of their lower risk for sedation, orthostasis, anticholinegic effects and cardiovascular adverse effects. (Gareri et al. 2000; Oshima and Higuchi 1999; Gerner 1985). In addition, novel antidepressants such as SSRIs appear to have a lower risk of inducing switch to mania compared with tricyclic antidepressants (TCAs) (Moller and Nasralla 2003). Antidepressants should be avoided in patients with rapid cycling. Older TCAs are not generally recommended in the elderly in view of their high potential to cause sedation, anticholineric, orthostatic and cardiovascular side effects. The World Federation of Societies of Biological Psychiatry (WFSBP) recommends the combination of an antidepressant and a mood stabilizer as a first line approach for all bipolar depressed patients (Grunze et al. 2002).

Lithium may have antidepressant effects in the elderly (Oshima and Higuchi 1999). Lamotrogine may also be a well-tolerated and effective treatment for bipolar depression in geriatric patients (Rhodes 2000). Recent data from the Stanley Bipolar Network indicate that the combination of lithium or other mood stabilizers with an antidepressant in a 1 -year follow up is superior in preventing depressive relapses compared with long term monotherapy with a mood stabilizer. (Altshuler, in press). The role of monoamine oxidase inhibitors in elderly bipolar depressed patients is limited, as in younger adults, because of their serious adverse effect profile, need for dietary restriction, and potential cycle acceleration or induction of mania in some patients. (Fuller and Sajatovic 2001, Altshuler et al. 1995). Stimulants such as methylphenidate may have moderate efficacy in geriatric mood disorder (Oshima and Higuchi 1999; Fuller and Sajatovic 2001), however the risk of precipitation of mania must be considered.

The combination of an atypical antipsychotic and an SSRI appears to be more effective than either agent alone for treatment resistant depression (Shelton et al. 2001). In a recent large international multisite, double- blind, 8- week randomized, controlled trial of olanzapine 5-20 mg/day (n=370) or olanzapine-fluoxetine combination, 6 and 25, 6 and 50, or 12 and 50 mg/day (n=86) or placebo (n=377), Tohen et al. (2003) found that olanzapine is more effective than placebo, and combined olanzapine-fluoxetine is more effective than olanzapine and placebo in the treatment of bipolar 1 depression without increased risk of developing mania symptoms.

Other medications used in bipolar disorders include benzodiazepines, thyroid hormones, nimodipine, omega-3 fatty acids, calcium channel blockers, inositol and buspirone. However their use is not well supported by controlled trials. Use of combination treatments is common in the elderly. This should be monitored closely in view of the age related pharmacokinetic and pharmacodynamic changes, comorbidities and other concomitant medications in the geriatric population.

Psychosocial Treatments

The last several decades have witnessed dramatic improvements in both the psychosocial and pharmacological treatment of mood disorders (Frank 2001). Although medication management is known to be an essential component of bipolar disorder treatment, specific forms of psychotherapy are also critical for many individuals with bipolar illness (American Psychiatric Association Guidelines, 2002). The primary goals of psychotherapeutic treatment are to reduce distress and improve the patient's inter-episode functioning as well as decrease the likelihood and severity of future episodes (Kahn 1993). Studies of psychotherapies that have been reported to be of benefit in older adults include family therapy, group therapy and cognitive behavioral therapy (Scogin and McElreath 1994, Teri et al., 1994, Kodar et al. 1996), however psychotherapeutic interventions specific to late-life bipolar disorder have not been well-studied. It is likely that successful therapeutic psychotherapeutic interventions for late-life bipolar disorder will need to clearly address common aging–related issues such as physical illness, retirement and job loss, loss of societal and financial status, and changes in interpersonal relationships due to illness or death. Treatment adherence, which is a major issue in mixed-age populations is likely to be a continued concern in late-life, perhaps complicated by increased medication administration complexity and reduced social support (Cloyd 1994, Beyer 2003).

Conclusions

The last decade has seen rapid growth in our understanding of bipolar disorder and proliferation of effective drug treatments as well as psychosocial interventions. Unfortunately there are still substantial gaps in understanding of illness phenomenology and treatment for late-life bipolar disorder. Understudied issues in the area of late-life bipolar disorder include a clear definition of early vs. late-onset illness, an adequate understanding of illness presentation and course among older adults with bipolar illness, as well as a clear consensus as to what constitutes best pharmacological treatments. Treatments for late-life bipolar disorder include medications as well as psychosocial interventions. There are very few published, controlled studies on drug treatments of bipolar disorder in older adults. The limited literature suggests that lithium; a mainstay of treatment in younger bipolar populations may have limited usefulness due to poor tolerability in older populations and possibly less efficacy in secondary manic states. Randomized, controlled trails comparing lithium to anticonvulsant therapy in geriatric patients with bipolar disorder are greatly needed to clarify clinical concerns regarding optimally effective pharmacologic agents in this population. Finally, there are additional aging –related modifiers that are understudied, yet critically affect treatment decisions for late-life bipolar illness including medical comorbidity, polypharmacy and access to care.

REFERENCES

Abilify (aripiprazole) product information. *Otsuka America Pharmaceutical Inc.*, Rockville M.D., 20850 U.S.A. and *Bristol-Myers Squibb Co.,* Princeton, N.J. 08543 U.S.A., November 2002.

Ahmed Z, Anderson IM. Treatment of bipolar affective disorder in clinical practice. *Journal of Psychopharmacology*. 2001; 15(1): 55-57.

Alexopoulos GS, Meyers BS, Young RC, Campbell S, Silbersweig D, Charlson M. 'Vascular depression' hypothesis. *Archives of General Psychiatry* 1997: 54: 915-922.

Alexopoulos FS, Young RC, Meyers BS, et al. Late onset depression. *Psychiatric Clin North America* 1988: 4: 329-337.

Almeida OP, Fenner S. Bipolar disorder: similarities and differences between patients with illness onset before and after 65 years of age. *International Psycho geriatrics*. 2002: 14(3): 311-22.

Altshuler LL, Suppes T, Black D, et al. Impact of antidepressant discontinuation after acute remission from bipolar depression on rates of depressive relapse on one-year follow-up. *Am J Psychiatry*, In press.

Altshuler LL, Post RM, Leverich GS, et al. Antidepressant-induced mania and cycle acceleration: a controversy revisited. *Am J Psychiatry* 1995; 152:1130-1138. .

Alvir JM, Lieberman JA, Safferman AZ, Schwimmer JL, Schaaf JA. Clozapine-induced agranulocytosis: incidence and risk factor in the United States. *N Engl J Med.* 1993; 329: 162-167.

Ameblas A. Life events and mania. *British Journal of Psychiatry* 1987: 150:235-240._.

American Psychiatric Association. APA online practice guidelines for the treatment of patients with bipolar disorder: disease definition, epidemiology, and natural history. vailable at: *http://www.pysch.org/clin_res/pg_bipolarL.html*. Accessed December 1999.

American Psychiatric Association. Practice Guideline for the Treatment of Patients With Bipolar Disorder [Revision]. *Am J Psychiatry* 2002; 159:1-50. .

Angst J. Clinical typology of bipolar illness, in *Mania: An Evolving Concept.* Edited by Belmaker RH, van Praag HM. Lancaster, MTP Press, 1980.

Angst F, Stassen HH, Clayton PJ, angst J. Mortality of patients with mood disorders: follow-up over 34-38 years. *Journal of Affective Disorders*. 2002: 68(2-3): 167-81.

Bartels SJ, Forester B, Miles KM, Joyce T. Mental health service use by elderly patients with bipolar disorder and unipolar major depression. *American Journal of Geriatric Psychiatry* 2000: 8:160-166.

Battino D, Corci D, Rossini A, et al. Serum carbamazepine concentrations in elderly patients: a case-matched pharmacokinetic evaluation based on therapeutic drug monitoring data. *Epilepsia*. 2003:44(7): 923-9.

Bayer JL, Siegal A, Kennedy JS, Kaiser C, Tohen K, Berg P, Street J, Baker R, Tohen M, Tollefson G, Breier A. *Olanzapine, divalproex, and placebo treatment, non-head to head comparisons of older adult acute mania. Institute on Psychiatric Services Annual Meeting. October, 2001. Orlando, FL.*

Berkowitz A. *Experience with ziprasidone in elderly patients: case series. Second Annual Dementia Congress*, September 2003, Washington, DC.

Bernus I, Dickenson RG, Hooper WD, Eadie MJ. Anticonvulsant therapy in aged patients. Clinical phamacokinetic considerations. *Drugs Aging* 1997; 10(4): 278-89.

Bernus I, Dickinson RG, Hooper WD, Eadie MJ. Anticonvulsant therapy in aged patients. *Clinical Pharmacology*.1997: 10(4): 278-289.

Beyer JL, Kuchibhatia M, Looney C, Engstrom E, Cassidy F, Krishnan Kr. Social support in elderly patients with bipolar disorder. *Bipolar Disorder* 2003: 5(1): 22-7.

Blow F, Sajatovic M, Ignacio R.*Substance abuse and post-traumatic stress disorder among individuals with bipolar disorder. Presented at the American Association of Geriatric Psychiatry 17th Annual Meeting, Baltimore, Maryland. Feb. 2004.*

Bourdon KH, Rae DS, Locke BZ, et al. *Estimating the prevalence of mental disorders in U.S. adults from the Epidemiologic Catchment Area Survey. Public Health rep* 1992: 107: 663-668.

Bourin M, Aubry P, Marcus RN et al. Aripiprazole versus haloperidol for maintained treatment effect in acute mania. In: *New Research Abstracts of the 156th Annual meeting of the American Psychiatric Association;* May 20, 2003; San Francisco, Calif. Abstract NR 467:175.

Bowden CL. Acute and maintenance treatment with mood stabilizers. *International Journal of Neuropsychopharmacology* 2003; 6(3): 269-75.

Bradley CJ, Zarkin GA. Inpatients stays for patients diagnosed with severe psychiatric disorders and substance abuse. *Health Services Research* 31: 387-408, 1996.

Brodie MJ, Overstall PW, Giorgi L. The UK Lamotrigine Elderly Study Group. Multicentre, double-blind, randomized comparison between lamotrigine and carbamazepine in elderly patients with newly diagnosed epilepsy. *Epilepsy Research* 1999; 37: 81-7.

Brook S, Lucey JV, Gunn KP. Intramuscular ziprasidone compared with intramuscular haloperidol in the treatment of acute psychosis. *J Clin Psychiatry* 2000; 61:933-941.

Burke KC, Burke JD, Regier DA, et al. Age at onset of selected mental disorder in five community populations. *Arc Gen Psychiatry* 1990: 47: 511-518.

Calabrese JR, et al. *A placebo-controlled study of topiramate in acute mania. Munich: European College of Neuropsychopharmacology (ECNP) annual meeting,* 2000.

Calabrese JR, Keck PE, McElroy SL, Shelton MD. A pilot study of topiramate as monotherapy in the treatment of acute mania. *J Clinical Psychopharmacology* 2001;21: 340-342.

Calabrese JR, Bowden CL, Sachs GS, et al., for the Lamictal 602 Study Group A double-blind placebo-controlled, prophylaxis study of lamotrigine in rapid-cycling bipolar disorder. *Journal of Clinical Psychiatry* 2000; 61: 841-850.

Calabrese, JR, Bowden CL, Sachs GS, et al., for the Lamictal 602 Study Group. A double-blind placebo-controlled study of lamotrigine monotherapy in outpatients with bipolar I depression. *Journal of Clinical Psychiatry* 1999; 60: 79-88.

Calabrese JR, Shelton MD, Rapport DJ, Kimmel SE. Bipolar disorders and the effectiveness of novel anticonvulsants. *Journal of Clinical Psychiatry* 2002; 63(suppl 3). 5-9.

Cassano GB, McElroy SL, Brady K, et al. Current issues in the identification and management of bipolar spectrum disorders in "special populations". *Journal of Affective Disorders* 2000; 59(suppl. 1): S69-S79.

Cassidy F, Carroll BJ. Vascular risk factors in late onset mania. *Psychological Medicine* 2002, 32, 359-362.

Cates M, Powers R. Concomitant rash and blood dyscrasia in geriatric psychiatry patients treated with carbamazepine. *Annals of Pharmacotherapy* 1998; 32(9): 884-7.

Chapron DJ. Comment on pharmacokinetics of lithium in the elderly. *Journal of Clinical Psychopharmacology* 1988; 8: 78.

Charney DS, Reynolds CF, Lebowitz BL, et al. Depression and bipolar support alliance consensus statement on the unmet needs in diagnosis and treatment of mood disorders in late life. *Archives of General Psychiatry* 2003; 60(7): 664-72.

Chen ST, Altshuler LL, Melnyk KA, et al. Efficacy of lithium vs. valproate in the treatment of mania in the elderly: a retrospective study. *Journal of Clinical Psychiatry* 1999; 60: 181-186.

Chengappa KNR, Gershon S, Levine J. The evolving role of topiramate among other mood stabilizers in the management of bipolar disorder. *Bipolar Disorder* 2001; 3: 215-232.

Colenda CC. Mania in late life: The challenges of treating older adults. *Geriatrics*.2002; 57(10)50-54.

Cloyd JC, Locker TE. Antiepileptic drugs in the elderly: pharmacoepidemiology and pharmacokinetics. *Archives of Family Medicine* 1994: 3: 589-98.

Daniel DG, Potkin SG, Reeves KR, Swift RH, Harrigan EP. Intramuscular (IM) ziprasidone 20mg is effective in reducing acute agitation associated with psychosis: a double-blind, randomized trial. *Psychopharmacology* (Berl) 2001; 155:128-134.

Davidson M, Harvey PD, Varvarcke J, et al. A long-term, multicenter, open-label study of risperidone in elderly patients with psychosis. *International Journal of Geriatric Psychiatry* 2000: 15: 506-514.

Dawling S, Crome P. Clinical pharmacokinetic considerations in the elderly: an update. *Clinical Pharmacokinetics* 1989: 17(4): 236-63.

DeDeyn P, Jeste DV, Auby P, et al. Aripiprazole in dementia of the Alzheimer's type. *American Association of Geriatric Psychiatry* March 2003 Honolulu, Hawaii.

Depakote® Tablet Product Information, 2001. Divalproex sodium delayed-release tablets, Abbott Laboratories, Abbott Park, IL.

Dhingra U, Rabins PV. Mania in the elderly: a 5-7 year follow-up. *Journal of the American Geriatrics Society* 1991:39:581-583.

Dickey B, Azeni H. Persons with dual diagnosis of substance abuse and major mental illness: their excess costs of psychiatric care. *American Journal of Public Health* 1996, 86: 973-977.

Eastham JH, Jeste DV, Young RD. Assessment and treatment of bipolar disorder in the elderly. *Drugs Aging* 1998; 12(3): 205-24.

Etemad B. *IM and oral ziprasidone in elderly patients with acute psychosis. American Psychiatric Association 55th Institute on Psychiatric Services, November 1, Boston, Massachusetts.*

Evans DL, Byerly MY, Greer RA. Secondary mania: diagnosis and treatment. *Journal of Clinical Psychiatry* 1995 ;56, 31-37.

Evans D. Bipolar disorder: diagnostic challenges and treatment consideration. *J Clin Psychiatry* 2000: 61(Suppl 13): 26-31.

Evins AE. *Efficacy of newer anticonvulsant medications in bipolar spectrum mood disorder.* 2003; 64 (suppl 8): 9-14.

Fielding S, Kerr S, Godber C. Lithium in the over-65s—a dedicated monitoring service leads to better quality of treatment supervision. *International Journal of Geriatric Psychiatry* 1999; 14(11): 985-7.

Foster JR. Use of lithium in elderly psychiatric patients: a review of the literature. *Lithium* 1992; 3: 77-93.

Frank E, Novick D. Progress in the psychotherapy of mood disorders: studies from the Western Psychiatric Institute and Clinic. *Epidemiology Psychiatry and Sociology* 2001: 10(4): 245-52.

Friedman SA, Raizner AE, Rosen H. Et al. Functional defects in the aging kidney. *Annals of Internal Medicine* 1972: 76: 41-45.

Fuller M, Sajatovic M. *Drug information handbook for psychiatry.* 3rd Edition. Lexi-Comp, Inc., Cleveland, Ohio 2002.

Fuller MA, Sajatovic M. 2001. *Drug Information for Mental Health. Lexi-Comp Inc.:* Cleveland, OH.

Gareri P, Falconi U, De Fazio P, De Sarro G. 2000. Conventional and new antidepressant drugs in the elderly. *Prog Neurobiol* 61(4): 353-396.

Gerner RH. 1985. Present status of drug therapy of depression in late life. *J Affect Disord* 1:S23-S31. .

Geodon® Prescribing Information. New York, NY: Pfizer Inc: 2003.

Goldberg JR. Treatment guidelines: current and future management of bipolar disorder. *Journal of Clinical Psychiatry* 2000; 61(Suppl. 13): 12-18.

Goldberg JF, Sacks MH, Kocsis JH. Low-dose lithium augmentation of divalproex in geriatric mania. *Journal of Clinical Psychiatry* 2000;61(4): 304.

Goodwin FK, Jamison KR, Post RM, et al. Eds. *The natural course of manic-depressive illness: neurobiology of mood disorders.* Baltimore: Williams and Wilkins, 1984.

Goodwin FK, Jamison KR. *Manic Depressive Illness*. Oxford University Press: Oxford. 1990.

Goodwin GM, Consensus Group for the British Association for Psychopharmacology. Evidence-based guidelines for treating bipolar disorder: recommendations from the British Association for Psychopharmacology. *Journal of Psychopharmacology* 2003: 17(2): 149-173 .

Greenblatt DJ, Abernathy DR, Shader RI. Pharmacokinetic aspects of drug therapy in the elderly. *Ther Drug Monitoring.* 1986: 8(3): 249-55.

Greil W, Kleindiest N, Erazo N, Muller-Oerlinghausen B. Differential response to lithium and carbamezepine in the prophylaxis of bipolar disorder *Journal of Clinical Psychopharmacol* 1998; 18(6): 455-60.

Grunze H, Kasper S, Goodwin G, et al. World Federation of Societies of Biological Psychiatry (WFSBP) Guidelines for Biological Treatment of Bipolar Disorder, pt 1: treatment of bipolar depression. *World J Biol Psychiatry* 2002; 3: 115-124.

Henderson DC, Caglerio E, Gray C, Nasralla RS, Hayden DL, Schoenfeld DA, Golf DC: Clozapine, diabetes mellitus, weight gain, and lipid abnormalities: A five year naturalistic study. *Am J Psychiatry* 2000; 157:975-981.

Hirsch E, Schmitz B, Carreno M. Epilepsy, antiepileptic drugs (AEDs) and cognition. *Acta Neurol Scan* 2003; 108 Suppl 180: 23-32.

Hirschfeld RMA. The efficacy of atypical antipsychotics in bipolar disorders. *J Clin Psychiatry* 2003; 64 (Suppl. 8): 15-21.

Hoff RA, Rosenheck RA: Long-term patterns of service use and cost among patients with both psychiatric and substance abuse disorders. *Medical Care* 36: 835-843, 1998.

Hoff RA, Rosenheck RA. The cost of treating substance abuse patients with and without comorbid psychiatric disorders. *Psychiatric Services* 1999: 50(10): 1309-15.

Hoffman WF, Ballard L, Turner EH, Casey DE. Three-year follow-up of older schophrenics: extrapyramidal syndromes, psychiatric symptoms, and ventricular brain ratio. *Biological Psychaitry* 1991:30(9): 913-26.

Hunt N., Silverstone T. Tardive dyskinesia in bipolar affective disorder: a catchment area study. *Int Clin Psychopharmacol* 1991; 6: 45-50.

James NM. Early and late-onset bipolar affective disorder. *Archives of General Psychiatry* 1977: 34: 511-518.

Jefferson JW, Griest JH, Ackerman DL, et al. *Lithium encyclopedia for clinical practice*, 2nd edn. American Psychiatric Press: Washington, DC, 1987.

Jeste DV, Barak Y, Madhusoodanan S, Grossman F, Gharebawi G. International multisite double blind trial of the atypical antipsychotics risperidone and olanzapine in 175 elderly patients with chronic schizophrenia. *Am J. Geriatric psychiatry* 2003; 11:6; 638-646.

Jeste DV, Lacro JP, Bailey A, Rockwell E, Harris MJ, Caligiuri MP. Lower incidence of tardive dyskinesia with risperidone compared with haloperidol in older patients. *J Am Geriatr Soc* 1999; 47(6): 716-719.

Jeste DV, Glazer WM, Morgenstern H, Pultz JA, Yeung PR. *Rarity of persistent tardive dyskinesia with quetiapine treatment of psychotic disorders in the elderly. Presented at the Annual Meeting of the American College of Neuropsychopharmacology December 12-16, 1999. Acapulco, Mexico.*

Kahn DA. The use of psychodynamic psychotherapy in manic-depressive illness. *Journal American Academy of Psychoanalysis* 1993: 21: 441-455.

Kanba S,Yagi G, Kamijiima K. The first open study of zonisamide, a novel anticonvulsant, shows efficacy in mania. *Progress in Neuropsychopharmacology and Biological Psychiatry* 1994: 189: 707-715.

Kando JC, Tohen M, Castillo J, et al. The use of valproate in an elderly population with affective symptoms. *Journal of Clinical Psychiatry* 1996; 57(6): 238-40.

Kane JM, McGlashan TH. Treatment of schizophrenia. *Lancet.* 1995: 34(8978): 820-5.

Keck PE, Saha AR, Iwamoto T, et al. Aripiprazole versus placebo in acute mania. In: *New Research Abstracts of the 155th Annual Meeting of the American Psychiatric Association: May 22, 2002;* Philadelphia, PA. Abstract NR 314:86.

Kodar K, Brodaty H, Anstey K. Cognitive therapy for depression in the elderly. International *Journal of Geriatric Psychiatry* 1996: 11: 97.

Koller EA, Doraiswamy PM: Olanzapine associated diabetes mellitus. *Pharmacotherapy* 2002: 22:841-852.

Krauthammer C, Klerman GL. Secondary manic: manic syndromes associated with antecedent physical illness or drugs. *Archives of General Psychiatry* 1978: 35: 1333-38.

Krishnan KRR. Biological risk factors in late life depression. *Biological Psychiatry* 2002: 52:185-192.

Lamictal (lamotrigine) product information. Research Triangle Par, NC: Glaxo Wellcome Inc., 2001.

Leadbetter R, Messenheimer J, Bentley B, et al. Mood –stabilizing properties of lamotrigine: A review of data from controlled clinical trials. *Psychiatric Annals* 2002; 32 (12): 766-772.

Leppik IE. Issues in the treatment of epilepsy. *Epilepsia* 2001; 42 (Suppl 4): 1-6.

Lesem MD, Zajecka JM, Swift RH, Reeves KR, Harrigan EP. Intramuscular ziprasisdone, 2 mg versus 10mg, in the short-term management of agitated psychotic patients. *J Clin Psychiatry* 2001; 62:12-18.

Levine J, Chengappa KN, Brar JS, et al. Psychotropic drug prescription patterns among patients with bipolar I disorder. *Bipolar disorder* 2000; 2(2): 120-30.

Loebel A, Siu CO, Romano SJ. *Overview of ziprasidone tolerability in older patients. Poster presented at the American Psychiatric Association 55th Institute on Psychiatric Services* 2003. Boston, MA. .

Loebel A, Mackell J, Leaderer M, Dybica SB, Erwin WG. *Utilization of ziprasidone in elderly nursing facility residents. American Psychiatric Association 55th Institute on Psychiatric Services*, November 1, 2003, Boston, Massachusetts.

Loranger AW, Levine PM. Age of onset of bipolar affective illness. *Archives of General Psychiatry* 1978: 35: 1345-1348.

Lyons JS, McGovern MP. Use of mental health services by dually diagnosed patients. *Hospital and Community Psychiatry* 40: 1067-1069, 1989.

Madhusoodanan S, Bogunovic O, Brenner R, Gupta S. Use of topiramate as an adjunctive medication in an elderly patients with treatment-resistant bipolar disorder. *American Journal of Geriatric Psychiatry*. 2002; 10(6): 759.

Madhusoodanan S, Bogunovic O, Gupta S, Steinmeyer C, Brenner R, Jeste DV. Use of atypical antipsychotics in elderly patients with schizophrenia and schizoaffective disorder. *Journal of Advances in schizophrenia and brain research* 2002; 4:4: 110-122.

Madhusoodanan S., Brenner R., Araujo L., Abaza A. Efficacy of risperidone treatment for psychosis associated with schizophrenia, schizoaffective disorder, bipolar disorder or senile dementia in 11 geriatric patients: A case series. *Journal of Clinical Psychiatry* 1995: 56: 514-518.

Madhusoodanan S., Suresh P., Brenner R., Pillai R. Experience with the atypical antipsychotics risperidone and olanzapine in the elderly. *Annals of Clinical Psychiatry* 1999: 11(3): 113-8.

Madhusoodanan S., Brenner R., Alcantre A., Clinical experience with quetiapine in elderly patients with psychotic disorders. *J Geriatric Psychiatry Neurol* 2000: 13: 28-32.

McDonald WM. Epidemiology, etiology, and treatment of geriatric mania. *J Clin Psychiatry* 2000: 61(Suppl 13): 3-11.

McDonald WM, Thompson TR. *Treatment of mania in dementia with electroconvulsive therapy. Psychopharmacology bulletin.* 2001, 35(2): 72-82.

McDonald WM, Nemeroff CB. The diagnosis and treatment of mania in the elderly. *Bull Menninger Clin* 1996: 60: 175-196.

McDonald WM, Tupler LA, Marsteller FA, Figiel GS, DiSouza S, Nemeroff CB, Krishnan KR. Hyper-intense lesions on magnetic resonance images in bipolar disorder. *Biological Psychiatry* 1999: 45: 965-971.

McElroy SL, Suppes T, Keck PE, et al. Open-label adjunctive topiramate in the treatment of bipolar disorders. *Biological Psychiatry* 2000; 47:1025-1033.

McElroy SL, Altshuler LL, Suppes T, Keck PE, Frye MA, Denicoff K, Nolen WA, Kupka RW, Leverich GS, Rochussen JR, Rush AJ, Post RM. Axis I psychiatric comorbidity and its relationship to historical illness variables in 288 patients with bipolar disorder. *Am J Psychiatry* 2001, 158(3): 420-6.

McFarland BH, Miller MR, Staumfjord E. Valproate use in the older manic patient. *Journal of Clinical Psychiatry.*1990; 51:479-481.

McManus DQ, Arvanitis LA, Kowalcyk GG, for the Seroquel Trial 48 Study Group. Quetiapine: a novel antipsychotic: experience in elderly patients with psychotic disorders. *J Clin Psych* 1999; 60(5): 292-298.

Meatherall R, Younes J; Fatality from olanzapine induced hyperglycemia. *J Forensic Sc* 2002; 47:893-896.

Mehta S, Pryor F, Rowan AJ, Uthman B, Ramsey RE. Tolerability and efficacy of topiramate in older patients. *Epilepsia*: 42(Suppl 7): 143 (Abs 2.125).

Mendlewicz J, Fieve RR, Rainer JD, et al. Manic-depressive illness: a comparative study of patients with and without family history. *British Journal of Psychiatry* 1972: 120: 523-530.

Messenheimer JA. Lamotrigine. *Epilepsia* 1995; 36, Suppl. 2. S87-94.

Messenheimer JA. Rash in adult and pediatric patients treated with lamotrigine. *Ca J Neurol Sci* 1998; 25: S14-S18.

Moller HJ, Grunze H. Have some guidelines for the treatment of acute bipolar depression gone too far in the restriction of antidepressants? *Eur Arch Psychiatry Clin Neurosci* 2000; 250: 57-68.

Moller HJ, Nasralla HA. Treatment of bipolar disorder. *J. Clinical Psychaitry* 2003: 64(Suppl 6): 9-17.

Moorhead SRJ, Young AH. Evidence for a late onset bipolar-I disorder sub-group from 50 years. *Journal of affective disorders.*2003; 73(3): 271-277.

Mordecai DJ, Sheikh JI, Glick ED. Divalproex for the treatment of geriatric bipolar discord. *International Journal of Geriatric Psychiatry.* 1999; 14: 494-496.

Mukherjee S., Rosen A.M., Caracci G. Shukla S. Persistent tardive dyskinesia in bipolar patients. *Arch Gen Psychiatry* 1986; 43: 342-346.

Onder G, Pedone C, Landi F, Cesari M, Della Vedova C, Bernabei R, Gambassi G. Adverse drug reactions as cause of hospital admissions: results from the Italian Group of Pharmacoepidemiology in the Elderly (GIFA). *Journal of the American Geriatrics Society* 2002: 50: 1962-1968. .

Oshima A, Higuchi T. Treatment guidelines for geriatric mood disorders. *Psychiatry Clinical Neuroscience* 1999; 53 suppl: S55-9.

Pfizer Inc. *Study Report of Ziprasidone Clinical Pharmacology protocol.* Rockville, M.D.: F.D.A. Center for Drug Evaluation and Research Division of Cardiorenal Drug Products Consultation; June 14, 2000.

Pirzada SR, Ries R, LoGerfo JP. Cost of comorbid alcohol and drug problems. *American Journal on Addictions*. 6: 193-204, 1997.

Pollock BG. Adverse drug reactions of antidepressants in elderly patients. *Journal of Clinical Psychiatry* 1999: 60, Suppl 20: 4-8.

Puryear LJ, Kunik ME, Workman RI. Tolerability of divalproex sodium in elderly psychiatric patients with mixed diagnoses. *Journal of Geriatric Psychiatry and Neurology*. 1995; 8(4): 234-237.

Rabins PV, Aylward E, Holroyd S, Pearlson G. MRI findings differentiate between late-onset schizophrenia and late-life mood disorder. *International Journal of Geriatric Psychiatry*. 2000; 15, 954-960.

Regier DA, Myers JK, Kramer M, et al. The NIMH Epidemiologic Catchment Area program: historical context, major objectives, and study population characteristics. *Archives of General Psychiatry* 1984: 41: 934-941.

Rhodes LJ. Maintenance ECT replaced with lamotrigine . *Am Journal of Psychiatry* 2000: 157(12): 2058.

Risinger RC, Risby ED, Risch SC. Safety and efficacy of divalproex sodium in elderly bipolar patients. *Journal of Clinical Psychiatry* 1994; 55(5): 215.

Risperidone (Risperdal) product information. Janssen Pharmaceutic Products, L.P., Titusville, NJ 08560, August 2003.

Robillard M, Conn DK. Lamotrigine use in geriatric patients with bipolar depression. *Canadian Journal of Psychiatry* 2002; 47(8): 767-70.

Russo P, Smith MW, Dirani R, et al. Pharmacotherapy patterns in the treatment of bipolar disorder. *Bipolar Disorder* 2002; 4(6): 366-77.

Sachs G. S., Thase M.E. Bipolar disorder therapeutics: maintenance treatment. *Biol Psychiatry* 2000; 48: 573-581.

Sachs GS, Printz DJ, Kahn DA, Carpenter D, Docherty JP. *The expert consensus guideline series: medication treatment of bipolar disorder 2000. Postgrad Med Special Issue* April: 1-104.

Sachs G, Mullen JA, Devine NA. *Quetiapine vs placebo as adjunct to mood stabilizer for the treatment of acute mania. Presented at the 3rd European Stanley Foundation conference on Bipolar Disorder;* Sept. 12, 2002; Freiburg, Germany.

Sajatovic M, Popli A, Semple W. Ten-year use of hospital-based services by geriatric veterans with schizophrenia and bipolar disorder. *Psychiatric Services* 1996: 47: 961-965.

Sajatovic M., Ramirez L.F., Garver D., Thompson P., Ripper G., Lehman L.S. Clozapine therapy for older veterans. *Psych Serv*. 1998; 49: 340-344. .

Sajatovic M, Blow FD, Ignacio RV, Kates HC. Bipolar Disorder in the Veterans Health Adminstration: Age-related modifiers of clinical presentation and health services use. *Psychiatric Services*. 2004; 55(9)1014-1021.

Sajatovic M. Aging-related issues in bipolar disorder: A health services perspective. *Journal of Geriatric Psychiatry and Neurology* 2002; 15: 128-133.

Sajatovic M, Hrouda, D, Davies, M. Adherence enhancement in bipolar disorder. *Psychiatric Services*. 2004; 55 (3):246-269.

Salzman C. Geriatric psychopharmacology. *Annual Reviews in Medicine*. 1985. 36: 217-228.

_____ . Medication compliance in the elderly. *Journal of Clinical Psychiatry* 1995;56 Suppl 1:18-22. .

Sanderson DR. Use of mood stabilizers by hospitalized geriatric patients with bipolar disorder. *Psychiatric Services*. 1998: 49(9). 1145-1147.

Schneider AL, Wilcox CS. Divalproate augmentation in lithium-resistant rapid cycling mania in four geriatric patients. *Journal of Affective Disorders*. 1998; 47: 201-205.

Schulman R.W., Singh A., Shulman K.I. 1997. Treatment of elderly institutionalized bipolar patients with clozapine. *Psychopharmacol Bull* 33: 113-118.

Scogin F, McElreath L. Efficacy of psychosocial treatments for geriatric depression: a quantitative review. *J Consult Clinical Psychology*. 1994: 62, 69.

Segal S, Reisenberg RA, Ice K, English P. *Ziprasidone in Mania: Double blind placebo controlled trial. Poster presented at the American Psychiatric Association 55th Institute on psychiatric services 2003;* Boston, MA USA.

Sernyak M. J., Griffin R.A., Johnson R.M., et al. Neuroleptic exposure following inpatient treatment of acute mania with lithium and neuroleptic. *Psychiatry* 1994; 151:133-135.

Sethi MA, Mehta R, Devanand DP. Gabapentin in geriatric mania. *Journal of Geriatric Psychiatry and Neurology* 2003; 16(2): 117-20.

Shelton RC, Tollefson GD, Tohen M, et al. A novel augmentation strategy for treating resistant major depression. *Am J Psychiatry* 2001; 158:131-134.

Shulman KI, Rochon P, Suykora K, et al. Changing prescription patterns for lithium and valproic acid in old age: shifting practice without evidence. *British Medical Journal*. 2003; 326 (7396): 960-961.

Shulman KI, Mackenzie S, Hardy B. The clinical use of lithium carbonate in old age: a review. *Prog Neuropsychopharmacol Biol Psychiatry* 1987; 11: 159-164.

Shulman KI. Mania and cerebrovascular disease. In *Vascular Disease and Affective Disorders*. Chiu E, Ames D, Katona C (eds). Martin Dunitz Ltd: London. 2002.

Shulman KI, Tohen M, Satlin A, Mallya G, Kalunian D. Mania compared to unipolar depression in old age. *American Journal of Psychiatry* 1992: 149:341-345. .

Shulman KI, Tohen M. Unipolar mania reconsidered: evidence from an elderly cohort. *British Journal of Psychiatry* 1994:164:547-549. .

Sibisi CDT. Sex differences in the age of onset of bipolar affective illness. *British Journal of Psychiatry* 1990: 156: 842-845.

Sicuro R. *Use of higher dose quetiapine in elderly patients: A chart review study. Poster presented at: 16th Annual Meeting of the American Association for Geriatric Psychiatry; March 1-4, 2003; Oahu H.L.*

Sicuro F. Treatment of bipolar disorder among older adults: a review of clinical cases using quetiapine. *Supplement to Annals of Long term care and clinical geriatrics*. Sept. 2003; 1-11.

Spicer CC, Hare EJ, Slater D. Neurotic and psychotic forms of depressive illness: evidence from age-incidence in a national sample. *Br J Psychiatry* 1973: 123: 535-541.

Sproule BA, Hardy BG, Shulman KI. Differential pharmacokinetics of lithium in elderly patients. *Drug Aging* 2000; 16(3): 165-77.

Steffens DC, Krishnan KR. Structural neuroimaging and mood disorders. Recent findings, implications for classification, and future directions. *Biological Psychiatry* 1998: 43:705-712.

Strakowski SM, Sax KW< McElroy SL, Keck PE, Hawkins JM, West SA. Course of psychiatric and substance abuse syndromes co-occuring with bipolar disorder after a first psychiatric hospitalization. *J Clin Psychiatry* 1998: 59(9): 465-71.

Street J, Tollefson GD, Tohen M, et al. Olanzapine for psychotic conditions in the elderly. *Psychiatric Annals* 2000; 30 (3): 191-6.

Tariot P, Salzman C, Yeung P, Pultz J, Raniwalla J. *Clinical improvement and tolerability is maintained long-term in elderly patients with psychotic disorders treated with quetiapine. Presented at the Annual Meeting of the American College of Neuropsychopharmacology December 12-16, 1999. Acapulco, Mexico.*

Tariot P.N., Salzman C., Yeung P.P. et al. Long term use of quetiapine in elderly patients with psychotic disorders. *Clin Ther* 2000; 22(9): 1068-1084.

Teri L, Logsdon R, Wagner A, Uomoto J. The caregiving role in behavioral treatment of depression in dementia patients. In: *Stress Effects on Family Caregivers of Alzheimer's Patients.* Light E, Niederehe G, Lebowitz BD. (eds). Springer Verlag: New York, New York,. 1994.

Tohen M, Goldberg JF, Arritaga AMGP, Azorin JM, Vieta E, Bayle MCH, Lawson WB, Emsley RA, Zang F, Baker RW, Risser RC, Namjoshi MA, Evans AR, Breier A. A 12 double blind comparison of olanzapine vs haloperidol in the treatment of acute mania; *Arch Gen Psychiatry* 2003; 60:1218-1226.

Tohen M, Vieta E, Calabrese J et al. Efficacy of olanzapine and olanzapine-fluoxetine combination in the treatment of bipolar 1 depression. *Arch Gen Psychiatry* 2003; 60:1079-1088.

Torney EF, Swalwell C. Fatal olanzapine-induced ketoacidosis. *Am J Psychiatry* 2003; 160:12,2241.

Tueth MJ, Murphy TK, Evans DL. Special considerations: use of lithium in children, adolescents, and elderly populations. *Journal of Clinical Psychiatry* 1998; 590(Suppl 6): 66-73.

U.S. Bureau of the Census. Resident population of the Unites States. Middle series projections. 2006-10 by age and sex. Washington: The Bureau, March 1996.

Vasudev K, Goswami U, Kohli K. Carbamazepine and valproate monotherapy: feasibility, relative safety and efficacy, and therapeutic drug monitoring in manic disorder. *Psychopharmacology* 2000: 150(1): 15-23.

Woerner MG, Alvir MJ, Saltz BL, Lieberman JA, Kane JM. Prospective study of tardive dyskinesia in the elderly: rates and risk factors. *American Journal of Psychiatry*. 1998: 155(11): 1521-8.

Yassa R, Nair NPV, Iskandar H. Late-onset bipolar disorder. *Psychiatric Clin North American* 1988; 11: 1171-113.

Yatham LN, Kusumakar V, Calabrese JR, et al. Third generation anticonvulsants in bipolar disorder: a review of efficacy and summary of clinical recommendations. *Journal of Clinical Psychiatry* 2002; 63(4): 275-83.

Yeung PR, Mintzer JE, Mullen JA, Sweitzer DE. *Extrapyramidal symptoms in elderly outpatients treated with either quetiapine or risperidone. Presented at the Annual Meeting of the American College of Neuropsychopharmacology December 12-16, 1999. Acapulco, Mexico.*

Young RC, Klerman GL. Mania in late life: focus on age of onset. *American Journal of Psychiatry* 1992: 49: 867-876.

Young RC, Falk NR. Age, manic psychopathology and treatment response. *International Journal of Geriatric Psychiatry* 1989: 4.

INDEX

U

V

W

Y

Z